Anger, Guilt, and the Psychology of the Self in *Clarissa*

American University Studies

Series IV
English Language and Literature

Vol. 191

PETER LANG
New York • Washington, D.C./Baltimore • Boston
Bern • Frankfurt am Main • Berlin • Vienna • Paris

Victor J. Lams

Anger, Guilt, and the Psychology of the Self in *Clarissa*

PETER LANG
New York • Washington, D.C./Baltimore • Boston
Bern • Frankfurt am Main • Berlin • Vienna • Paris

Library of Congress Cataloging-in-Publication Data

Lams, Victor J.
Anger, guilt, and the psychology of the self in Clarissa / Victor J. Lams.
p. cm. — (American university studies. Series IV:
English language and literature; vol. 191)
Includes bibliographical references and index.
1. Richardson, Samuel, 1689–1761. Clarissa. 2. Psychological fiction,
English—History and criticism. 3. Epistolary fiction, English—History and
criticism. 4. Young women in literature. 5. Psychology
in literature. 6. Anger in literature. 7. Guilt in literature.
8. Self in literature. I. Title. II. Series.
PR3664.C43L36 823'.6—dc21   98-27378
1999   ISBN 0-8204-4160-0
ISSN 0741-0700

Die Deutsche Bibliothek-CIP-Einheitsaufnahme

Lams, Victor J.:
Anger, guilt, and the psychology of the self in Clarissa / Victor J. Lams.
–New York; Washington, D.C./Baltimore; Boston; Bern;
Frankfurt am Main; Berlin; Vienna; Paris: Lang.
(American university studies: Ser. 4; English
language and literature; Vol. 191)
ISBN 0-8204-4160-0

The paper in this book meets the guidelines for permanence and durability
of the Committee on Production Guidelines for Book Longevity
of the Council of Library Resources.

Printed in the United States of America

TO
BARBARA WRIGHT LAMS

Acknowledgments

Gratitude requires that I thank the people who helped during the writing of this book. My sisters Mary Sue Jaspers and Sylvia Jaspers, both of Eden, South Dakota, the former for declaring the awkward second draft intelligible, the latter for bibliographical assistance; my colleagues Robert Burton and Stan Felver, who both read early drafts; Sally Peltier Harvey, my former student and an eventual colleague, for reading various drafts while busy writing her own study of Willa Cather; another colleague, Clifford Minor, for help with the Latin and Greek inscriptions on engravings that appear in the Wither emblems in Chapter 8; my good friends Murray Markland and Paul Petersen, both now deceased, for being patient and supportive auditors during the early, or haranguing, stage of the study's development; David Downes, for his collegial counsel, and for advice about publication; Gabrial Hornstein, President of AMS Press in New York, for his encouragement and support, as well as for helping to make the AMS *Clarissa* available to us all; to Heinz Kohut and Paul Ricoeur and those who published their books, for intellectual guidance without which this book would have been literally unthinkable; to my colleague and officemate Gil Prince, for countless acts of kindness, and for encouraging me to please stop making the book sound like Professor Hector lecturing them.

My greatest debt is to my friend and colleague Lois Bueler, for her diligent and painstaking assistance in *writing* the book. Her characteristic belief was that I should not approach, assume, imply or insinuate a point but make it, which I generally thought I already had done. My own presumption was that, when I did make a point, I ought to hammer it several times so that readers would notice, while her view was that I should make it briefly and move on to another point—which would make for a shorter book but that couldn't be helped. There was never any contest, though, because the more clearly anyone observes the most essential truth and the more quickly and accurately sees and explains the reasons for it, the more understanding and wise [Cicero's phrase: "*prudentissimus et sapientissimus*" (I, v)] she will be esteemed. And rightly so. We have both worked hard to make this book briefer and easier to read than it would have been without her gracious, and tireless, effort on its behalf. Thanks, Lois.

Victor Lams

* * *

I would like to acknowledge the permission given by © **The British Museum** to reproduce the drawing of Dame Elizabeth Carteret's funeral monument in Ackermann's *Westminister Abbey* (1812). The three emblems found in Chapter 8 are taken from George Wither's *A Collection of Emblemes*, London, 1636, pages 45, 102 and 157; these items are reproduced by permission of *The Huntington Library, San Marino, California*.

Table of Contents

Introduction

Although *Clarissa* appears to be a story about courtship and attempted seduction, it is really a narrative phenomenology which examines the operations of anger on Lovelace and the Harlowes and its quelling and extinction in Clarissa. Lovelace's courtship of Clarissa is fraudulent, and his attempted seduction is a disguise which conceals the real nature of his transaction with her. This transaction, driven by his anger towards women in general, is his way of taking narcissistic revenge for the improperly structured self which causes that anger. When in her first letter Clarissa says that her family "has been in *tumults*" since the duel between her brother and Lovelace "and I have borne all the blame" (I.5; 1.3-4),[1] she sounds the theme of anger and guilt. When Lovelace in his first letter to Belford calls himself a "*tempestuous soul*" that"*ev'ry windy passion blows*" (I.200; 1.147), he identifies himself as the cause of the tumults for which Clarissa is blamed.

The anger which drives the novel's action is focused on the issue of guilt, for anger points the finger of accusation towards the person who is presumed guilty of a wrongdoing. Examining the issue of guilt brings to light several partly obscure patterns of meaning which help illuminate the action. The Harlowes' violence exemplifies the self-defensive psychic dynamic that operates when any threatened social group protects itself by making one of its members its scapegoat. Lovelace's brutality, intended to punish Clarissa's alleged mistreatment, reveals a pattern of compulsive actions that replicates the symptoms of pathological narcissism. Understanding these two meaning patterns helps situate this book within recent criticism. In "The Rise of Richardson Criticism," Siobhán Kilfeather describes three "trends" which have emerged since the midcentury studies of Dorothy Van Ghent and Ian Watt, two of which are pertinent:

The first of these is a revolution in attitudes to the representation of women, and particularly of violence against women. A second trend is a reversal of the tendency to seek archetypal patterns which would codify and unify Richardson's unwieldy texts into a tendency to celebrate their diversity and disjunction. (251)

This book combines exploration of the representation of violence against women with the unearthing of psychological matrices that largely account for such behavior. Because the violence done to Clarissa reaches beyond the parameters of her particular century and circumstances to exemplify violence generally, something like archetypal patterns emerge from analysis of how she is treated by her family and Lovelace and how she responds.

If one cannot understand the Harlowes without comprehending the scapegoat dynamic, or understand Lovelace without seeing his pathological narcissism, neither can one grasp the psychology of Clarissa's self without attending to her theological reflections on her devastating experience. Kilfeather calls the attempt to explore Richardson's religious themes "theoretically undesirable as well as impossible" (206). Terry Castle, Terry Eagleton and William Beatty Warner appear in their different ways to support that view.[2] Unfortunately, when one ignores Clarissa's religious actions, one ignores what is arguably the most important portion of the novel. If one is correct to inquire about the Harlowes "What are they doing and why?" and of Lovelace "What is he doing and why?," one must surely pose the same question of Clarissa.

The need for this book rises from the fact that Richardson's characters often are only imperfectly aware of the real nature of their actions and motives. Samuel Johnson calls them characters of nature and contrasts them to the flatter, less independent and complex characters of manners invented by Fielding. "'Characters of manners are very entertaining; but they are to be understood by a more superficial observer than characters of nature, where a man must dive into the recesses of the human heart'" (Boswell 389). To explicate those "recesses" which Richardson explores, I decided to employ what Stanley Hyman describes as the "organized use of non-literary techniques and bodies of knowledge to obtain insights into literature" (3). Rather than confining myself to any one interpretive point of view, I utilize many non-literary tools to investigate problems arising at specific points. Thus, Thomas Aquinas's and John Norris's descriptions of prudence help us understand Clarissa's aspirations to excellence, John Bowlby's analysis of mourning clarifies her self-restoration efforts after the rape, and Gabriel Marcel's phenomenological description of a hope that is born out of hopeless situations explains the "better hope" which she achieves before her death. Crucially important interpretive help has been given by René Girard, who analyzes the scapegoat dynamic which propels the Harlowes into their family-defensive sacrifice of Clarissa; Heinz Kohut, whose analysis of pathological narcissism is the key to understanding Lovelace's conduct; and Paul Ricoeur, whose phenomenology of religion is essential to realizing the precise nature of Clarissa's religious actions after the rape. The purpose in using these interpretive tools is always to achieve for *Clarissa's* readers the goal which Herbert Fingarette sets in *Self-Deception*: "I aim to present the texture of our experience, not just coherently, but with the patterns more visible and their significance more clearly displayed than before" (7).

These numerous and disparate interpretive aids are necessary because the novel's principal letter writers are only partially to be trusted as interpreters of the actions they recount. For instance, Clarissa, who is both naive and deceived, has virtually complete control over the story during the Harlowe Place events. Letters written by her family are subsumed into the interpretive maelstrom of her correspondence with Miss Howe, while Lovelace's three letters to Belford are too few and appear too belatedly for those letters to affect the interpretive hegemony of her version. Since readers must rely on her account of the meaning of events, they are deceived about Lovelace's intentions along with Clarissa herself. When after the flight the epistolary control gradually shifts to Lovelace, readers are no better off than they were with Clarissa, since Lovelace is *self*-deceived about the nature of his transaction with her and continually invents cover-stories which craftily maintain his self-ignorance.

The interpretive problems posed by the novel have determined the book's organizational structure. The initial three chapters, prompted by the need to explain why Clarissa defends her family, show that Lovelace deliberately angers the Harlowes, transforming them into his tools, while he misleads Clarissa about his purpose and prepares her for abduction. The next three chapters explore Lovelace as a pathological narcissist self-deceived with respect to the nature of his interactions with Clarissa. Chapters 7 and 8 recount the process by which Clarissa after the rape mourns her losses, restructures her self, and comes to terms with her life's meaning. Chapters 9 and 10 explicate Lovelace's psychic collapse because of Clarissa's death, show his success in learning to bear guilt, and explain his final effort to be reconciled to Clarissa.

This study presumes that the primary action of *Clarissa* is the speech action found in the characters' letters, not the off-stage events which they write about. Kilfeather says it briefly: "The letters are the action" (253). The crucial events that take place in the novel occur when the letter writers' inner states of self-reflection are enacted within social reality through speech, or rather, by the transcribed speech of epistolary prose in which they evaluate past actions and anticipate the future. The mental projects of the principal characters and the reflections in which they monitor successes and losses in light of their goals ARE the novel's action.

This idea of action is implicit in Margaret Doody's comment that "the narration in letters is in this novel an image of the material world transformed into consciousness, and the characters present themselves and all that concerns them as consciousness engaged in activity" (152). What Doody calls "transforming into consciousness" is the activity pursued by Clarissa and Lovelace throughout the novel. They are the only characters who, in self-reflection, transform their world into consciousness. That they do so is what *makes* them the main characters. Their action is primarily their letter writing, the self-transforming activity by which they live. Thus there are two stories in Clarissa. As Tom Keymer says, "There is the story of events. . . . And there is a second story, which in many ways outgrows the first." In this "second story" one encounters characters "struggling to fix their experiences adequately in prose and so define and assert their own conflicting senses, psychologically, epistemologically and above all morally, of what is happening in their world" (1992, 48). Though the "second story" grows from the "story of events," that second story is not secondary in its importance. It is the central action of the novel.

Since the work of Clarissa and Lovelace to fix their mental states in prose is the core action of the novel, it follows that the main characters' most crucial acts are speech acts: stating, requesting, promising, and declaring. The important terms here are *act* and *action,* both of which signify doing. Before writing, Clarissa and Lovelace experience various states of mind, but such experiencing does not constitute genuine action. The states of mind in which one hopes, fears, believes or means things "are not acts," says John Searle. But *stating is* an action, and stating, whether they are addressing one another or Miss Howe and Belford, is what Clarissa and Lovelace do. The transaction between them is the battle between their antithetical Intentionalities,[3] their wholly contrary ways of perceiving—and stating—the world. When Clarissa writes Miss Howe describing her most recent rejection of Solmes, she is enacting "Intentional states," that is, her mental states of being relieved that she has not yet succumbed to family demands, of feeling terrified by the prospects still before her, of hoping that Lovelace has a good heart, and of fearing that he does not. By doing these things, Clarissa is engaging in self-enactment, the process by which she lives her life.

To say that the characters' enactments of their Intentional states in epistolary prose is the primary action of the novel is not to say that external events are unimportant, but that their importance is secondary to the characters' *interpretations* of the events. Yet this is the situation which makes Richardson's novel difficult to understand accurately. Because the chief characters harbor such radically different viewpoints, their interpretations of the events cannot help being contradictory. How is the reader to deal with the fact that Clarissa's and Lovelace's readings of events are so diametrically opposed? One could conclude that the novel's meaning is indeterminate because opposing interpretations effectively void each other, and this is Terry Castle's approach. Castle thinks that events are "human actions" but *interpretation* is mere "comment on action." She says "The significance of human actions in *Clarissa* does not inhere, seemingly, in the actions themselves, but is promoted, retroactively, by interpreters . . . who witness and comment on action" (20–1). She calls *Clarissa* "a cacophany of voices, a multiplicity of exegetes struggling to articulate different 'constructions' of the world" (21), but this cacophanous multiplicity can only travel down the slippery slope into semantic nihilism: "The tragedy is that this opacity in the realm of events, the inaccessibility of any single human truth, breeds a kind of hermeneutical anarchy" (21). Such a conclusion can be arrived at only if one began with it.

Yet Castle is correct to discover "hermeneutical anarchy" in the text, though far from being caused by "the inaccessibility of any single human truth" (21), that anarchy is caused by Lovelace. He invents fraudulent facts to trap Clarissa, his most effective deceptions being the social events which appear to occur despite his intention. These events are designed to mislead Clarissa's community into falsehoods that redound to her disadvantage. They function like speech acts because they are directed at audiences Lovelace wishes to deceive and because they have what John Searle calls an "illocutionary point"—

the untrue meaning which Lovelace intends his audience to believe true. The story of the novel is the battle between Lovelace's attempt to falsify Clarissa's world and transform her into a creature of narcissistic desire, and her determination to discover, articulate and embrace the truth about herself.

Notes

1 Volume and page numbers from the AMS "Clarissa Project" third edition are provided first (I.5), followed by those from the Dent "Everyman" third edition (1.3–4).

2 Castle says of Clarissa that she is "an exemplary victim of hermeneutic violence," that "her experience finally is a paradigm of oppression," and that her response to the violence done her is "of a piece with that of the political victim: self-condemnation, demoralization" (22, 25–6). But violence and the sacred, as René Girard explains, are interrelated, and Castle cannot account for Clarissa's self-description as "all blessed hope" when she dies.

Rather than deny Clarissa's religious action, Terry Eagleton reads it as prefiguring the secular faith which looks forward to a day when violence and injustice give way before enlightenment: "What societies cannot yet accomplish historically, they often nurture in the realm of myth; this seems to me the most relevant contemporary reading of Clarissa's religious faith" (93).

William Warner prefers to simply ignore Clarissa's religious dimension, obliterating it through counter-interpretation. As he says, "though the first text may remain the 'same,' the rules for reading steadily change; the pen that writes the readings of the text passes from reader to reader and generation to generation. And this pen will inevitably be guided by the will and desire of the one who holds it" (264).

3 *Intentionality* 1983, 29. As Searle uses "Intentionality," the word refers to mental states which are "directed at . . . states of affairs in the world" (1). The term is not limited to mental states of intending to perform some act. Rather, it includes all mental states which are "directed at" social realities, including hopes and fears, beliefs and desires. Because Intentional states have their existence in the mind, their reality is purely mental. Intentional states are not "acts" because acts are things that we do. But Intentional states become Intentional acts when we enact them by bodily gestures or speech acts.

Chapter 1

The Harlowes Corrupted

From the first letter beginning the novel, our impression of the Harlowes is a bad one. Miss Howe describes them as truculent people who have already mistreated Lovelace and are now preparing to mistreat Clarissa, so from the outset one sees the Harlowes as the hateful family who have become "a byword for cruelty, gloomy hypocrisy, and greed," as Mark Kinkead-Weekes puts it (126). In contrast, our first impression of Lovelace is positive. He seems decent and magnanimous, since, as Miss Howe says, he had tried to avoid the duel with James, and, that attempt failing, nicked him only enough to cool his desire to fight, "helped him off with his coat and waistcoat, and bound up his arm, till the Surgeon could come" (I.2; 1.2). It is hard not to like Lovelace, and it seems appropriate to dislike the Harlowes for treating him "with high indignity" (I.3; 1.2) when he visits to express his concern about James's wound. One easily believes those eye witnesses who, Miss Howe reports, "blame your family for the treatment they gave him" (I.2; 1.1). Yet while everyone else blames her family, Clarissa, who has the most to blame them for, not only is reluctant to do so but vigorously defends them. Miss Howe calls their behavior "a point you will not permit me to expatiate upon" (I.4; 1.3). One can understand Clarissa's reluctance to accuse the Harlowes, which is easily explained by her experience and her temperament: knowing that they have always loved her, she expects to be again beloved when calm returns, and her charitable nature always makes her more forgiving than accusatory. But her continuing defense of the Harlowes as their brutality increases puzzles readers and makes them curious whether she is disingenuous or simply obtuse. George Sherburn puts it well when he refers to "the need of frank criticism of her family by Clarissa" (954).

What is at issue in Sherburn's complaint is Clarissa's intellectual honesty, her ability to face and accept the truth. If she has reason to

respect her family, it must be because of what they were like before
the novel opens—or, more accurately, before Lovelace comes. And
that is information readers need, for it is the basis of Clarissa's behavior toward them throughout the novel. Fortunately, thanks to Clarissa's
thorough account in her early letters, one can reconstruct the Harlowes
as they had lived before Lovelace by reading the palimpsest of their
family conduct which remains in the text. One finds that the family's
treatment of Clarissa after Lovelace arrives is highly untypical of
Harlowe Place as it had once functioned; behind its current condition
of increasing violence, one can find evidence of its earlier orderly and
well-integrated familial operation. Now this account differs from common explanations of the family, in which their brutality is seen as
rooted in their nature as greedy, ambitious people who love riches
above everything.[1] That the Harlowes love money and are very ambitious is undeniable. Yet the common interpretation, although it contains truth, is only partly accurate, because the family's reaction to the
threat posed by Lovelace is nuanced and complex. The place to begin
understanding the Harlowes is, then, to examine the extensive textual
evidence which demonstrates that Clarissa's family are ordinary people
rather than villainous folk and that Lovelace's influence helps bring
about their corruption. Kinkead-Weekes is right to say "nowhere in
the eighteenth century is there such a penetrating analysis of the worst
tendencies of bourgeois ambition" as that found in *Clarissa,* though
he shrewdly recognizes that "both our understanding and their own
development are gradual processes" (126). It is that gradual process
whereby the Harlowes stop being Clarissa's friends and become fulmi-
nating enemies that needs to be better understood if one is to recognize the psychological complexity of the Harlowe Place action.

The textual evidence shows that, until Lovelace angers them, the
Harlowes are a successful economic and social unit who assign family
work according to a conventional eighteenth-century model, the men
investing their effort in entrepreneurial tasks while the women mainly
attend to domestic relationships. The Harlowes are prosperous. But,
more than that, they live together contentedly, they discuss and decide matters of mutual importance frankly and fairly, and, despite their
flaws, they are not only a happy, but a *loving* family, as Clarissa herself tells us. Their wealth and their expectations of continuing happiness are linked, for years ago the elder Harlowes decided to pool their
financial resources in order to "raise" the family to social eminence;
this datum has always been extrapolated to produce a "money-grub-

bing" caricature which radically falsifies the real human complexity of the action in Harlowe Place. Contrary to the presumption that the Harlowes are so obsessed with desire to "break into the peerage" that they concentrate their wealth on young James to prevent "the dispersal of their fortune among their children" (Kinkead-Weekes 127), one knows from Clarissa's report that her uncles "extended" the plan of raising the family "to each of us three children; urging, that as they themselves intended not to marry, we each of us might be so portioned . . . as that our posterity, if not ourselves, might make a first figure in the country" (I.73; 1.53–4). Uncle Antony for example, "thought there was wealth enough in their own family to build up three considerable ones." And when Uncle Harlowe too endorses the decision to bankroll the Clarissa/Lovelace alliance, "Especially as so much could be done for Miss Bella and for my brother, too, by my Father" (I.78; 1.57), one realizes that their two views are complementary, Antony's design to triple the chance of "raising" the family being balanced by Uncle Harlowe's stress on the need of fair and equitable distribution of Harlowe wealth. James, Antony and John Harlowe are architects, "investors" in the future who are setting the foundation of an edifice that can only be finished if it is competently begun. To reduce that vision to "bourgeois ambition" is to condemn or trivialize an activity that in itself is not heinous or contemptible. As Uncle Antony tells Clarissa in a long letter (I.216–225; 1.159–66), the family goal requires cooperation and sacrifice by all, and he offers himself and his brother John, both remaining bachelors to benefit James's children, as role models (I.224; 1.165) of family self-sacrifice.

Miss Howe, who never liked the Harlowes, despises the vision that warms the hearts of the older generation. She reduces them all to grumbling malcontents driven by insatiable greed:

> Is true happiness any part of your family view? So far from it, that none of your family but yourself could be happy were they not rich. So let them fret on, grumble and grudge, and accumulate; and wondering what ails them that they have not happiness when they have riches, think the cause is want of more. . . . (I.56; 1.41–2)

But Clarissa dislikes the rhetoric of belittlement that Miss Howe turns against the Harlowes ("you have so very strong a manner of expression where you take a distaste" (I.180; 1.132)) because she knows hers is a loving family despite their wealth and ambition. Clarissa's defense of the people she knows best carries with it the authority of her personal experience, which ought to deserve our investigative respect, particularly since Miss Howe is often provoked into overstatement.

Sane people live by amalgamating complementary values, not by focusing monomaniacally on any one value, and in this respect the Harlowes are sane. That they value other things than wealth is clear from their response to Lovelace's putative courtships of Arabella and Clarissa. If money were their single value and the daughters mere chattel to be traded for wealth, one of the girls would have to wed Lovelace, for, not only is he of noble family, he has two thousand pounds a year, he is the "presumptive heir" of Lord M's "large Estate," and he has "great expectations" (I.6; 1.5) from his aunts. If the older, plainer and nastier sister, Arabella, refused him, her family, were they greedy hypocrites, would make her marry him. Yet when she does refuse him they do not object. When he is reintroduced, this time as a suitor to Clarissa, the Harlowes deliberate rather than rejoice that they have a second chance to marry Lovelace's fortune. Aunt Hervey thinks Clarissa and he will make the "finest couple in England," Mrs. Harlowe worries about Lovelace's "reputed faulty morals," but Uncle John believes that Clarissa would reform him "if any woman in the world could" (I.13; 1.9). When one considers the three domains in which human desires are most often fulfilled—money, personal excellence and power—one sees that the Harlowes are weighing Lovelace in all three respects in order to reach a balanced judgment. His title and his wealth matter to them, of course, but they also show concern about his personal qualities, his "reputed faulty morals." They also understand that a woman should have the power to pick her husband, or at least to reject unwelcome suitors. Like his wife, Mr. Harlowe is more concerned about Lovelace's personal conduct than his wealth, but he is most concerned about James's hatred of him, because, as the father, it is his responsibility "to prevent all occasions of disunion and animosity in his family" (I.14; 1.10). Before Lovelace arrives, the family attend to many things, including peace and happiness.

The Harlowes' essential sanity is conspicuously evident when we compare them with Roger Solmes. Solmes inherited the fortune that he did not deserve and will not share; he "knows nothing but the value of Estates, and how to improve them, and what belongs to Land-jobbing and Husbandry" (I.44; 1.33). The Harlowes do not focus their efforts exclusively on accumulation of wealth for its own sake. The three brothers inherited their father's financial talent (the estate he wills to Clarissa is "principally of my own raising"): one assumes that John's "new-found mines" were "found" by diligent search, Antony's "East-India traffick, and successful voyages" are evidence of his financial competence, and, although Clarissa's father raised his capital through marriage ("the very large portion" his wife brought) and subsequent inheritance (the deaths of "several" of her "relations" (I.28; 1.21)), he probably enhanced his wealth by sound capital investment, until gout took "from the most active of minds . . . all power of activity . . . his extra-ordinary prosperity adding to his impatiency" (I.32; 1.23). The Harlowe males are clearly interested in making money, and in that respect they share much with Solmes as entrepreneurs, but the difference is that they do not moneygrub to the exclusion of everything else, for their affections are settled upon people. They are not miserly accumulators, but to the contrary have built an elegant dwelling with private rooms and personal libraries for Arabella and Clarissa, knowing that money is valuable for what it can buy. They are looking ahead to the social opportunities that wealth can make possible. With the important exception of young James, they have more generous family instincts than Solmes, who got his inheritance at the expense of poorer relatives ("immense riches . . . left by one niggard to another, in injury to the next heir" (I.81; 1.59)). Were the Harlowes greedy, why did they not embrace Solmes's initial request to become Clarissa's suitor? Yet Solmes's "application has not met with the attention of one single soul" (I.33; 1.25). Though Miss Howe says that they are "too rich to be happy" (I.56; 1.41), it is only after the Harlowe family have been infuriated by Lovelace that they begin thinking of Solmes as a husband for Clarissa.

This is not to say that the older Harlowes' entrepreneurial energies have had wholly good effects. Their wealth has had the unintended result of deflating the younger generation's worth by making them beneficiaries, not contributors. When Mr. Harlowe's children are referred to as worthy and hopeful young people, one senses that money has become a yardstick to measure other values. What makes them worthy? Why are they hopeful? Because, at some time in the future, they stand to inherit the "worth" that older Harlowes have accumulated and will bestow upon them. James and Arabella are covertly resentful about their less than essential place in Harlowe Place. Indeed, one can guess that James's wish to inherit the entire family fortune is motivated by his personal insecurity—his need to compensate for the sense of being "worth" little by acquiring all the "worth" the Harlowes have accumulated ("Nothing less would satisfy his ambition" (I.73; 1.54), Clarissa says). Clearly, James's arrogance and ill-nature derive from his having little to do except to inherit the Harlowe fortune and try to rule the family's decisions. Likewise, Arabella's bitterness, her ineffectuality and above all her jealousy of Clarissa suggest that she, too, is not satisfied by her position in Harlowe Place. James and Arabella have suffered from the family's overvaluation of wealth, for their character defects are caused and would only be tolerated by people who are accumulating money with the single purpose of enriching their children. Clarissa's happier attitude is the fruit of her concern about other people and her desire to distribute some of the Harlowes' wealth to the neighborhood poor; she values money because it can alleviate the distresses of those who lack it, rather than for its specious benefit of raising the self-importance of those who already have enough.

In addition to leaving James and Arabella with no work to do, the family's entrepreneurial energies have had another, even more dangerous, ill-effect: love and wealth are so intertwined in the Harlowes' real scheme of values as in practice to have become interchangeable. Love and wealth are psychologically equivalent to them. Grandfather Harlowe's Will is crucial in revealing this defect, for it activates the Harlowes' incipient anxieties about being adequately loved. When her grandfather willed Clarissa his estate, "No-body indeed was pleased," she says, because "altho' every-one loved me, yet being the youngest child, Father, Uncles, Brother, Sister, all thought themselves postponed" (I.74; 1.54). In willing her an estate, her grandfather ignores the conventions of patriarchal inheritance, which understandably dismays his sons because it changes the rules he raised them to observe. Yet more is being destabilized than inheritance procedures, for the family understand his bequest as the deliberately intended symbol of his personal love for Clarissa—his Will explicitly says so. That is what most angers the Harlowes; the old man makes it transparently clear that money and love are equivalent. Grandfather's Will has intermingled financial generosity and personal affection; one can infer that, after he retired from business, his attention shifted from money towards people, because Clarissa (the "precious child" whose "kind and tender regards" (I.29; 1.21) taught him to value personal affection) is given love by being given an estate.

The problem is that by giving wealth as a token of affection Grandfather Harlowe undermines the hierarchical ground upon which

Harlowe Place stands. His incoherent Will instructs his sons to obey patriarchal convention by obeying the father's will, at the same time that he violates the rules for inheritance of property with the set purpose of turning his wealth into a token of love. Grandfather Harlowe employs the vocabulary of compulsion when he commands his sons not to "impugn or contest" his Will. But then he shifts into a vocabulary of affection when he calls Clarissa "the delight of my Old age," reordering Harlowe values by giving his estate in exchange for her "amiable duty and kind and tender regards" (I.29; 1.21). The Harlowes' reaction to grandfather's Will is the key to understanding that they are suffering a love deficit, as one can put it—an affectional deficiency which has, for one thing, soured the natures of James and Arabella and made them envy Clarissa for being loved more deeply than they.

Once one realizes that wealth and love are interchangeable in Harlowe Place, one can perceive why the family are concerned about estates, whether it be Solmes's or Clarissa's, because the cardinal issue is not the property itself (wealth), but Clarissa (love). Clearly, the Harlowes are ambitious and acquisitive in their very bone-marrow, but they are more than that. They are Clarissa's loving family, and that truth is important if we are to understand the complexity of their motivations. Love, angry love reflecting the Harlowes' disturbed affections for Clarissa rather than simply their hunger for Solmes's estate, will be at stake once Lovelace's threat amplifies the problem of personal worth that grandfather's Will so powerfully brings to light.

Nevertheless, despite this evidence of incipient pathology, the Harlowes would not have become "a byword for cruelty, gloomy hypocrisy, and greed" (Kinkead-Weekes 126) without the malignant influence of Lovelace, whose intention we do not know because we have yet to meet him directly. One has to rely upon Clarissa for information about Lovelace, but she is wholly in error because he lies to her, and Richardson (for the moment) allows those lies to go unnoticed. Lovelace's effect on the Harlowes can be expressed by the metaphor of the parasite. A parasite works by introducing into an operating system an unobserved, apparently insignificant alteration which, without seeming to change that system, permits the invading parasite to prosper by feeding on its host. Michel Serres's extended example of how the social parasite operates is Tartuffe's corrupting the host family who unwittingly contribute to their own corruption; convinced that Tartuffe truly is what he seems to be, they are wholly controlled by the intrusive parasite who governs them. Like Tartuffe, Lovelace's intention in Harlowe Place is to play the role that Serres calls the "thermal exciter": "The flows accelerate; the ganglia swell; the defensive system is mobilized; the fever goes up" (190, 196). Lovelace infects the Harlowes by making them feverish, mobilizing their "defensive system," though he uses anger, not admiration, to do it. Whether in his mocking courtship of Arabella, his duel with James or his confrontation with the older Harlowe males, Lovelace follows the same procedure of making his victims angry so that they appear to be the aggressors, their subsequent reactions overshadowing his deliberate provocations.

The evidence that Lovelace manipulates the social situation in Harlowe Place in order to produce the duel and the altercation that follows is seen in Clarissa's earliest letters, although one has to interpret them with more understanding than she is capable of. Blinded by Lovelace's deceptions, she informs Miss Howe that he and the Harlowes were about equally to blame for their falling out. Actually, her family understand full well that Lovelace was at fault, although they would be hard pressed to explain exactly how he managed to move them so quickly into so towering a frenzy. But Clarissa, separated from them by the very rage that Lovelace has generated in them, no longer sees from the same point of view as they. She considers that some of James's affronts to Lovelace were "too flagrant to be excused" (I.22; 1.16), she learns "from Mr. Symmes's Brother, that he [Lovelace] was really insulted into the act of drawing his sword" (I.27; 1.20), and, since she trusts her own observations and the testimony of reliable witnesses, she concludes that her relatives caused Lovelace's outrage and hatred against them. And readers—presuming that Clarissa's narrative is trustworthy because she is truthful—divide the blame, as she does, and suppose the Harlowes and Lovelace equally at fault.

The fact is, however, that Clarissa's little history of the events leading up to the duel is not reliable, for it rests upon the foundation of lies which Lovelace has manufactured to mislead her, her family and their community about the essential truths of their situation. It is he—not chance, not accident—who brings about the swordfight with James. It is he who deliberately and with studied purpose manufactures the subsequent altercation with the older Harlowe males—playing the victim to prove them tyrants who insult their betters and interrupt the course of his faithful love for the woman of whom their entire vile family are unworthy. Through such poseur's pretenses as these, Lovelace is making the Harlowes dance like puppets "upon my own wires" (I.200;1.147), as he tells Belford, once the reader at last gains belated access to their correspondence. And Clarissa is one of those puppets. For when the poor woman informs Miss Howe that she "will recite facts only" (I.6;1.4), the "facts" she recounts—not all of them to be sure, but enough to falsify the rest—have already been distorted by Lovelace. In effect, she acts as Lovelace's scribe, narrating the radically corrupted version of public events which he himself has orchestrated and authorized.

Lovelace's pretended courtship of Arabella is the first of the carefully contrived pretenses that turn Clarissa's relatives from friends into implacable enemies. The perceptive reader can observe in his mockcourtship of her older sister the first sign of the bottomless insincerity which Lovelace skillfully conceals behind his semblance of openness, candor and concern for others. His make-believe courtship is initiated by Uncle Antony's mistake in supposing Arabella the intended bride, rather than her younger sister, an error that Lovelace deftly shapes into the opportunity to disappoint and humiliate Arabella. When marriage negotiations have been opened by Uncle Antony and Lord M (Mr. and Mrs. Harlowe "not forbidding" (I.6; 1.4)), Lovelace is introduced to Arabella and his pretended courtship begins. If one recollects how people normally correct social errors, one sees that courtship addressed to the wrong sister would be unlikely to occur. One would expect a normal suitor, unless too embarrassed to do so, to inform Uncle Antony that he had wanted Clarissa, request the substitution, and stop his visits until that correction is made. The evidence that Lovelace is radically insincere in his pretended courtship of the older sister—and that this insincerity is malevolent rather than thoughtless—lies in the fact that his mock courtship insults and humiliates Arabella into turning against Clarissa; thus, Lovelace adroitly transforms her disappointed sister into an ardent enemy.

Clarissa's narrative of the courtship of Arabella is focused on her sister's foolish vanity rather than on Lovelace's deceit, which she has no reason to suspect. In design, her narrative is a simple moral exemplum that begins with Arabella's visit to the Dairy-house to brag and preen because Lovelace has preferred her over Clarissa ("stepping to the glass, she complimented herself" (I.7; 1.5)). The moralistic narrator recognizes that Arabella's vanity is the pride that cometh before an inevitable fall. And because she is making a familiar and important moral point, she focuses on Arabella's folly rather than on Lovelace's deception, though she does observe his manipulations: "One would be tempted to think by the issue, that Mr. Lovelace was ungenerous enough to seek the occasion" for Arabella's irritation "and to improve it" (I.10; 1.7). To the Clarissa who narrates this moral exemplum, what happens to Arabella seems a painful way for her sister to learn the hard but useful lesson that vanity will harm a woman. That being the center of her attention, Clarissa overlooks what Lovelace did to Arabella, which is why readers tend not quite to assimilate the genuinely contemptible nature of his conduct. The parasite has invisibly contaminated the accuracy of Clarissa's account. To the degree that one can grasp Lovelace's falsehood, one excuses it because Arabella's bad temper ("my poor Sister is not naturally good-humoured" (I.10; 1.7)) is presented as a fault that justifies the disappointment he makes her suffer. Moreover, readers share Clarissa's complacency—the complacency of knowing she is the better match for Lovelace, which makes her ignore the insult to Arabella because of its implied compliment to her.

Lovelace's manipulation of her is so smoothly conducted that Arabella never does figure out how he managed to get her to "such a pitch of displeasure" (I.10; 1.7) that she rejects his proposal twice. As Clarissa presents the scene, Lovelace uses Arabella's outraged emotion to elicit her second refusal: he

> re-urged his question, as expecting a definitive answer, without waiting for the return of her temper, or endeavouring to mollify her; so that she was under a necessity of persisting in her denial: Yet gave him reason to think she did not dislike his address, only the *manner* of it, . . . (I.10–11; 1.7–8)

Because Clarissa describes Lovelace's "thermal exciter" effects so accurately, she obviously grasps them. But understanding the significance of what she grasps is quite another thing, and more than she can do. Absorbed by her sister's vanity, she lacks any reason to think Lovelace insincere, so she does not examine what she clearly apprehends. But she knows that he has not genuinely proposed, because for a marriage proposal to occur the woman must plausibly be able to accept the offer. If circumstances are such that Arabella cannot accept, the words themselves are not enough. Clarissa realizes that Lovelace has not really proposed, because nobody with his social penetration would keep silent during many visits when "opportunity was given him for it" (I.8; 1.5) only to make a marriage proposal when he knows Arabella cannot accept it. Nevertheless, the question "What is Lovelace doing?" never occurs to Clarissa because she has already presumed that Lovelace wishes to correct Uncle Antony's error. In other words, she has assumed that Lovelace, though he surely is not cooperating with Arabella, *is* tacitly cooperating with *her*.

Lovelace's narrative of his actions confirms the suspicion that he misleads and humiliates Arabella and deceives her family with the intention of elevating himself. In his earliest letter to Belford, he says, with tongue in cheek, "much difficulty had I, so fond and so forward my Lady! to get off without forfeiting All" (I.197; 1.145) with her family. By stressing "difficulty," he highlights for Belford's admiration the boldness required to pretend courtship while nevertheless ensuring that the "fond and forward" Arabella will refuse him. But the deeper motive for his courtship is the wish to provoke her anxiety and disappointment. He enjoys monitoring her discomfort, observing her as irritation rises along with determination to force him to make his proposal. The hopes he raises in order to disappoint are not limited to her expectation of having him for her husband. He wants Arabella to be humiliated by seeing that his bashful reserve, his politeness and deference, are deliberate mockery. He wants her to feel the contempt implied by his parody of respect. What makes Arabella an especially effective carrier of Lovelace's parasitic effect, however, is the constraint of silence which he forces upon her. She is too embarrassed to confess that she still desires him as her husband, so she pretends indifference, and by doing so finds herself cooperating in her own humiliation. Lovelace has created a truthful falsehood (she refused him), one so expertly tailored to fit her vanity that she cannot dispute it. The parasite stays invisible by silencing his hosts, robbing them of both speech and honesty.

When Lovelace returns to court the younger sister, Clarissa once again observes the evidence of fraudulence but is unable to unmask the fraud itself because she lacks the necessary context to interpret that evidence. After he attempts but fails to win her heart directly, Lovelace attempts to form an attachment with Clarissa by arguing with her brother and sister, hoping she will either thank him for enduring their contempt or request that he be patient with them. Realizing that either course would lay her under some obligation, Clarissa rejects both, so that Lovelace's indirect effort to win her fails. In the meantime, however, she notices an important clue to his deceit: "one might have expected from a man of his politeness, and from his pretensions, you know [coming as her suitor], that he would have been willing to *try*" (I.24; 1.17) not to quarrel with her siblings. Clearly, she sees the absence of "fit" between what he does and what he pretends to be doing: he is not acting the way a sincere suitor ought to act.

Lovelace has to invent the duel with James because Clarissa and her family fail to encourage visits and he loses his socially plausible reason for continuing them. Like the mock courtship of Arabella, the duel hinges on the trick of making something happen and then making the opposite seem to have happened: James seems the aggressor when he draws his sword and attacks while Lovelace is trying to conciliate him, as Arabella seems to have refused him when he proposed. In these exchanges Lovelace demonstrates his superb strategic patience, for he waits until disabling anger has overwhelmed his adversaries and then reverses their emotions against them. In both cases Lovelace robs his victim of self-esteem, humiliating Arabella by pretending humble admiration and emasculating James by taking away his sword.

Lovelace is the director of and the lead actor in the duel, which is a carefully scripted drama intended to persuade everyone that he and Clarissa are in love; he invents the duel because she is *not* in love with him and therefore must be made to *seem* so. Lovelace's procedure is first to taunt James to raise his anger, and then to select a time and location that make James appear the aggressor and himself the victim. The family's doorway is a good place to push past James as he defends his home (making him chafe "like a hunted boar at bay" (I.25; 1.18)), but it is not a proper place for the duel, since Lovelace would seem the aggressor while James would seem to be rightly defending his sister and his turf. But at Mr. Symmes's, James will seem the aggressor, Lovelace the designated victim who "could not avoid drawing his Sword" (I.2; 1.1). To the delight of the onlookers who dislike James for his arrogance and temper, Lovelace provokes the duel without seeming to do so; more than that, he orchestrates the duel in such a way that it seems to demonstrate his affection towards Clarissa. An exultant Miss Howe reports the story that everybody is listening to and repeating throughout the community:

> This, I am told, was what Mr. Lovelace said upon it; retreating as he spoke: "Have a care, Mr. Harlowe—Your violence puts you out of your defence. You give me too much advantage. For your Sister's sake I will pass by every thing:— if—"
>
> But this the more provoked his rashness, to lay himself open to the advantage of his adversary,—Who, after a slight wound given him in the arm, took away his Sword. (I.2; 1.1)

Miss Howe reports not only the event but also its significance as spontaneous, and apparently reliable, evidence of Lovelace's love for James's sister. Lovelace is forgiven for taunting his victim because the community know James's vile temper and enjoy watching him receive the humiliation he deserves.

The duel is a brilliant strategic device on Lovelace's part, for it raises James's personal hate into a whole family's enmity. Arabella's humiliation had been private, but James is embarrassed by a public demonstration of his fatuous ineptness, and his wound is suffered by all the Harlowe males. The shock wave of the duel divides the family into those who protect Harlowe Place and those who are perceived as threatening its safety, namely, the Clarissa desired by their enemy; Lovelace's "for your sister's sake I will pass by everything" has the effect of a call to arms. The deeper wound suffered by the Harlowe males, sexual humiliation, is clear to Clarissa. For when Miss Howe says that blusterers like James "are generally cravens among men" (II.15; 1.248) she chastens her for making "so light" both of James's brush with death and of his loss of honor: "his credit in the eye of the mischievous sex has received a still deeper wound than he *personally* sustained" (II.59–60; 1.281). Although Clarissa is loyal, the Harlowes have been made too exasperated to believe that she is entirely loyal. When Uncle Antony denounces "the crime which it would be in [her] to encourage a man who is to wade into her favour . . . thro' the blood of her Brother" (I.3; 1.2), we recognize the thinly veiled threat that "encouraging" Lovelace will not be tolerated.

As the next step in his campaign, Lovelace uses his "thermal exciter" effect upon Clarissa's father and uncles, orchestrating the altercation at Harlowe Place in which no sword draws blood because "a door [is] held fast locked between" the combatants. This altercation is the last element in Lovelace's plan to split Clarissa from her family in order to take possession of her for himself. Understanding how indignant the Harlowe males have been rendered by the duel, he makes them even more furious by sending messengers to inquire about James's arm. As always, his action is expertly timed so that the confrontation he orchestrates will have the meaning he intends. Once six messengers in three days have raised the temperature to fever pitch, Lovelace "thought fit on the fourth day to make in person the same inquiries" (I.26; 1.19). Clarissa, who cannot see the parasite whose effects she is describing, narrates the scene that Lovelace is conducting:

I fainted away with terror, seeing every one so violent, and hearing Mr. Lovelace swear that he would not depart till he had made my Uncles ask his pardon for the indignities he had received at their hands; a door being held fast locked between him and them. (I.26; 1.19)

Clarissa faints out of fear for her family's safety, and the same motive will later persuade her into correspondence with Lovelace. To complete the web of deceit which he has been weaving, Lovelace immediately grows calm and leaves in a parody of concern for her wellbeing: "when Mr. Lovelace was told how ill I was he departed" (I.26; 1.19).

Lovelace departs when and in the manner he does so that her family will take Clarissa's faint as evidence that she does love him despite her denials, and everyone will take his departure as obvious evidence of his affection. As it happens, everyone does. Clarissa believes the falsehood that Lovelace loves her, since he jeopardized his own life ("for your sister's sake I will pass by everything") instead of killing her brother. Her family believe that Lovelace loves her, for James is still alive because of his adversary's lenience. Moreover, they conclude that Clarissa must love Lovelace, because her faint followed by his departure seems to demonstrate their mutual love. Even the public are deceived, for they believe the Harlowes are to blame. Thus, when Miss Howe reports that the public "blame your family for the treatment they gave him," we cannot be startled, because they are the same eye witnesses who "say that Mr. Lovelace could not avoid drawing his sword" (I.2; 1.1). By activating the "thermal exciter" effect, the Lovelace parasite has corrupted that network of assumptions which the community relies upon to learn the truth by answering these questions: what happened? who was to blame?

Once Lovelace has driven them into tumults, the Harlowes are reduced to house imprisonment while their enemy constantly makes revenge threats. It is James who finds a way out of their crisis with the plan that Clarissa marry Solmes. The difficulties with this plan are that Clarissa will not want to, and the Harlowes do not habitually use force against their members. James overcomes these problems by a double effort: he convinces the Harlowe males that Solmes's estate is indispensable, and he generates suspicion against his sister.

James designs his strategy during the month from January 20, when Clarissa gets permission to visit with Miss Howe ("Every one thinks it best" (I.34; 1.25) so that Lovelace will not renew his visits to Harlowe Place), until February 20, when she is summoned back to stand trial for her disobedience to Mr. Harlowe's command not to "see" Lovelace. During that period, the weight of their dilemma makes the Harlowes deceive themselves: James persuades his father and uncles that if Clarissa marries Lovelace they will lose the daughter and her inherited estate, though if she marries Solmes they will retain her estate and eventually get Solmes's as well. Once they have accepted James's proposition, they use the subterranean equivalence of money and love which maintains inside Harlowe Place to further deceive themselves: they come to believe that marrying Clarissa to Solmes will enrich the family, protect Clarissa from Lovelace's desire to take her, and persuade him to leave them alone.

The Harlowes have already started to deceive themselves when they give Clarissa permission to visit Miss Howe. Permission to visit constitutes entrapment, for Clarissa cannot stop Lovelace from visiting Miss Howe's or fail to "see" him there. Since the Harlowes understand that, her father's order not to see him "on pain of [his] displeasure" (I.37; 1.27) is made in bad faith. It is not inevitable that Clarissa's seeing Lovelace will be taken as disobedience, but it becomes expedient to interpret it in that way after Solmes has been selected to be her husband. The family abruptly demand that Clarissa return home because they intend to accuse her of disobedience so that, in restitution, she will be likely to withdraw the objections to Solmes that they anticipate. Putting her in the wrong is the purpose of her trial, because the Harlowes want the moral high ground for themselves. When accused of undutiful conduct, she will more likely obey her father's next command to compensate for the trespass of "seeing" Lovelace.

If the Harlowes' first step towards corrupting the family is to charge Clarissa with disobedience in seeing Lovelace, the next step is to present Solmes as her suitor in a way that puts her in the wrong should she refuse him; with that intention, they revise family history and accuse Clarissa of having obstinately remained single by refusing her earlier suitors, though in truth one knows that she always had the freedom to accept or reject them. "I had interest enough to disengage myself from the addresses of those gentlemen [Mr. Symmes and Mr. Mullins], as I had (before [James] went to Scotland, and before Mr. Lovelace visited here) of Mr. Wyerley's" (I.25–6; 1.19). Their anxiety over Lovelace's threats of violence persuades the Harlowes that Clarissa's wish to choose her own husband is a luxury too dangerous for them to afford, and at that point Mr. Harlowe invents the story about the undutiful daughter who yet remains obstinately unmarried: "My Father, with a vehemence both of action and voice . . . told me, that I had met with too much indulgence in being allowed to refuse *this* gentleman, and the *other* gentleman; and it was now *his* turn to be obeyed" (I.41; 1.30). By accusing her of obstinacy in refusing earlier suitors, her father encourages Clarissa to cooperate with them and accept their dictate rather than lose their affection: agreeing to marry Solmes will again make her "*the pride of their hearts*" (I.43; 1.31).

The Harlowes' self-deception infects their business sense as well, for, disoriented by Lovelace's threats, they abandon their good judgment and think Solmes's "*noble Settlements*" (I.80; 1.59) are to their advantage. Clarissa's better intelligence tells her that Solmes is "smiling no doubt to himself at a hope so remote" as the Harlowes' hope of gaining his estate; on the contrary, he "doubts not" that he will acquire the estate she is "envied for" (I.81; 1.60). Thus the putatively avaricious Harlowes cast dull eyes upon Lovelace's large annual income and eventual fortune and break all rules of family conduct in exchange for the precarious hope of getting Solmes's estate, disregarding the real likelihood of forfeiting Clarissa's.

The Harlowes now stand on the brink of a precipitous slide into unprecedented brutality towards Clarissa. Why do her family violate all rules of familial justice and forfeit their financial judgments to brutalize the member they all love best? A partial explanation is given by John Bowlby, who describes the aggressive acts by which families protect ties of affection. Such acts take two forms: attacks on intruders to drive them off, and punishment of offending members to renew their allegiance. "Any attempt by a third party to separate" individuals tied together by affective bonds "is strenuously resisted," and "much aggressive behavior of a puzzling and pathological kind" makes sense once its purpose of defending love-ties is understood (1979, 69). Thus the Harlowes, seeing that Lovelace will not go away, threaten Clarissa instead.

What triggers the Harlowes' turn to brutality is Clarissa's refusal to cooperate with them, which evokes a pathological form of self-defensive activity that René Girard calls the Scapegoat. Persecution narratives, historical texts which narrate campaigns of social violence from the viewpoint of the persecutors, always assume that the victims are guilty. Such narratives, Girard has found, always describe some historical communal crisis reflected in the collapse of rules of conduct, the loss of group stability, and the disappearance of the differences in hierarchical status and roles that typify well-ordered communities. Once a breakdown occurs, healthier exchanges are replaced by the "reciprocity of negative exchanges" such as insults, blows and revenge. Because these "conflictual and solipsistic" reactions worsen the crisis, people come to feel helpless and "disconcerted by the immensity of the disaster" (1986, 13–4). The corruption of the Harlowes is a scapegoat reaction. Mr. Harlowe surrenders paternal authority; James assumes authority not his own. Arabella erupts in what, to Clarissa, is masculine rage and violence. Mrs. Harlowe is forced to implement policy which she knows to be tyrannical. Clarissa's faithful servant, Hannah, is replaced by the arrogant, presuming, dishonest maid Betty. Clarissa is imprisoned in her home, denied permission to attend church, forbidden even to have pen and ink. Above all, she loses not just the freedom to choose her husband, but the power to reject a distasteful suitor.

Persecution narratives have three characteristics, all of which can be seen in operation inside Harlowe Place in reaction to the Lovelace threat. One characteristic is that persecution narratives always describe violence directed at those members of a society "whom it is most criminal to attack," especially kings or fathers as "symbols of supreme authority," though the violence may also be focused on "the weakest and most defenseless" members (1986, 15). It is irrelevant whether the violence has its source outside or inside the society, since in either case the defenders of the threatened group locate and expel those few persons or the one individual whom they believe "extremely harmful to the whole" of the clan (15). The "hierarchical differences" stabilizing the foundations of communal order are always the target of the attack (Girard 1986, 15). Lovelace attacks Mr. Harlowe, who is "held by force from going to him with his sword in his hand" (I.26; 1.19), when he comes to Harlowe Place pretending solicitude for James's wounded arm; Lovelace attacks the most defenseless member of the family when he promises to take her despite their opposition, and the Harlowes understand him, even though Clarissa herself remains oblivious that his courtship is just a disguise for his violence.

A second characteristic of persecution narratives, according to Girard, is that its victims are accused of abominations such as incest, bestiality, sacrilege and participation in Satanic rites. The usefulness of these charges is that the anxieties of the group are shifted onto the individuals who are identified as unfaithful to the community's values and a menace to its safety. Incest is not charged against Clarissa, yet the incest motif is present when James courts her on behalf of Solmes. Disobedience to her father's will resembles religious profanation because her family know she accepts obedience as her religious duty, so they interpret her correspondence with Lovelace as her collusion with the Satanic intruder. Her clandestine letters to him strike her family as the continuation of the disloyal spirit they first saw when she inherited her grandfather's estate.

The third characteristic of persecution narratives, the one most critical for Harlowe Place, is that victims of persecution are always chosen for sacrifice because they are marked by some abnormal, marginal status: Clarissa's extraordinary prudence and the family's pride in her reputation mark her. Since the average sets the norm, divergence from "normal social status of whatever kind" (18) increases one's chance of being the victim. If "Every eye . . . is upon [Clarissa] with the expectation of an example" (I.4; 1.3), "every eye" will incline to think her guilty when the family needs a scapegoat. For as Girard notes, "crowds commonly turn on those who originally held exceptional power over them" (19); the girl who persuaded tightfisted uncles to provide money for her charities ("This girl by her charities will bring down a blessing upon us all" (VIII.213; 4.503), says Uncle Antony) had "exceptional power" over them, and thus one can expect that her elders would "turn on" her when threatened. Arabella unleashes her long pent up fury against the "Specious little witch" whose "cunning *fetches*" and sly "*hook-in's*" made Clarissa the more popular daughter, "curling, like a serpent, about [her] Mamma" (I.294; 1.217) to make the adults love her. James is outraged by her "exceptional power" over their elders, he having been "*out-grandfather'd*" (I.79; 1.58) when Clarissa inherited the estate he himself desires. And the older Harlowes are angry because of the way Clarissa lords it over the rest of the family, even while she languishes in solitary confinement; on March 27, for example, her heart "disturbed at every foot I hear stir" downstairs, where the Harlowes engage in "close debate" to decide her fate, Clarissa is in effect banished from the family, for she can follow the debate only as Maid Betty reports it, superciliously, to "teaze and vex" her:

> Then the insolence—the confidence . . . that she, who was so justly in disgrace for downright rebellion, should pretend to prescribe to the whole family!—should name a Husband for her elder Sister! What a triumph would her obstinacy go away with, to delegate her commands, not as from a Prison, as she called it, but as from her Throne, to her Elders and Betters; and to her Father and Mother too! (II.97; 1.309)

Girard's description of the scapegoat dynamic that corrupts the family also applies to the motives that cause their violence. Persecutors develop an "appetite for violence" that is satisfied only by a cleansing sacrifice. After identifying the "accessible cause" of the community's distress, they satisfy their "dream of purging the community" of those "traitors who undermine" it (16). Though it is Lovelace who has raised the threat of disorder, the Harlowes are helpless against him. Clarissa, however, is within their power, so they sacrifice her, not only to protect against his threats but to satisfy their appetite for revenge. One can recognize a desire for revenge in Arabella's question, "Will not t'other man [Lovelace] flame out, and roar most horribly, upon the snatching from his paws a prey he thought himself sure of?" (I.297; 1.219).

Whenever a community sacrifices a scapegoat to shield itself from a threat, its motive is always to limit violence as much as is possible but "to turn to it, if necessary, as a last resort to avoid an even greater violence" (Girard 1986, 113). The Harlowe family's debate about granting Clarissa permission to visit Miss Howe clearly is a first step towards the acceptance of "limiting" violence against Clarissa; they must decide one way or the other, but both decisions are wrong because neither one will remove the threat. This stalemate is crucial, Girard observes, since there is always an impasse and Caiaphas (to whom it is "expedient that one man should die for the people" (John 18:14)) is called upon to break it (112-13). James Harlowe enacts the role of Caiaphas the tie-breaker who cuts the knot and presents a plan of action.

Still, while one can understand why her family use violence against Clarissa, how can they not see that they are sacrificing her? Why do they not understand what is evident to all readers? The reason is that, like all persecutors, they believe they are innocent victims who are neutralizing the guilty party, and the story they tell cannot tell them otherwise. If one had a Harlowe narrative in which they explain their conduct to themselves, that story would be a true persecution narrative because it would show what occurred from the distinctive viewpoint of the persecutors, who always believe that their victims are guilty. They would not perceive the scapegoat which is "the *hidden* structural principle" (Girard 119, my italics) behind any persecution narrative.[2] But since they have Clarissa's narrative, readers see what her family cannot. Readers can easily see that she is being persecuted, for her innocent-victim point of view belies the self-justifications found in the Harlowes' letters. While Clarissa cannot comprehend that Lovelace purposely angered them to mobilize their opposition against her, she sees that the Harlowes are her persecutors. She also knows that their anger is somehow connected with their love.

Notes

1 Since the aim of Chapter 1 is to demonstrate that conventional interpretations of the Harlowes are insufficiently nuanced, this footnote documents representative readings which have appeared in recent decades.

Ian Watt, (*The Rise of the Novel* 1957): "the combination of family authority with the attitude of economic individualism not only denies Clarissa any freedom of choice, but even leads her family to treat her with calculated cruelty" (223).

Margaret Anne Doody (*A Natural Passion* 1974): "The domestic atmosphere of the Harlowe family is evil, and Richardson knows it is. The incapacity of this money-grubbing family to love . . ." (178–9).

Christina Marsden Gillis (*The Paradox of Privacy* 1983): "The plan to marry off Clarissa to the 'odious Solmes' derives, then, from a net of negative motives: jealousy, hatred, avarice" (26).

Angus Wilson ("Clarissa," in *Samuel Richardson*, ed. Myer, 1986): The Harlowes "are superbly portrayed as a hardhearted, avaricious, city merchant family that has made its pile and established itself at Harlowe Place" [which, says Lovelace,] "is sprung up from a dunghill" (45).

Jocelyn Harris (*Samuel Richardson* 1987): "Traditional emblems of avarice, they 'fret on, grumble and grudge . . . .' They hate Clarissa's moderation and generosity" (53).

John Allen Stevenson ("The Courtship of the Family," *ELH* 48:4 (1981), 757–77), who knows better than to believe that "The Harlowes are nasty because they are so greedy," believes that her relatives are using "what appears to be a property marriage to disguise their true aim . . . , to keep Clarissa for themselves." Marrying her to Solmes "offers no transition out of the family, but rather a kind of marriage into the family, a particularly literal form of endogamy which has, at times, stongly incestuous overtones" (757,760-1).

By contrast, Rita Goldberg (*Sex and Enlightenment* 1984) gets it right when she says "The senior Harlowes are characterized not so much by conscious hypocrisy, or even by greed, as by blindness [the Harlowe males] and passivity [Mrs. Harlowe and Aunt Hervey]" (71). Goldberg correctly rejects greed as their motive, and she accurately identifies "blindness" as the condition which permits Clarissa's family to turn her into their scapegoat.

2. Girard helps us to characterize *Clarissa* as a scapegoat novel when he says that "with respect to the scapegoat mechanism" all texts which contain it belong to either of these two categories: those in which "the mechanism is nowhere apparent," and those in which "this same mechanism is revealed. The innocence of the victim is proclaimed; the scapegoat is clearly seen as such but the persecutors . . . are no longer there to reveal for us the structural effect that the process exercises on their language, their vision and their behavior" (1997, 31). In fact, *Clarissa* is an amalgam of the two types, because Clarissa's Harlow Place narrative *reveals* the scapegoat mechanism *by throwing attention upon* "the language, vision and behavior" of her persecutors.

Chapter 2

The Contest of Passion and Prudence

One can best think of Clarissa's struggle with her family as the contest of their passion, which cripples their intelligence, and her prudence, which stiffens her to defend not simply her own genuine interests but those of her family as well. The Harlowes are such decent people in so many ways that nothing short of some emotional explosion could turn them into savage persecutors. And the most pitiful thing about their situation is that Lovelace has so completely falsified Clarissa that the harder she struggles to be absolutely truthful with them, the more outrageously dishonest she appears to be. While Lovelace waits patiently for them to do his work, the Harlowes tear Harlowe Place apart in self-defense.

Passion and Prudence

Lovelace's emotional destabilizing of the Harlowe family by wounding James, threatening his father and uncles and vowing to take Clarissa away from them is the cause of the family's upset. Yet since they are very unwilling to passively accept Lovelace's abuse, the Harlowes bestir themselves for counterattack in order to overcome the anguish their threatener has caused them and to recover the peaceful condition which the family formerly enjoyed. Such a counteroffensive hinges on their capacity not only to feel but to propagate and heighten self-defensive and family-defensive passions. In Thomas Aquinas's schema of human emotions—a schema that makes better sense than modern descriptions of the passions' purposes—there are two kinds of passions. There are those which seek good and flee evil directly (such as love and hatred, desire and aversion, joy and sadness), and there are other passions that pursue good and flee evil through indirection, thereby helping to achieve the aims of the first set. If one examines the Harlowes' situation, one sees that they are angry at Lovelace for insulting and humiliating them. But at the same time they fear him because they believe that he means those threats he constantly directs at them, James's bloody arm being a constant reminder of the reality of his violence. On the other hand, they hope to pay back insult for insult, especially by denying and frustrating Lovelace's wish to take Clarissa from them, which they mean to effect by marrying her to Solmes. Having observed one nobleman in action, they turn towards a bourgeois merchant, a member of their own social class, as Clarissa's husband. Aquinas calls the indirect "effectuating" exciters (including anger, fear and hope, which help achieve the aims of the direct passions like love and hatred) the "irascible" passions (IIaIIae, 23.1). It is precisely the irascible passions anger, fear and hope that stand firm in defense of Harlowe Place. In Clarissa's home, anger, fear and hope operate like white blood cells attacking Lovelace's infection, or like a defensive militia driving him away. She opposes those passions at her peril, since the wellbeing of the entire family is at stake. However, because the events which occur in Harlowe Place are narrated by Clarissa, readers have to make intelligible for themselves the excitements which transform the reasonable Harlowes into violently irrational persecutors.

As Clarissa tells Miss Howe in her first letter, she herself is being blamed for the "tumults" in her home, although she never did anything to cause them. The Harlowes see it differently, for they accept Lovelace's untruth that Clarissa is in love with him, and they suspect and fear that she really is the enemy inside the walls, her past good behavior notwithstanding. What passions are they feeling toward her? The Harlowes are angry with her because they *love* her. At the beginning of the contest between them, her family feel anxious because they value her love, feel slighted by her presumed disloyalty to them, and need her current allegiance. Thus, at the outset the family's passion is the anger of friends. Yet there is a problem, for people bound by affectional ties can become enemies when anger—which is meant to restore strained or ruptured relations—endures too long and carries the angry party across what Bowlby calls "the narrow boundary" between deterrence and revenge. When that occurs, a love that is occasionally laced with "hot displeasure" can turn into "a deep-running resentment" (1973, 249). Lovelace infects the Harlowes' love for Clarissa in this way, activating a vicious circle of "intense possessiveness, intense anxiety, and intense anger" (254); the family's affection gradually becomes resentment, and then turns into revenge because of what they see as her ungrateful behavior. It is not only that the Harlowes' upset is redirected from the Lovelace who cannot be controlled to the Clarissa who is in their power. It is that she herself becomes the center of their resentment when they begin to convince themselves that she has turned renegade.

The reason why the Harlowes become so angry with Clarissa is that she seems to be harming them *deliberately*; they believe that she is not acting through ignorance, for she knows the situation, nor through passion, because she resists them week by week with a sturdy conviction not based in transient emotion. She must, they infer, be deliberately insulting them. As Aquinas points out, we most quickly forgive people who harm us unknowingly, or those who offend us because they are temporarily upset. But it is difficult not to retaliate against those who, "in our opinion, have hurt us on purpose," for those who hurt us deliberately "seem to sin from contempt" of us (IaIIae, 47.2). That is the Harlowes' situation: the conviction that Clarissa is ungrateful provokes the vitriolic bitterness that increasingly overtakes her relatives.

Like her family, Clarissa is motivated by powerful fears and anxious hopes, but she is not driven out of her right mind as are her relatives. Clarissa is the only Harlowe who firmly holds her course and keeps her prior goals in sight regardless of the upset swirling around her. In fact, it is clear from the nature of the conflicts she faces that Clarissa was intended to be a novelistic dramatization of prudence, the Aristotelian character virtue that had been subsumed into Christian thought by Augustine and Aquinas and was still alive for moral reflection in Richardson's England. John Norris's *Treatise Concerning Christian Prudence* (1710) is a philosophical study that recapitulates Aristotle's and Aquinas's understanding; Norris knows the classical tradition and endorses it wholeheartedly, at a time when, as Alasdair MacIntyre informs us, the character virtue schema was starting to founder (229–33). Clarissa, in fact, dramatizes an understanding of prudence which is intelligible only in light of a conception of human character as based on prominent virtues (prudence, justice, temperance and fortitude) that are instilled by proper training and discipline. Clarissa, then, dramatizes an understanding of prudence that was disappearing, even as the word *prudence* was assuming a different meaning. Fielding's Lady Booby and Sheridan's Joseph Surface, satiric exemplars of prudence corrupted into Norris's "cunning," prepare the way for William Blake's

"rich, ugly old maid courted by incapacity," in which the cardinal virtue has degenerated to its demonic parody. Because Richardson's novel
harkens back to Aristotelian character virtues, readers need to recognize that in Clarissa prudence undergoes its ultimate challenge—to
make wise choices even when one's freedom of action is wholly constrained.

The centrality of the prudence theme is clear from the first letter,
where Miss Howe reminds Clarissa that "your present trial is but pro-
portioned to your prudence" (I.3; 1.2). And her mother begins persuading Clarissa to marry Solmes by reminding her that she is "a
dutiful, a prudent, and a *wise* child" (I.96; 1.70). Thus the women
who know Clarissa most intimately acknowledge and celebrate her
prudence, although they wholly disagree on whether marrying Solmes
really would constitute prudent action. Aquinas provides a definition
of prudence that well describes Clarissa's characteristic manner of
conducting herself throughout the novel. Like any virtue, prudence is
a habit of right action directed to the "doing [of] good deeds." It is
"essentially an intellectual virtue" because its essence is "right reason
about things to be done" (IaIIae, 58.3). Prudence is a necessary virtue
because to live well means to act well, or to deliberate upon one's life
and to make "right choices" based upon careful deliberations rather
than "merely from impulse or passion." Not that the passions are to
be choked into submission, however, because without them there would
be nothing for one to deliberate and make prudent choices *about*.
Prudence begins with taking counsel, "which belongs to discovery," in
order to arrive at a right judgment. When a right judgment has been
made, prudence commands the will to carry out the decision by using
the appropriate means, thus "applying to action the things counselled
and judged" (IIaIIae, 47.8). Though always "on the alert to do whatever has to be done," prudence is not hasty, for, as Aristotle advises
us, it is better to be "slow in taking counsel" but "quick in carrying out
the counsel taken" (IIaIIae, 47.9).

The prudence for which Clarissa has earned her reputation is her
ability to reason properly, to think carefully and to beware, as Milton's
Adam instructs Eve, "lest by some fair appeering good surpris'd" her
intellect should "dictate false" (*PL* IX, 354–5). Cicero says that the
"peculiar province" of prudence or wisdom is the effort to discover
the truth. In fact,

the more clearly anyone observes the most essential truth in any given case
and the more quickly and accurately he can see and explain the reasons for it,

the more understanding and wise [*prudentissimus et sapientissimus*] he is generally esteemed, and justly so. (I, v)

Clarissa tries to arrive at two "essential truths": to explain to her family why it is a mistake to force her to marry Solmes, and to come to an informed judgment about Lovelace's trustworthiness. Whenever we have access to Clarissa's mind, she is either giving her reasons for not marrying Solmes or weighing the evidence that can lead to sound reasons for marrying or not marrying Lovelace.

But a virtue can fulfil its meaning and purpose only within some practice. As Alasdair MacIntyre uses that term, a practice is any complex, cooperative enterprise (like research chemistry or professional skating) in which the enterprise itself can be improved through the efforts of its members, who strive to raise the "standards of excellence" which help to define that activity (187). A virtue is an acquired capability needed for the proper conduct of the practice that depends on it (191). And prudence is necessary in both of Clarissa's practices, family living and her friendship in virtue with Miss Howe. In her home, Clarissa reminds her relatives that they are obliged to treat her better if they would avoid the "distresses" caused by the "misconduct" of intemperate families (Ross 33). Her friendship with Miss Howe is complementary to her family practice—both its furtherance in herself and its extension to the community. "She was the nearest perfection of any creature I ever knew" (VIII.222; 4.510), Miss Howe says, and her approach to perfection was not accidental: her "*early* correspondence" with Dr. Lewen and other "learned Divines" (VIII.203; 4.495) was part of her training, as was the financial competence of holding "a reserve" of ready money "for unforeseen cases, and for accidental distresses" (VIII.212; 4.503) befalling the neighboring poor. But any practice, says MacIntyre, requires social cooperation for its successful conduct; thus when Clarissa sets herself the goal of living an exemplary human life, she asks Miss Howe's help, for self-flattery and self-justification lie in wait for the foolish person who does not seek the aid of others:

> I charge you (as I have often done) that if you observe any-thing in me so very faulty as would require from you to others in my behalf the palliation of friendly and partial Love, you acquaint me with it: For methinks I would so conduct myself as not to give reason even for an *adversary* to censure me: And how shall so weak and so young a creature avoid the censure of *such*, if my *friend* will not hold a looking-glass before me to let me see my imperfections? (I.65; 1.48)

In the "practice" of personal excellence, the cooperative effort of correcting one another's faults encourages self-knowledge and discourages the kind of complacency one sees in Arabella when she gazes in her mirror. Therefore, Clarissa asks Miss Howe to "hold a looking glass before me," the better, as Hamlet instructed the players, to show Virtue her own feature.

The Contest

When Clarissa begins her resistance against her family, she sees that she "*must* oppose" them and "must without delay *declare*" her opposition (I.83; 1.61), for not to declare herself would be taken as her tacit intent to comply. She knows that her family, having always found her compliant, expect her to obey them. But the gentlest spirits, she tells Miss Howe, are "most determined" when provoked because "their very deliberation," the deliberation which is at the core of prudence, "makes them the more immovable" (I.86; 1.63). Though the Harlowes think her proud and stubborn, she is being sensible; she is "immovable" because she knows what Cicero would call "the most essential truth" about Solmes as a potential husband—that he has none of the proper qualifications. The mismatch between them was obvious to the Harlowes earlier on, since none of them attended to Solmes's initial application, but now what is obvious has to be argued. Vexed, Clarissa asks Miss Howe, "when a point is clear and self-evident, how can one with patience think of entering into an argument or contention upon it?" (I.86; 1.63).

The contest between Clarissa and her family operates within the scapegoat mechanism that Lovelace has activated inside their home, and the three stages of the contest are controlled by him. In the first stage, the Harlowes try to gain Clarissa's consent without arousing the resistance they anticipate. Mrs. Harlowe's initial effort (seven conversations on March 3–4) having failed, James takes control, "by command of" (I.155; 1.114) his parents, and Mrs. Harlowe's tactfulness gives way to deliberate abuse and humiliation. During this mid-March stage, as James and Arabella insult her mercilessly, Clarissa writes letters appealing to her parents and uncles. By March 24th, the apparent arrogance of her opposition has so incensed her family that they abandon even the pretense that she is being treated reasonably. They increasingly adopt physical and psychological compulsion, indeed, outright and evident aggression. This final stage—during which the Harlowes' passions are continuously fired by the absent Lovelace who works them like puppets—lasts from March 26th until Clarissa's flight from Harlowe Place on April 10th.

Mrs. Harlowe, who is emotionally close to Clarissa and knows how to manage people tactfully, opens the first stage on March 3. Because opposition to her husband's wishes would tear the family apart, Mrs. Harlowe suppresses her own judgment and supports him. First she calms Clarissa. Then she assumes the position that her daughter's marriage to Solmes is a *fait accompli,* for if Clarissa does not cooperate, she misunderstands the role of women in their family: "You know, my dear, what I every day forego, and undergo, for the sake of peace. Your Papa is a very good man, and means well; but he will not be controuled, nor yet persuaded (I.96; 1.70). Hoping to limit Clarissa's pain and avoid the opposition that too much clarity might provoke, she does not directly state the purpose of their meeting. "I am glad," she says, that "you can guess at what I have to say to you" (I.95; 1.70); this is an indirect speech act which means, You are shrewd enough to see the inevitable outcome, so don't foolishly oppose your father's will. Mr. Harlowe is inflexibly determined, counter-arguments would be pointless, and Clarissa's swift compliance is best for everybody. The scapegoat is being asked to sacrifice herself, in order that her sacrificers need not shoulder the guilt of having done it.

Mrs. Harlowe's strategy is to insist upon what she carefully avoids saying outright—a strategy designed to deflect Clarissa's attention from the damage that marrying Solmes would cause her to the advantages that her compliance would provide the family. She "would not wilfully break that peace which costs [her] Mother so much to preserve" (I.96; 1.70), for instance; she would not upset the family by giving a wrong impression that she might refuse to marry Solmes. Such "would not's" offer Clarissa the opportunity to disavow her own intention to oppose the Harlowes' will, which, as the Harlowes realize perfectly well, Clarissa is likely to do; that is why they select Mrs. Harlowe to deal with her. So rather than insist on Clarissa's compliance, all that her mother asks is the "act of omission," i.e., not *stating,* not even *implying,* the adamant refusal her family fear. Mrs. Harlowe's politic approach includes the strategic conditional that she has been coached by other Harlowes to give: if Clarissa's heart truly were free, then obstinacy must be all that keeps her from wedding Solmes. When such indirection fails, Mrs. Harlowe uses a more direct approach, telling Clarissa that her mother's peace of mind, the Harlowes' satisfaction, and her own safety are adequate reasons why she must marry Solmes.

When Clarissa tries to give reasons why she should *not* have to marry Solmes, she discovers that reasons are not wanted, since hers will not be heard. Such behavior is uncharacteristic of the Harlowes because, until recently, the family council has been the forum in which family members meet and decide things rationally. Their deafness to Clarissa is a novel phenomenon. In her second interview, for example, Mrs. Harlowe tires of having to overrule Clarissa's efforts to state her views: "Answer me not . . . I am not prepared for your irresistible expostulation . . . I won't be interrupted . . . Again interrupted! . . . Am I to be questioned and argued with?" (I.96–99; 1.71–73). Growing weary of silencing her daughter, "Condition thus with your father," she says. "Will he bear, do you think, to be thus dialogued with?" One realizes how deeply Lovelace has upset the family, for discussion had been Mr. Harlowe's ordinary way of informing himself before endorsing decisions; we see him hearing and weighing the pertinent evidence in the early stage of Lovelace's visits when her family consider whether he should be permitted to court Clarissa.[1] The Harlowes' refusal to allow her to articulate the reasons why she should not be mistreated is highly untypical, but the scapegoat dynamic has so energized their passions that she is "permitted" to speak her mind *only,* Mr. Harlowe says, "if it be to ease her heart, and not to dispute *my* will" (I.105; 1.77).

The pretense that they are being reasonable towards Clarissa leads the Harlowes into obvious inconsistencies. Because testing and evaluating the practical wisdom of those with whom one shares a common practice is the work of prudence, Clarissa is engaged in prudential work when in a remarkable text she shows her family's inconsistencies to reveal their bad faith; she insists that their stated motives in forcing Solmes upon her cannot be their genuine motives and that they are going to undermine and ruin her future.

PERSON in a man is nothing, because I am supposed to be prudent: So my eye is to be disgusted, and my reason not convinced—. . . Thus are my imputed good qualities to be made my punishment; and I am to be wedded to a *monster*—. . . And that I may be induced to bear this treatment, I am to be complimented with being indifferent to all men: Yet, at other times, and to serve other purposes, be thought prepossessed in favour of a man against whose moral character lie *just* objections.—Confined as if, like the giddiest of creatures, I would run away with this man, and disgrace my whole family! (I.108; 1.79–80)

Here, Clarissa articulates the truth which her family disavow by self-deception, that when they determined to marry her to Solmes, the squat, ugly "monster," they meant to be revenged on Lovelace, the handsome man who is not going to enjoy her. Solmes's sexual monstrousness is not fortuitous in the Harlowes' design. On the other hand, Clarissa is unable to recognize what is crystal clear to her relatives, which is that, unless they can somehow prevent her, she *will* "run away with this man" and bring disgrace on her family! The Lovelace parasite has so affected family perceptions that none of them can see the entire picture—her relatives being blind to Clarissa's truthfulness, while she remains oblivious to the imminent danger that provokes their anxiety and brutality.

The opening stage of the Harlowes' campaign goes bankrupt in Mrs. Harlowe's sixth conversation (Letter 20, March 4), in which she delivers a strong peroration on the outcome of disobedience; seeing that rational arguments are not allowed, Clarissa listens in silence, punctuating her mother's monologue with observations to Miss Howe. When, for instance, she is told that her father's "good opinion" of her prompted him, while she was visiting Miss Howe, to arrange her marriage to Solmes with "finished contracts" which cannot now "be made void, or cancelled," Clarissa is silent to Mrs. Harlowe but outspoken to Miss Howe: "Why then, thought I, did they receive me, on my return . . . with so much intimidating solemnity?—To be sure, my dear, this argument as well as the rest, was obtruded upon my Mother" (I.135; 1.99). Clarissa knows that her mother is not advancing sincere arguments but delivering rote forms, all of which reduce to the Harlowes' fear of Lovelace and determination that *he will not have her.* Given the part that her mother must play in the family drama, she and Clarissa cannot do anything useful but must simply endure the suffering together, for they cannot influence events. Her mother's peroration having ended, Clarissa pauses silently and brings up within recollection numerous reasons why she should not marry Solmes; in Tom Keymer's count, she offers "at least seven distinct reasons for exemption, drawing on natural law, divine law, expediency and sentiment to build the case for refusal" (1992, 132–33). She does not "build" that case to her mother, however, but instead she "enacts" those unspoken reflections into social reality by writing them to Miss Howe. What one finds here is the first occasion when Clarissa's freedom to engage with her relatives in that family "practice" to which her prudence is directed is overruled, since she is reduced to silence in Harlowe Place—even though personal excellence, her other project, remains open in her correspondence with Miss Howe.

As the Harlowes' frustration and anger mount, their strategy with Clarissa changes. Mrs. Harlowe having failed in her gentler approach, James takes charge of the next stage in the second week of March, and the Harlowes' effort to gain Clarissa's compliance becomes more impatient and harsh. Earlier she was not allowed to dialogue with Mrs. Harlowe; now James forbids her to send letters to any of her family. Clarissa, who knows that communication is needed to solicit aid, writes anyway, since silence is surrender. Her letters to her relatives in this second stage are based upon her double confidence in their continuing love and her persuasive talent. Since the parents in a well-conducted family should care for their children, Clarissa sends letters to each of hers asking their aid. Torn between her husband's command and her daughter's effort to enlist her as mediator, Mrs. Harlowe's only response is to lament the wholesale destruction of civility in the family she has worked so diligently to render peaceable. Clarissa writes to her father next, but he thunders in reply "It is *my* authority you defy" and signs himself "*A justly incensed Father.*" This father is angered by Clarissa's rejection of family feeling, her evident preference for the libertine whom they hate. Mr. Harlowe's style is autocratic, his temper inflexible, his feeling gout-stiffened. His bitterness is caused by his conviction that she has failed to reciprocate her family's love and solicitude:

> I see how light all Relationship sits upon *you*. The *cause* I guess at, too. I cannot bear the reflections that naturally arise from this consideration. Your behavior to your too indulgent, and too fond Mother—But, I have no patience— (I.164; 1.120)

While Clarissa's relationship with her relatives turns worse by the minute, Lovelace monitors the disaster through his corrupt informant, Joseph Leman, tailoring his threats against the family and his protestations of passionate love to the daughter to match the case which hourly develops. Clarissa, naturally, cannot know that Lovelace intends to abduct and deflower her, because he lies to her about his intentions. Neither can she comprehend that his actions around Harlowe Place are intended to continue stirring up her relatives' anger and fear—to ensure their imprisoning tyranny to her. Consequently, there is no way that either she or readers of the novel would recognize Lovelace's parasitic effect upon her uncles in his March 12 visit to their church. By such a visit he deliberately stirs their anger to a higher pitch because he knows from Leman that Clarissa has written to them asking their help.

Forgetting that Lovelace knows everything that occurs inside their house, Clarissa writes her uncles on March 11 asking their help. Lovelace's response is to visit their church, on March 12, "in hopes to see me" as she thinks; she infers that his informant must have "failed him" (I.192; 1.141), since he seems not to know that she is forbidden to go to church. Yet Clarissa clearly sees the inappropriateness of that visit; "What did the man come for," she wonders, "if he intended to look challenge and defiance, as Shorey says he did, and as others, it seems, thought he did, as well as she. Did he come for *my* sake; and, by behaving in such a manner to those present of my family, imagine he was doing me either service or pleasure?—He knows how they hate him: Nor will he take pains, would pains do, to obviate their hatred" (I.193; 1.142). Unable to conceive of the elaborate snare that Lovelace intends, yet driven to account for his actions by some plausible explanation, she attributes his conduct first to pride and then to rashness. She cannot understand that he visits them with the express purpose of infuriating her uncles—and readers, of course, are as unable as she to sniff out Lovelace's motives.

Continuing to think about this church visit, Clarissa says, "My Uncles had my Letters in the morning. They, as well as my Father, are more incensed against me, it seems. Their Answers, if they vouchsafe to answer me, will demonstrate, I doubt not, the unseasonableness of this rash man's presence at our church" (I.194; 1.143). The evidence makes it clear, though hindsight is required, that Lovelace planned his visit to undermine Clarissa's request for her uncles' help. And, though she cannot understand that he intends it, she knows what its effects will be: "I shall suffer: And in what will the rash man have benefited himself, or mended his propects [that is, his prospects of having her as his wife]?" (I.195; 1.143). Yet readers who understand that Lovelace is irritating the Harlowes in order to undermine Clarissa can see that he will have "mended his prospects"—not of marrying her but of further entangling her—by angering her uncles on the very day they sit down in a sour humor to answer her letters.

When Clarissa writes her uncles, she focuses her argument in each case upon the justice that should guide family practice, but she tailors her appeals individually to tender-hearted Uncle John and to plain-spoken Uncle Antony. She asks Uncle John to imagine her future un-happiness as Solmes's wife, to "picture" that misery and share it with her father in the light her "tender years" will not allow. Because she is a Harlowe, her future is a part of the family's own, and her tender uncle surely would not want it to be spoiled. Uncle John, beside him-self because of Lovelace's visit and convinced that she is in cahoots with the rake they all hate, tells her "we are an *embattled phalanx* . . . you will see by that expression, that we are not to be pierced by your persuasions, and invincible persistence" (I.210; 1.154). Using a pugnacious, confrontational approach for her plain-speaking Uncle Antony, she enumerates the catalogue of the injustices that the Harlowes have perpetrated: her uncles' "sternness," her brother's "con-temptuous usage," Arabella's "unkindness," Clarissa's own confine-ment "like a prisoner," the replacement of Hannah by the supercilious Betty Barnes, and the general disgrace they are causing her, as well as themselves. And she boldly inquires, "Are these steps necessary to reduce me to a level so low, as to make me a fit Wife for this man?" (I.212; 1.156). Clarissa provides Uncle Antony the family-centered perspective on the Harlowe disorder. Knowing that Uncle Antony val-ues wealth yet is not niggardly, she attacks Solmes for the economic injustices that he perpetrates, ones that her family would not nor-mally admire nor imitate:

> Does not his own Sister live unhappily, for want of a little of his superfluities? And suffers he not his aged Uncle, the Brother of his own Mother, to owe to the generosity of strangers the poor subsistence he picks up from half-a-dozen families?—You know, Sir, my open, free, communicative temper: How un-happy must I be, circumscribed in his narrow, selfish circle! out of which, being with-held by this diabolical parsimony, he dare no more stir, than a conjurer out of his; nor would let me.
>
> Such a man as this, *love!*—Yes, perhaps he may, my Grandfather's Estate, and an alliance which would do credit to his obscurity and narrowness, may make him think he can love. . . . (I.215; 1.158)

In her catalogue of family disorders and her comments on Solmes's sordid motives, Clarissa is not being impudent or irreverent; she is really being prudent, describing the "most essential truth" of her situ-ation to those who might help her.

Clarissa stings Uncle Antony into impassioned eloquence, for he knows the seriousness of her challenge, questioning as it does the justice, decency and good sense of current family leadership. Clarissa and her uncle disagree about the family project's proper goals, however. His darling scheme is to "raise" the family, and he and his brothers have deceived themselves into believing they will do that by marrying her to Solmes. Uncle Antony responds by defending paternal authority—but also by appealing to "the good, and honour, and prosperity" (I.217; 1.160) of the family—values he thinks vulnerable in her. For Antony, family wisdom requires that individuals sacrifice for the advancement of the whole clan; thus the battle between the family's temporary madness (disguised as family acquisitiveness) and the more legitimate Harlowe values which used to prevail (defended by Clarissa) is joined in Uncle Antony's response:

> O but You can't love Mr. Solmes! —But, I say, you know not *what* you can do. You *encourage* yourself in your dislike. You *permit* your heart . . . to *recoil*. Take it to task, Niece; *drive it on* as fast as it *recoils* . . . and we are all sure you will overcome it. And why? Because you *ought*. So we think, whatever *you* think: And whose thoughts are to be preferred? (I.224; 1.165)

Uncle Antony's affection for Clarissa is evident in spite of his exasperation and a habit of expressing affection in the language of commerce. When he complains that a Harlowe estate may be "run away with," his anxiety is over losing the niece more than losing the property. Wanting Clarissa's cooperation, he speaks his mind as he would during any family council, since he is loath to think that "the noblest plan that ever was laid down for the honour of the family you are come of" (I.224; 1.164) might collapse because of her refusal. His devotion to family rings out in a rhetorical question celebrating the unselfish spirit that originally marked the Harlowes: "What must we think of any one of it [the family], who would not promote the good of the whole? . . . and would set one part against another?" (I.224: 1.165). The scapegoat effect that Lovelace generates works as strongly as it does because the passion that drives it seeks to protect things worth our respect.

Clarissa's concentration on the essential elements of family practice is as prominent in her letters to James and Arabella, on March 11, as in those to her uncles. To James she complains that if he thinks politeness and civility are not required of brothers to sisters, surely justice is; she reminds him that the goal of a university education is to instruct a man "to reason justly, and to subdue the violence of his passions" (I.187; 1.138). To her sister she points out that, even if James's tyrannical masculine passions should be expected, particularly if his antipathies and ambition can be gratified, sisters should support each other and not ruin one another's reputations with their relatives: "Indeed, my Bella, this is not pretty in you" (I.190; 1.140), she writes.

In James and Arabella one finds a passion different from the anger, fear and hope which motivate their elders. Envy, which as Aquinas describes it is a kind of sadness about oneself caused by others' good fortune, drives them. Clarissa says that James and Bella always loved her, but when she inherits their grandfather's estate, jealousy "now-and-then overshadows" that love (I.5; 1.4). Kinkead-Weekes surely has Clarissa's siblings in mind in stating that "What is finally liberated in the Harlowes is sadism" (141), because it is in James and Arabella that sadism first appears and most flourishes. At the outset they are cruel because they both hate Lovelace, and one suspects that his proximity is required to remind them of his abuse in order to blame her. But eventually, abusing Clarissa gives them sadistic pleasure. Once Grandfather Harlowe's bequest weakens their love for Clarissa and Lovelace's insults annul it, love is replaced by their delight in giving her grief. Once they come to believe that Clarissa has always been a hypocrite, they are freed from their sense of inferiority to her, although that freedom makes them feel worse, not better; the more they torture her, the angrier and more bloodthirsty they become.

James and Arabella celebrate their new-found superiority in expressions of contempt. Although both have the same purpose, to inflict great pain on her, they have different styles of torture. James holds up the mirror so that she will recognize that she has been falsely masking as an angel of light. Arabella, the family archaeologist, charges Clarissa with dissimulating since infancy; though her sarcastic and caustic rhetoric of contempt is far less inventive than James's, the absence of all finesse is compensated by her hot indignation. James's irony has broader scope and cuts deeper with a keener edge. By assuming authority over Clarissa, he is able to explore a wide range of rhetorical strategies and personae and thereby abuse her in a number of tonalities. He is supercilious, mock-solicitous, scoffing, and coldly appraising. Indifferent to the lacerating anguish he is causing, he plays the magistrate unilaterally sealing her fate, picturing scenarios in which her obduracy is crushed out of her. Perhaps they will send her to live in Antony's moated house with Solmes, "unhardened by" letters from Lovelace, and if, after two weeks, she *still* wants Lovelace, the family can then determine "whether to humour [her], or to renounce [her] for ever" (II.26; 1.256).

James's continuing abuse has the two-fold effect on Clarissa of provoking despondent reflections ("What a world is this! . . . one half of
mankind tormenting the other, and being tormented themselves in
tormenting!" (II.38; 1.265)) and of stimulating her to find an avenue
leading out of the impasse. Here again we note the gradual rifting and
separation of her two practices—personal excellence and familial life—
because her freedom to act has been taken away in Harlowe Place.
The only avenue of effective action which she has is speech enactment
of her mental states in letters to Miss Howe. Her family cannot stop
her from "enacting" herself in her letters, even while she is stymied in
her home because the scapegoat dynamic has overcome her relatives'
reason. Letters to them simply provoke their fury, for they believe she
will destroy the family unless her opposition is overcome, while Clarissa,
who knows herself innocent, keeps on searching for a compromise.
She answers James with four proposals and the personal challenge
that he state in writing his reasons for thinking that he is right and she
is wrong. She appeals from force to reason, since, as Cicero says, the
person who best explains the truth will be thought the most prudent.
The judgment between them, she suggests, should be made by neutral
evaluators who decide "according to the force of the arguments" presented (II.44; 1.269).

Clarissa's March 24 challenge to James after overhearing her main
antagonists "triumphing together" in the garden earlier that morning,
followed by Arabella's furious response to her proposals (Bella "almost foaming with passion" (II.39,45; 1.266,271) as she responds),
precipitates the third and final stage of the contest. The harder Clarissa
struggles to overcome her incipient expulsion from the family, the
more calamitous is the result. For example, the last straw for the
Harlowes is her proposal that Arabella wed Solmes, in exchange for
which she will promise to stop writing to Lovelace, and once again
enjoy that "Love and Favour which I used for eighteen years together
to rejoice in" (II.94; 1.307); such a proposal cannot help but further
exasperate her relatives, for by satisfying their putative purpose of
gaining Solmes's estate, and by renouncing ownership of her
Grandfather's estate, Clarissa has focused attention upon their injustice and cruelty. Yet, because persecutors are always convinced that
they are innocent and their victims are guilty, the family are more
incensed than ever. They explode indignantly over Clarissa's "inso-
lence" in prescribing a cure for the familial disease she appears to be
causing. They are infuriated at her speaking "not as from a Prison

. . . but as from her Throne" (II.97; 1.309). Paradoxically, in the scapegoat dynamic the weakest member seems the strongest and most dangerous member of the community. That is why her family take her to be a tyrannical monarch, a Lord of Female Misrule who has inverted the hierarchies of power within Harlowe Place, and who must therefore be toppled from her throne. Worse, in their estimation her power is not indigenous to the family, as is James's usurped authority, but emanates—as do all her initiatives—from Lovelace. Thus the Harlowes inexorably move onward from psychological cruelty to the verge of open violence to crush her resistance. That they return unopened and ripped Clarissa's request not be thrust out of doors expresses their determination to cleanse the family of the member they hold responsible for their unhappy state. By expelling her from the Harlowe speech community, they declare her alienated.

In the conclusion of the contest, James is the minister who presides over the ritual sacrifice of the Harlowes' scapegoat by enacting the sparagmos, or the dismembering of the doomed animal. "You shall be redeemed," he assures Clarissa, for Solmes "will be so good as to redeem you from ruin," trying to transfer her hand to Solmes', from whom "I snatched my hand away," while James with "unmanly gripings" holds her close, until "He tossed my hand from him with a whirl that pained my very shoulder" (II.194–5; 1.381). When one considers the evidence of both text and context, one can grasp that James's intention is to sacrifice Clarissa by marrying her to the sexual monster whose sadistic erotic enormities on her will punish her for desiring Lovelace; Clarissa feels that she is "an animal to be baited" by James, Arabella and Roger Solmes—who "loves you the better for your cruel usage of him." Aunt Hervey, too, says, "He is in raptures about you" (II.226; 1.404), and, as Clarissa informs Miss Howe, Betty Barnes "hinted to me, that the cruel wretch [Solmes] took pleasure in seeing me; altho' so much to my disgust—And so wanted to see me again" (II.229; 1.407). James "presents" her as the unblemished victim being offered in sacrifice: "Look at her person! [And he gazed at me, from head to foot, pointing at me, as he referred to Mr. Solmes] Think of her fine qualities! . . . we all gloried in her till now. She is worth saving. . ." (II.195; 1.382). The unblemished Clarissa is presented and publicly transformed, through the frenzy of her family's accusations, into the defiled member who can be expelled in order to purify Harlowe Place of the stain which her relatives attribute to her. The scapegoat dynamic moves to its completion.

As minister of the ritual sacrifice, James supposes himself an instrument of Harlowe family policy who is protecting Clarissa from her foolish attachment to Lovelace. Yet his most compelling motive is the desire of defeating his arch-rival, which clarifies his quasi-incestuous "courtship" of Clarissa on behalf of Solmes. As his opposition to Lovelace grows increasingly more obsessive, James's reason for forcing Clarissa to marry Solmes changes. In the family's earliest cover story Solmes represents the prospect of more property, but when the scapegoat dynamic moves toward its completion Solmes becomes the instrument for punishing the woman whose disloyalty inpugns the family honor. James spearheads the attack because his most fervent desire is to frustrate Lovelace, denying him sexual access to Clarissa and disposing of her sexual favors elsewhere. One notices that the James who earlier claims that he can "never be easy and satisfied" until Clarissa has been married cannot in the final analysis be "satisfied" unless she is married to the sexual monster whose sadistic embraces will punish her for her erotic attraction towards Lovelace.

Behind his pretense of doing the right thing for his family, James's genuine motive for cruelty is his continuing rivalry with Lovelace. He is stung not just by old memories of humiliation at the university and the bloodier one of being wounded during their duel. James is also lacerated by the likelihood that if Lovelace were to marry his sister, he himself would be overshadowed as the dominant male in his own family. Because he *cannot* allow that to happen, Clarissa has to marry Solmes. Evidence that this rivalry with Lovelace is his operative motive appears when James coarsely insults Clarissa by alluding to Dryden's translation of Virgil's Third Georgic, on raising livestock. On its face, James's "*Amor omnibus idem*" allusion derides the animal desire he attributes to Clarissa,[2] which approximates the bestiality charged against the scapegoat (Girard 1986, 17). Using Dryden's book that way proves dangerous to its user, however, because the Georgic which insults Clarissa thus egregiously is equally effective in dramatizing the condition of James's own desire, i.e., his fear of being rendered impotent by Lovelace.

James's anxiety is presented in Dryden's translation by both of the Sister Arts, for the poetic description is accompanied by a full-page illustration of two bulls engaged in a rutting combat to determine who shall take possession of that "beauteous Heifer" who looks on and awaits the outcome. James's desires are focused upon Lovelace, whose opposition provokes James into the mirroring antagonism which is the root of his brutal treatment of Clarissa. The two men go head-to-head like Dryden's bulls, with their tails beating the air while their inter-locked horns and ramping bodies prove their determination.[3] James corresponds to Dryden's beaten bull—humiliated and unforgiving—who "resents his Wounds,"

> His ignominious Flight, the Victor's boast,
> And more than both, the Loves, which unreveng'd he lost. (220)

When one transfers the disappointment of Dryden's vanquished bull from the Georgic to James's second "*Amor*" letter to Clarissa, one sees that his passion is accurately imaged by the rutting contest in Dryden's book; James looks beyond Clarissa to Lovelace, and to his galling inferiority when measured against his arch-rival. He cannot beat Lovelace directly, but he *may* overcome him indirectly by controlling his sister and so denying him possession of her.

> He says you are *His,* and shall be *His,* and he will be the death of any man who robs him of his PROPERTY. So, Miss, we have a mind to try this point with him. My Father, supposing he has the right of a Father in his child, is absolutely determined not to be bullied out of that right. And what must that child be, who prefers the Rake to a Father?
> This is the light in which this whole debate ought to be taken. Blush, then, Delicacy, that cannot bear the poet's *Amor omnibus idem!* Blush then, Purity! Be ashamed, Virgin modesty! (II.35-6; 1.263).

Furious over his loss in the duel, anticipating further losses in the future, James is compelled to "try *this* point," ownership of Clarissa, with Lovelace; his personal humiliation has turned into the anxiety of all the family males that Lovelace will emasculate them by taking her. Possessed by an insatiable desire to possess what his rival desires,[4] James is the faithful steward who enacts on Clarissa Lovelace's own sadistic brutality until such time as Lovelace can inflict that brutality by his own hand.

Notes

1   Mr. Harlowe's original condition as a thoughtful, prudent man is described in Clarissa's "little history" (I.13–4;1.10), while the beginnings of his change into an irascible tyrant are seen in her account of the January 20 family meeting (I.35–6;1.26).

2   On March 22, when the Harlowes are planning to move Clarissa to Antony's moated house, James writes his sister promising her a "fortnight's conversation" with Solmes in her family's presence. If, during that period of sequestration,

> unhardened by clandestine correspondence, you shall convince [the Harlowes], that Virgil's *Amor omnibus idem* (for the application of which I refer you to the Georgic as translated by Dryden) is verified in you, as well as in the rest of the animal creation; and that you cannot, or will not, forego your prepossession in favour of the *moral,* the *virtuous,* the *pious* Lovelace . . . it will then be considered whether to humour you, or to renounce you for ever. (II.26; 1.256)

Clarissa recognizes the allusion instantly, since she "had begun to apply herself to Latin" and "had re'd the best translations of the Latin Classics" (VIII.203,219; 4.496,504). Resenting James's "vile hint from the Georgic," she answers by telling him that "if Humanity were a branch of your studies at the University [she is alluding to James's college relationship with Lovelace, in answer to his implicit boast about being a better Latinist than she], it has not found a genius in you for mastering it" (II.27; 1.257). Dryden thus translates the "Amor" remark which she resents:

> Thus every Creature, and of every Kind,
> The secret Joys of sweet Coition find:
> Nor only Man's Imperial Race; but they
> That wing the liquid Air; or swim the Sea,
> Or haunt the Desart, rush into the flame:
> For Love is Lord of all; and is in all the same. (221)

One recalls that James draws attention less to Dryden's "Amor" text than to the "application" which follows, in which Clarissa is expected to recognize her self and situation (imprisoned in her room to keep her away from Lovelace) in the "furious Mare," tied up in the stable to keep her away from the stallion:

> far above the rest, the furious Mare,
> Barr'd from the Male, is frantick with despair.
> For when her pouting Vent declares her pain,
> She tears her Harness, and she rends the Reyn; (222)

3   The full text of Dryden's bulls contest is as follows:

> A beauteous Heifer in the Woods is bred;
> The stooping Warriours, aiming Head to Head,
> Engage their clashing Horns, with dreadful Sound
> The Forest rattles, and the Rocks rebound.
> They fence, they push, and pushing loudly roar;
> Their Dewlaps and their Sides are Bath'd in Gore.
> Nor when the War is over, is it Peace;
> Nor will the vanquish'd Bull his Claim release:
> But feeding in his Breast his ancient Fires,
> And cursing Fate, from his proud Foe retires.
> Driv'n from his Native Land, to foreign Grounds,
> He with a gen'rous Rage resents his Wounds;
> His ignominious Flight, the Victor's boast,
> And more than both, the Loves, with unreveng'd he lost.
> (220)

4   This discussion of James's treatment of Clarissa is indebted to Girard's analysis of mimetic rivalry: "This is the terrible paradox of human desires. They can never be reconciled in the preservation of their object but only through its destruction" (1986, 146).

Chapter 3

The Contest of Prudence and Fraud

Clarissa's struggle with the Harlowes is an equal contest in the sense that she *knows* they want to make her violate reason and conscience by marrying Solmes, an act which would spoil her life. To the contrary, her struggle with Lovelace is an unequal contest because she is unable to know that the cooperation he extends is feigned and that his purpose is to defraud her into performing an action which would ruin her life. Having threatened the Harlowes to turn them into her persecutors, Lovelace offers himself as her fellow-sufferer, her friend and protector, a basically decent man who would benefit from her generosity in reforming him. In other words, while Lovelace energizes the Harlowes into action by means of their anger, he elicits Clarissa's cooperation by appealing to her generosity and corrupting her prudence through false facts he invents with the intention of undermining her judgments about his moral character.

The most amazing thing about the history of reader reactions to *Clarissa* is the remarkable success Lovelace has always had in persuading readers that he is a decent person. The Harlowes, of course, think him a very bad fellow, but that is the judgment we would expect from a family who have become "a byword for cruelty, gloomy hypocrisy, and greed" (Kinkead-Weekes 126), the family who treat him "with high indignity" (I.3; 1.2) when he visits them to express concern about James's wounded arm. On the other hand, Mrs. Norton, who is not affected by the scapegoat dynamic which drives the Harlowes out of their better judgment, says about him "Mr. Lovelace, I doubt, is not a man that will justify *your* choice so much as he will their dislike" (I.266; 1.196), and Aunt Hervey, who is likewise unaffected by Lovelace in evaluating him, says "let me tell you, Niece, if he had the respect of you which he pretends to have, he would not throw out defiances as he does" (I.312; 1.230). But Clarissa cannot see the truth about

Lovelace which these two mature women recognize and try to share with her, and this is partly his doing, partly her own. He is a supremely astute confidence man who knows how to turn her strengths against her. Yet what occurs is partly her fault, for as Cynthia Griffin Wolff says, "Immersed as she is in her own needs," she perceives him "merely as a figure in her fantasies." Further, because she does not think Lovelace "an important moral force, she mistakenly assumes that he is incapable of having an adverse effect on her" (99). Wolff's insight is important because this wrong assumption about him makes Clarissa vulnerable to Lovelace's deceptions, the fulcrum of which is his pretense to being truthful and generous.

The reason, then, why so many readers have for so long been made fools of by Lovelace is twofold: he is very good at it, and the Clarissa who aspires to become a secondary means cooperating with divine grace in reforming him is our narrator. Richardson has created a double difficulty, one that is designed to draw us into Clarissa's error in order that, with her, we may emerge from such errors and see him as he really is, i.e., a Satanic tempter. Tom Keymer makes that point when he says, "The onus remains with the reader to discover Lovelace's foot for himself" (196), since the novel's text "clearly invites its reader to share Clarissa's perception of Lovelace's seeming benevolence, and thus also to share, in what ultimately will prove an educative way, a part at least of her error" (1992, 79). The problem readers face is that because Lovelace's own narrative is belatedly introduced into the novel's first installment, the Lovelace writing openly to Belford remains hidden, while the Lovelace who presents his false self to Clarissa moves like a virus in the bloodstream of *her* narrative. What one can call "Clarissa's Lovelace," or the Lovelace deceiver as she misperceives him, is an illusion whose success is gauged by her mistaking of falsehoods for genuine realities. To dispel the pretenses which Lovelace generates by means of his manifold self-misrepresentations, it is essential to trace carefully the stages through which he disables Clarissa's prudence—by producing false facts which so well deceive her that she falls in love with him.

Lovelace as Confidence Man

A confidence man works by gaining the trust of the people he uses as tools to achieve his own aims, and Lovelace is a con man. When Clarissa refuses to become infatuated with him after he has been pre-

sented as her suitor, he invents the duel with James and the altercation with the more elder Harlowes. Then he skillfully transforms
Clarissa's swoon out of fear for her relatives' safety into the implicit
evidence of a love relationship between himself and her. Realizing
from her faint how powerfully she is moved by her concern for family
safety, Lovelace turns that concern to use by blackmail when he tacitly
threatens continued violence unless she begins a correspondence with
him. The correspondence itself, a serious violation of prudence on
Clarissa's part, is Lovelace's greatest invention because it provides
him with continuing access to her mind and sensibility during the time
when she is becoming further isolated from the friends he is turning
into her enemies. The correspondence is remarkably effective because,
regardless of what is written in any given letter, the mere fact that they
are communicating operates to his advantage, for the Harlowes' anger grows stronger while Lovelace's influence on Clarissa continues.

Lovelace's correspondence with Clarissa is a channel through which
his parasitic effect on her intellect can operate. He uses it to flatter
her, to misinform her and to offer specious comfort after she becomes
entangled in the web of deceit which he weaves. Unlike the Harlowes,
whose error is to try to overcome Clarissa's will by opposing it, Lovelace
overcomes her by eliciting her free cooperation through the flattery of
promising "to govern himself entirely by [her] will" (I.27; 1.19). Realizing that prudence is her strength and understanding that judgment
lies at the heart of prudence, Lovelace promises that he will "govern
himself" just as she wishes; telling Clarissa that her wish is his command because her judgment is superior to his is the essence of his
flattery, and her sense of her own superiority makes her vulnerable to it.

Lovelace also uses the correspondence to misinform Clarissa. For
his strategy to succeed, he must know what is going on inside Harlowe
Place, concurrently with giving her family disinformation about his
own intentions. Joseph Leman (the agent hired by James to spy on
Lovelace, who turns him against his employers) channels information
to Lovelace while he channels disinformation into the family home.
His designs will work if Lovelace uses his superior knowledge effectively against Clarissa, and for this he needs the correspondence, a
tool for strategically misrepresenting himself: whenever the Harlowes
move against her, he immediately sends her a letter offering comfort
and assistance. The first instance of this continuing strategy of firing
off a letter to Clarissa at a moment of crisis that he himself has deliberately invented occurs when Mrs. Harlowe's persuasive efforts have

collapsed; Lovelace's letter following on the heels of that collapse complains bitterly of his and of her bad treatment by the Harlowes, insists upon his love for her and his conciliatory attitude towards her implacable relatives, and offers to rescue her from her untenable situation.

Indeed, this *zippering together* of the Harlowes' escalating moves against Clarissa with his own letters offering condolence and assistance, at moments of crisis which he has generated, is the heart of Lovelace's epistolary deception of Clarissa. It is the means by which, as Clarissa realizes, and says, she is "*drawn* on one hand, and *driven* on the other" (I.149; 1.110). When one examines this earliest example of Lovelace's zippering technique, one sees that a crisis occurs when the first stage of the Harlowe effort to gain Clarissa's consent to marry Solmes fails; in their final interview, on the night of Saturday, March 4, Mrs. Harlowe, says Clarissa, "flung from me with high indignation," after which "My Father is come home," and then at midnight, "This moment the keys of every-thing are taken from me" (I.147; 1.108). Informed of this crisis by Joseph Leman, Lovelace reponds immediately, for the following morning (March 5) Clarissa writes, "Hannah has just brought . . . a letter from Mr. Lovelace, deposited last night, signed also by Lord M," from which she infers that "not one thing escapes him that is said or done in this house" (I.148; 1.109). His letter, of course, does not refer to the conferences between mother and daughter reported to him by his informant, because he wishes to create an impression of spontaneous love uncontaminated by the malevolence he disguises. To conceal the fact that Joseph Leman provided him with the information that prompted his letter, Lovelace provides her a plausible extra-mural source: "My sister, he says, reports the same things; and that with such particular aggravations of insult upon him . . ." (I.148; 1.109).

Notice that in the story Lovelace is telling Clarissa they both suffer her family's tyrannical abuse; they are its victims. Clarissa cannot but wonder "Really, my dear, were you to see his Letter, you would think I had given him great encouragement, and that I am in direct treaty with him; or that he is sure that my friends will drive me into a foreign protection; for he has the boldness to offer, in my Lord [M]'s, an asylum to me, should I be tyrannically treated in Solmes behalf" (I.149; 1.109–10). Is it just a coincidence, this snug fit, this tailor-tight matching of Lovelace's moves to her family's moves? It is the uncanny sense that the world is not generally so full of these coincidences as her home has now become that makes Clarissa "very uneasy to think how

I have been *drawn* on one hand, and *driven* on the other, into a clandestine correspondence, which my heart condemns" (I.149; 1.110). In the story that Lovelace is writing for her, Clarissa is not choosing her part. She is being assigned the role that he intends her to play; he is coaxing her to believe that the two of them are equally the victims of family tyranny, but that there is a way for her to escape it, i.e., the "foreign asylum" into which Lovelace has from the first intended the Harlowes to "drive" her. The worse Clarissa's situation becomes, the better Lovelace seems to understand it. Immediately after her father's March 8 "*Justly incensed*" letter arrives (I.164; 1.120) Clarissa receives another Lovelace letter, offering comfort and describing those expedients which she ought to consider as solutions—to the problems which he himself has created for her.

Embarrassed and defensive about her correspondence with him, and wholly preoccupied by her opposition to Solmes, Clarissa does not focus on Lovelace's letters in hers to Miss Howe until rather late in the Harlowe Place action. She does not fear his letters, for she does not realize that he is working on her through them. Though she is suspicious of his intentions, she fails to see that her very suspicions advance Lovelace's designs by making her more attentive to him. She is caught in a correspondence she believes she has freely entered but cannot now terminate with safety. Her father forbids it, yet her mother has tacitly blessed it because, realizing that "the case is difficult" (I.117; 1.86), she assigns Clarissa the responsibility of determining for herself whether to continue. Yet because defending the family is the parents' role, the fact that Clarissa tries to do it herself means that order in the family continues its rapid degeneration. Knowing she "shall be more and more entangled" (I.149; 1.110) by continuing to write him, she deplores the error of having "thrust [her]self into the gap between such uncontroulable spirits!—To the interception perhaps of the designs of Providence, which may intend to make these hostile spirits their own punishers" (II.237–8; 1.110). But that "gap" exists because Lovelace intended it: to entangle her, raise the family's anger, and make her dependent upon him.

Lovelace's letters provide Clarissa the orientation time she needs to feel comfortable with him, and their March 18 meeting at the family woodhouse goes far to convince her that she can safely put confidence in him, which is his chief intention in setting up their meeting ("I shall then see what I may depend upon from her favour. . . . If I thought I had no prospect of that, I should be tempted to carry her off" (I.237; 1.175)). Though Clarissa is startled by the "rustling as of somebody behind a stack of wood" (I.238; 1.176) and surprised to find herself alone with Lovelace, he quickly calms her, and his gentle demeanor belies the ferocity he shows the Harlowes. His pretended meekness flatters her, just as did his pretended obedience to her will, and she is vulnerable because she does not suspect fraud. By pretending cooperation in their meeting Lovelace easily gains Clarissa's confidence, and he further uses the occasion to excite irritation and anger, because he knows that anger can establish emotional ties as well as love. This is why he continues in person the same device that irritates her during their correspondence: he complains that she has failed to be generous, while he thanks her profusely for a generosity he falsely attributes to her. He wishes Clarissa to argue with him, for her irritation at his attempt to "suppose" her into love has the effect of enticing her into cooperation with him. Thus, when he accuses her for being indifferent despite his "passionate and obsequious devotion," Clarissa strengthens her attachment to him by giving him a sound tongue lashing: "Why don't you let me know, in terms as high as your implication, that a perseverance I have not wished for, which has set all my relations at variance with me, is a merit that throws upon me the guilt of ingratitude for not answering it as you seem to expect?" (I.240; 1.177).

Another outcome of meeting Lovelace in the flesh is that his presence increases his sexual attraction. When Clarissa suddenly faces him, she is not merely surprised, but physically shaken and emotionally disabled by his personal presence ("had I not caught hold of a prop which supported the old roof, I should have sunk" I.238; 1.176)). One cannot be certain from her reconstruction of the event that her reaction is not simply surprise and fear. But after their meeting Clarissa shows more personal interest in him than before it, and her later reflections offer evidence that her involuntary near-collapse has a sexual side. Clarissa's prudence is not intended to extinguish her involuntary sexual desires, but on the contrary to foster and validate them when they prove their reasonableness in light of her overall aims in life[1]; that is the reason why Clarissa begins evaluating Lovelace more carefully as her potential husband after their meeting outside the woodhouse. Her overwhelming involuntary reaction to him must in significant part be attributed to their correspondence, for by their language interactions she has developed stronger admiration for his mind.

As Clarissa begins to evaluate Lovelace with more interest, she begins to take seriously his feigned wish to reform himself. From this point forward, her expostulations with him become more vigorous and one sees evidence of increasing emotional intimacy. She is now "ready to infer" that if Lovelace and her family were reconciled, he might, as she delicately puts it, "be affected by arguments apparently calculated for his present and future good," because, as he says, he is "heartily sick of the courses he had followed" (I.244; 1.180). But setting aside for the moment both the sexual attraction she feels and the bait of reformation that Lovelace offers, there is something else to be recognized in the woodhouse meeting, and that is the sense of security—even though tempered by anxiety—which Clarissa feels in Lovelace's presence. Cynthia Griffin Wolff shrewdly remarks that Clarissa's father had always been "the very symbol of steadiness, strength, protection, and order" for her. But he has since abdicated that role, and so Clarissa is "desperately seeking a man who is strong" in the ways her father had been. "Only by finding such a man and subjecting herself to his authority can she revert to the passive role which she finds familiar and gratifying" (95–6). And how is Lovelace's reformation relevant to the recovery of security that preoccupies Clarissa? Here too Wolff is instructive: his *faults* attract her, because "they are the means by which she can again assert her own moral superiority (as she had asserted it before with her brother and sister)" (98–9).

Already half persuaded of his honesty and confident that his masculine strength can be profitable for her, in exchange for her moral service to him, she accepts Lovelace's explanation that his visit to their church was well intended. "He did not *expect* to see me there," she explains, "But hoped to have an opportunity to address himself to my Father, and to be permitted to attend him home." However, Dr. Lewen "persuaded him not to attempt speaking to any of the family at that time; observing to him the emotions into which his presence had put everybody." Haughtiness was not his intention, and, Clarissa tells Miss Howe,

> the attributing such to him was the effect of that ill will which he had the mortification to find insuperable: Adding, That when he bowed to my Mother, it was a compliment that he intended generally to every one in the pew, as well as to *her*." (I.251; 1.185)

Lovelace's account is untrue, yet Clarissa accepts it even though she knows "there would hardly be a guilty person in the world" if the explanations of accused people were believed (I.251; 1.186). He has again given her a version of his usual story: he proposed marriage but

Arabella would not have him; he attempted to act in a conciliatory manner but James drew his sword; he visited their church to express his charity towards "every one in the pew" but the Harlowes publicly refused to treat him with common courtesy. Another sign of the extent to which Lovelace is already replacing her parents as the guarantors of her security is her failure to speak up and defend them when he tells her "You are to consider, Madam, you have not now an option; and to whom it is owing that you have not; and that you are in the power of those (Parents why should I call them?) who are determined, that you shall *not* have an option" (I.248; 1.182–3). The woman who swooned at seeing her father draw a sword against Lovelace is shifting her allegiance.

Clarissa Falls in Love

The process by which Clarissa falls in love with Lovelace is so subtle and unobtrusive that she herself is unaware that it is happening. Lovelace's design to grow in her regard by displacing her relatives and becoming her only available object of affection works as he intended it to. Worn down by her family's continuing attacks, Clarissa finds it increasingly easy to feel gratified by his expressed concerns for her well-being, his offers of help and his promises of obedience to her will. When the family's Solmes offensive against her gets hotter on March 22 (II.45–7; 1.270–1), Lovelace's letters become more frequent. And Clarissa gives them more attention, as one might expect, because her family's efforts to press Solmes upon her are being guided by Lovelace in order to ensure that his own letters will have the greater impact on her.

Sometimes the evidence of Clarissa's developing affection is found in the circuitous syntax that helps her conceal it from her own insight. After her "new proposals" to James on March 24 have raised the anger and emotional disturbance which she overcomes by "composing" herself using her "Ode to Wisdom" music, Clarissa has a "calmer moment" to weigh her situation. Here one sees evidence that Lovelace is growing in her regard, for while she is "utterly displeased with" him (II.58; 1.281), she confidently assumes that his conduct in the duel is unassailable evidence of his love, and she then modulates from moral reflections on duelling to feelings of anxiety for his safety. Indeed, when she tells Miss Howe that it is "more *manly* to *despise*, than to *resent*, an injury," she is not addressing Miss Howe, or herself, but rather the Lovelace who is on her mind while she reflects; worrying about his well-being, she speaks as if she were speaking in his own person:

> Were I a man [Lovelace], methinks, I should have too much scorn for a person, who could wilfully do me a mean wrong [James], to put a value upon *his* life, equal to what I put upon *my own*. (II.60; 1.282)

The evidentiary value of Clarissa's concern for Lovelace's safety is clear when, after learning that Lovelace threatens to "visit" James and Solmes, she scolds him on March 26 for jeopardizing his safety. "Very extraordinary, I tell him," sharing with Miss Howe her scolding letter, "that a violent spirit shall threaten to do a rash and unjustifiable thing, which concerns me but little, and himself a great deal," unless she herself acts as rashly to stop him (II.69; 1.288).

Clarissa shifts her affectional allegiance from the Harlowes to Lovelace during the week between March 26 and April 1, and the chronology of that transfer needs to be traced to comprehend how it happens. Her mother and father having returned her letters to them unopened and shredded, she writes Uncle Harlowe on March 26 that "if deaf-eared anger will neither grant *me* a hearing, nor, *what I write* a perusal, some time hence the hard-heartedness may be regretted" (II.89; 1.303); when Uncle Harlowe answers with the last expression of affection that any of the family extend to her ("Every-body loves you; and you know they do" (II.90; 1.304)), an emboldened Clarissa offers her March 27 proposal that Bella marry Solmes and take her estate, which provokes the Harlowes' renewed anger. One sees that March 27 marks the definitive split between the Harlowes and the uncooperative woman whom they will sacrifice to protect themselves from Lovelace's violence. And her March 28 letter from Lovelace signals the transfer of affective dependence to him, for he "has got a great cold" waiting in the rain and she is "sorry he has suffered for my sake" (II.105; 1.314–15).

Another piece of the evidence for her March 27–8 transfer of affection to Lovelace is that when she continues her negotiations with her family by agreeing to a visit from Mr. Solmes—the price being that she needs to cancel her promised meeting with Lovelace ("inconvenient to meet him" for the risk "could not be justified" (II.119-20; 1.325))—, his letter denouncing her promise-breaking explodes into Clarissa's narrative with the epistolary equivalent of his physical effect in the woodhouse meeting. What happens is that the Harlowes' withdrawal of affection from Clarissa produces an affection-vacuum, as it were.

And Lovelace's complaint letter projects itself into the vacuum with palpable strength and force. His complaint about the cancelled meeting is the first letter she quotes in *his own words* and not her paraphrase: "Good God! . . . How shall I support this disappointment . . . My heart desponding from the barbarous methods . . . taken with you in malice to me!" (II.122–4; 1.327–8). The sober fact, of course, is that Lovelace is *not* "desponding" because of the "barbarous methods" of her family, for, to the contrary, he always intended and now controls every move they make against Clarissa.

At the very moment when Lovelace is writing the letter which will overwhelm her with its expression of compassionating anxiety for the brutality that she suffers "in malice to me," Clarissa is asking Miss Howe to "make enquiry" about him, because he "must by his conduct either give scandal, or hope of reformation" (II.121; 1.326). One can see that Clarissa intends to find the objective evidence that he can be trusted, yet Lovelace has anticipated the usefulness of such evidence and has preempted Miss Howe's inquiry by inventing the falsehoods that Clarissa wishes to believe true. The March 30 report that "your abominable wretch" (II.153; 1.350) seduced a village girl is news bad enough to "incense, alarm, and terrify" Clarissa (II.156; 1.352), who refuses to read his latest letter until she knows more. But Miss Howe's more welcome report on March 31 is that he proved generous, not promiscuous, and thus the disappointment and sexual jealousy which Clarissa experienced are transformed on April-fool's Day into euphoric satisfaction.

Presuming that Lovelace has started to reform himself by her example, Clarissa rejoices to find him "*capable* of so good and bountiful a manner of thinking" (II.161; 1.356); she believes him since he "puts his present and his future happiness 'with regard to both worlds, entirely upon me.'" Here for the first time, she incorporates Lovelace's words into her own sentence. Why? "The ardour with which he vows and promises, I think the heart only can dictate" (II.163; 1.358). As Tom Keymer says, the reader who admires Lovelace for his generosity and restraint in the Rosebud action "is at the top of a slippery slope" (78–9) as is Clarissa herself, since "Rosebud" is Lovelace's bait to secure her heart.

Authorized by her growing affection, Clarissa undertakes on April 1 to improve Lovelace's conduct by giving him a lecture on the immorality of corrupting servants: "A stand must be made by somebody, turn round the evil as many as may, or virtue will be lost" (II.165;

1.359). Blind to his fraudulence, Clarissa cannot now suspect that he corrupted Joseph Leman in order to undermine her. Concurrently with giving him moral advice, she practices in his regard a certain patience, enduring his imperfections in the expectation that his conduct will eventually improve. Realizing that her sermonizing means Clarissa is falling in love with him, and trusting that she will misinterpret his actions as motivated by affection, Lovelace now interferes with the Harlowes much more vigorously—making threats to keep them from moving her to Uncle Antony's moated house. Lovelace judges her accurately, since she attributes those threats to rashness, not malevolence. Lamenting the error in judgment that she imputes to him, Clarissa overlooks the tell-tale zippering of his actions and her family's reaction. On April 5, she reports that "indiscreet measures are fallen upon by the rash man, before I, who am so much concerned in the event of the present contentions, can be consulted" (II.237; 1.413), as though she and Lovelace were acting in cooperative collaboration.

Falling in love with him annihilates Clarissa's suspicion of Lovelace's intentions. When, for example, his menacing dissuades the family from moving her to Antony's house, Clarissa suffers as the result, yet she has lost the capacity to suspect chicanery in him, despite the wonderful confluence of coincidences which ought to raise her wondering disbelief:

> The rash man has indeed so far gained his point, as to intimidate them from attempting to carry me away: But he has put them upon a surer and a more desperate measure: And this has driven me also into one as desperate; the consequence of which, altho' he could not foresee it (a), may perhaps too well answer his great end [marrying her], little as he deserves to have it answered. (II.253; 1.425)

Clarissa's continuing presumption that "his great end" is to have her as his wife—a falsehood that his pretended courtship renders indisputable—is now strengthened by her inclination to interpret all his actions favorably. Her suspicions have been surrendered, and what she wishes now is the opportunity to direct their common affairs more tactfully than *he* knows how to do. In other words, Clarissa thinks she knows how to manage angry people better than he—which is a sorry mistake because angering people in order to manage them is his constant occupation. Given her circumstances, the best she can do is endure his rashness patiently, hoping, as her very circuitous syntax shows, that his conduct might "answer his great end, little as he deserves to have it answered."

The most ominous result of the collapse of her suspicion is that Clarissa begins siding with Lovelace against a family whose harsh treatment she cannot endure indefinitely. It is true that she continues to be worried about the Harlowes' safety, for when Lovelace pushes them into their most vigorous confrontation with him, Clarissa asks that he "presume not to offer violence to any of my friends" (II.180; 1.370–1), a hint which he improves on in the manner by which he provokes her flight. However, if concern for her family's safety motivates her first imprudence (agreeing to a correspondence), it is anger against James and Arabella that motivates her second error, the April 6 letter promising to leave with Lovelace; this is the "most rash thing that ever I did in my life" (II.253; 1.425), she later tells Miss Howe. Reflecting on her siblings' contemptuous brutality towards her, Clarissa turns against them and, to make the Harlowes suffer in return for their abuse of her, decides to leave with Lovelace: "I dwelt upon their triumphings over me; and found rise in my mind a rancour that was new to me; and which I could not withstand" (II.261; 1.431). Her violent reaction against her tormentors mirrors the violence they aim at her, which ultimately originates in Lovelace. Clarissa is sending herself down the road to grief by this instinctive action of striking back at her persecutors, for that is what carries her into the cycle of retribution which she had resisted until now.

Despite this momentary triumph of rancorous passions against her habitual prudence, Clarissa's reliable good judgment animates her April 6 promising letter to Lovelace. Considering her state of mind, one can easily see that she is evaluating Lovelace as a potential husband. And, because her judgment necessarily depends on the misinformation that he creates, he seems a prudent choice. She wants to escape from Solmes and guide Lovelace's reformation. Going with Lovelace (who promised to obey her and so would follow the conditions her letter specifies) appears to be a wise action. That it would be a bold act does not argue its imprudence. As it may be difficult to avoid giving a wrong social impression about her motives for leaving Harlowe Place with Lovelace, however, she insists, first, that after they leave Harlowe Place she will live with his family while Lovelace lives somewhere else, and, second, that he is not to broach the subject of marriage unless she gives him permission. Clarissa means these injunctions to ease the way to their marriage by securing for herself the time she will need to sooth her family and to be decorously received by his.

But although Clarissa is certainly preparing for marriage to Lovelace, she will not admit that to herself but instead disavows her own operative intention. Doing so puts her in bad faith with herself, the evidence of which is her dream of being murdered and buried by Lovelace. The dream articulates the self-division that exists between her habit of ethical self-scrutiny and her current refusal to examine her motives, which is why her mind "dreadfully misgave" her the night of April 6, after she deposited her "rash" letter agreeing to leave home with Lovelace. The nightmare which she experiences early the next morning dramatizes his malevolence toward her, thus contradicting the evidence of his presumed love. "Disturbed imagination" fashions this dream by "huddling together wildly" her current concerns—including her unwillingness to face and examine Lovelace's pattern of faithless seductions, which her Uncle Antony, Solmes and Aunt Hervey repeatedly try to share with her (II.227,256–7; 1.406,427). When she learned about Lovelace's apparent generosity to Rosebud, Clarissa surrendered suspicion of his motives, but now she has gone past surrendering her suspicion to actively refusing to examine unwelcome evidence.

Needing an explanation for the malevolence that she intuits behind Lovelace's protestations of love for her, Clarissa dreams that his murderous conduct is motivated by anger directed against the Harlowes and Solmes for their "plot to destroy" him, and that he turns to her as a surrogate victim because his genuine enemies have fled "into foreign parts." Lovelace carries her

> into a churchyard; and there, notwithstanding all my prayers and tears, and protestations of innocence, stabbed me to the heart, and then tumbled me into a deep grave ready dug, throwing in the dirt and earth upon me with his hands, and trampling it down with his feet. (II.264–5; 1.433)

The murder is to be accomplished sexually, as the dream narrative ("Stabbed me to the heart") makes evident. When, earlier on, her mother commands her "think of being Mrs. Solmes," she responds to Miss Howe "*There* went the dagger to my heart, and down I sunk" (I.97; 1.71). The "dagger to" her heart is semantically the same as the dream knife, for in truth it matters little whether Solmes or Lovelace seizes her: Solmes is her suitor because the Harlowes are trying to protect themselves from Lovelace's violence, and he himself means to punish her for reasons to be given in subsequent chapters, so in either case Lovelace holds the sacrificial knife. The dream does not mean that sexuality is death to Clarissa, but that the instrument Lovelace uses for the murder will be sexual. The "already dug" grave implies Lovelace's forethought, and "Two or three half-dissolved carcasses" suggests that such "murders" are habitual with him.

Awaking from her nightmare, Clarissa pushes it from her mind and recovers the conscious state of believing that Lovelace means her well. But though she has buried suspicion, she is remarkably anxious to have Miss Howe's advice about her escape plans. With trepidation, she reports the "strange diligence" (II.265; 1.431) that Lovelace exhibits by inundating her on April 7 with letters (at 8, at 1, and 9 o'clock) which contain "transports, vows, and promises" (II.269; 1.436), letters filled with "alternatives and proposals" for her to consider. Shaken by the strange diligence that would signal his insincerity were she suspicious, she begs Miss Howe to "advise me in this dreadful crisis" (II.275; 1.441) even though she insists that "I can have no room to doubt of his sincerity" (II.278; 1.443).

By this time Clarissa has become emotionally destabilized by the scissors force of being pressured to marry Solmes while being equally pressured by Lovelace's rash of promises and admonitions. Were she permitted time for unhindered reflection, which Lovelace denies her, she might raise her dream's intuitions into conscious awareness and combine that dream's insight with Mrs. Norton's and Aunt Hervey's testimony that her family's low opinion of Lovelace is accurate. Needing advice, she is fortunate to have Miss Howe as counsellor: familiar with Clarissa's temper and situation, she knows that her friend is neglecting to recognize the crucial fact about her situation (that she loves Lovelace); she has the steely courage to risk Clarissa's displeasure by helping her to know the truth. Miss Howe shoulders the task, not of informing her friend that she loves Lovelace, but of helping her to realize it herself by allowing that disavowed love to enter into her self-awareness.

Clarissa's self-ignorance about Lovelace is made clearer by Herbert Fingarette, who states that consciousness is best thought of not "as a kind of mental mirror" reflecting everything before it, but as "the exercise of the (learned) skill of 'spelling-out' some feature of the world as we are engaged in it." To spell-out something is, colloquially, "to make it explicit, to say it in a clearly and fully elaborated way, to make it perfectly apparent" (39). But spelling-out her attitude toward Lovelace is the point Clarissa has neglected, so Miss Howe undertakes to help her make "apparent" to herself the love she disavows. As Fingarette says, "we are selective" in what we tell ourselves about our intentions in the world, "but not arbitrarily so" (41), and *that* is the fact Miss Howe relies on to persuade her friend; she writes on April 8 that, were it not the scrupulously honest Clarissa who is finding excuses for refusing non-Lovelace aid in leaving home, "I, who am ever, as you have often remarked, endeavouring to trace effects to their causes,"

> should be ready to suspect, that there was a latent, unowned inclination, which balancing, or *preponderating*, rather, made the issue of the alternative [means of escape] sit more lightly upon the excuser's mind than she cared to own.
>
> You will understand me, my dear. But if you do not, it may be as well for me; for I am afraid I shall *have it* from you, for but starting such a notion, or giving a hint, which perhaps, as you did once in another case, you will reprimandingly call, 'Not being able to forego the ostentation of sagacity, tho' at the expence of that tenderness which is due to friendship and charity.' (II.289; 1.451)

Miss Howe's double argument is, first, that actions speak louder than words (even Clarissa's words), and second, that calling the kettle black or beating the messenger are nothing to the point.

Unfortunately, Clarissa refuses to accept the evidence which her friend presents. Instead, she sticks with the same story she told on March 1 when there was no reason to believe that love had yet found her: "My heart *throbs* not after him. I *glow* not, but with indignation against myself for having given room for such an imputation" (I.64; 1.47). This account is acceptable on March 1, but the situation has changed by March 18, when, reporting on the woodhouse meeting, she anticipates Miss Howe's charge by refusing to admit what her own subsequent language appears to insist upon:

> "Will you not question me about *throbs* and *glows*", she asks, if, from such instances of a command over his fiery temper, for my sake, I am ready to infer, that were my friends capable of a Reconciliation with him, he might be affected by arguments apparently calculated for his present and future good?" (I.244; 1.180)

Anyone who understands the mother tongue would find it difficult not to see in this sentence a three-point scenario that includes (1) the family are reconciled to us, (2) he reforms himself, and then (3) we marry. If this case went to court, one would be hard pressed not to take her "will you not question me about" lead-in as an expression of anxiety; her intention of remaining Lovelace neutral is belied by her own actions, which she disavows because those actions interfere with her conception of herself as morally unsuspect. The self-story that was acceptable on March 1 but had become devious by March 18 is even more obviously running against the evidence of her actions by

April 9, when she utterly disavows any "*latent* or *un-owned inclina-tion*" towards Lovelace because to harbor such an inclination would "leave me utterly inexcuseable" (II.294; 1.455) were she to leave home with him.

Clarissa's April 9 letter answering Miss Howe by denying her love for Lovelace provides further evidence that she is deceiving herself. Not "randomly," but in "adherence to a policy (tacitly) adopted" (Fingarette 48). That "policy" appears to be based upon a distinction that she implies but does not examine outright, the distinction be-tween erotic passion and moral passion—which could even be re-described as moral purpose. Clarissa on March 1 and on March 18 denies having "glows" or "throbs" for Lovelace, by which she evi-dently means the flushed visage and quickened heartbeat of sexual interest, which is the upheaval that animates "those giddy girls" whom Clarissa has "censured most severely," who the moment they have run away from home come before the Altar that witnesses "their undutiful rashness" (II.198; 1.458). If those "glows" and "throbs" which Clarissa denies experiencing for Lovelace indicate the impulsive action that produces "undutiful rashness," Clarissa is truthful in denying them, for, excepting her involuntary near-collapse in the woodhouse meet-ing, her erotic passions are under the strict control of her own pur-poses.

Now "glows" and "throbs" are not words that Clarissa uses in her April 9 letter, nor had Miss Howe chosen them for her April 8 letter. And yet the contrast Clarissa feels it important to draw between her-self—her own intentions and actions—and those of the "giddy girls" she has "censured" tells us that she considers *her* intentions towards Lovelace as motivated rather by moral passion, which is an intellectual desire, than by the personal emotion for which she often expresses low regard in making decisions. And so when Clarissa tells Miss Howe "I know not my own heart, if I have any of that *latent* or *un-owned inclination,* which you would impute . . ." (II.294; 1.455), she be-lieves that she is reporting her own conduct truthfully. This, however, is one of those times when, as Tom Keymer says, Clarissa "succumbs to [the] hazards" of casuistry defined as "a quibbling or evasive way of dealing with difficult cases of duty" (*OED* as quoted by Keymer, 1992, 89). At such moments "Her letters seem determined not by 'reality' but by the self-image she prefers to project, and they are based on a model of daughterly exemplariness that is increasingly at odds with her actual state," with the result that Clarissa's narrative becomes "an anxious construction, addressed to the good opinion of the reader, of the person she ought to be" (135).

Although Miss Howe cannot bring Clarissa to confess her love for Lovelace, she does help her friend to realize that she cannot leave Harlowe Place with him. One of her reasons for not leaving suggests that Clarissa's "(tacitly) adopted" policy is motivated partly by concern for her own reputation and her unwillingness to be thought "giddy" and "undutiful": "If *You*, my dear, think . . . that my *inclination* is faulty; the *World* would treat me much less scrupulously" (II.297; 1.457), she says—as one would expect from someone jealous of her reputation. When one contrasts Clarissa's "promising" letter with her reasons for withdrawing that promise, one sees that the thing she most wishes to avoid is an appearance of impropriety. But that aside, her core intention still is what it had been. Miss Howe's letter helps her recognize that a wrong impression WOULD be made by leaving with him, and that impression would obstruct the route towards their marriage. Her position is that marriage is possible only after Lovelace's moral reformation justifies that action, and therefore the public's perception must be that she has acted impeccably since one cannot reform a man by joining him in the gutter. Given Lovelace's proven rashness, his tendency to act without thinking about his action's implications, Clarissa sees that she will have to struggle even harder to make correct choices for both of them. She evidently understands that the terms described in her promising letter are ill-suited to her purpose, which is to so situate herself that marriage to Lovelace can be approached in an unobjectionable manner.

The argument Clarissa uses to persuades herself to remain in Harlowe Place includes three constituent reasons. First, she has "stipulated with" Lovelace "*for time, and for an ultimate option whether to accept or refuse him,*" but she now sees that leaving with him will inevitably imply her acceptance. Secondly, she has "stipulated . . . for his *leaving me as soon as I am in a place of safety* (which, as you observe, *he* must be the judge of)," but Lovelace's rashness makes it imprudent for her to depend upon his judgment in any delicate matter. And third, he has "*signified to me his compliance with these terms,*" so that she believes herself bound by her promise and unable to recall the terms he has agreed to and "suddenly marry" him—as Miss Howe counsels Clarissa to do immediately when she leaves with him. In summation, to "suddenly marry" would be to prove herself a "giddy girl"; to rely upon the un-reformed judgment of Lovelace in a matter so concerning would be foolish; to abandon her "ultimate option whether to accept or refuse him" *before* he has reformed would also be ill advised. Clarissa must therefore stay in Harlowe Place: "You see, my dear, that I have nothing left me, but to resolve not to go away with him" (II.298; 1.458).

The Flight From Harlowe Place

Having thus determined that she must stay in Harlowe Place, Clarissa begins worrying about how she will tell Lovelace: "how on this revocation of my appointment, shall I be able to pacify him?" Pacifying him is clearly a problem not of prudence, but of affection, for it is love that tells her not to break her promise without explaining herself. He will become angry, but "Is there a man living, who ought to be angry that a woman whom he hopes one day to call his, shall refuse to keep a rash promise, when, on the maturest deliberation, she is convinced that it was a rash one?" (II.298–9; 1.458–9). On April 9 she writes him her "Letter of Revocation," being determined to let him "take it as he will" (II.300; 1.460), but Lovelace does not take it at all:

> He is busied, I suppose . . . But then he has servants. Does the man think he is so *secure* of me, that having appointed, he need not give himself any further concern . . . I *might* be ill . . . The correspondence *might* be discovered . . . Yet it shall lie; for if he has it any time before the appointed hour, it will save me declaring to him personally my change of purpose, and the trouble of contending with him on that score. (II.302–3; 1.461.2)

The Clarissa one remembers from the outset—the Lovelace-neutral woman who had been "capable *by the* EGG . . . *of judging of the* BIRD" (VIII.215; 4.505)—would not have been taken by Lovelace's pitiful device of leaving her letter unclaimed—especially after that great flurry of letters which had inundated her immediately prior to her Revocation. But the Clarissa of early April thinks that she and Lovelace are cooperating to build a life in common, and so she does keep their appointment, unbolting the garden door and stepping outside Harlowe Place to "hand" Lovelace the letter he himself had refused to accept. That she keeps the appointment does not mean she intends to leave with him, however, and all the evidence endorses her veracity when she tells Miss Howe that she had been "*tricked away* . . . not only *against my judgment, but my inclination*" (III.46–7; 2.10–11).

Clarissa's determination to remain at home is the reason why Lovelace must design his abduction carefully—so that she will go with him despite her intention to the contrary, and so her family will believe she has gone away willingly. Her declared intention is to hand her revocation letter to Lovelace. She is "fixed and resolved" not to leave, and further reasons will follow the ones stated in the letter she presses upon him. When he ignores her efforts, she tells him "I am resolved not to go with you —And I will convince you that I *ought* not" (II.324; 1.477). But his aim is to take advantage of the rash promise she is trying to retract by abducting her. Her unpreparedness for travel signals him that "her intention [was] once more to disappoint" him, although even before her arrival he knew she would refuse to leave: "had I not happily provided for such a struggle [by Leman's alarm], knowing whom I had to deal with, I had certainly failed in my design" (III.29; 1.512).

The contest that concludes with Clarissa's flight features two opposed plans of action, one sincere, the other duplicitous. Clarissa is the Prudent Woman determined to overcome by her good judgment the disastrous course of action that is insisted upon by the Rash Man, while Lovelace the Confidence Man finesses her into seeming to have participated in his Escape from Parental Tyranny. While she endures his burgeoning obfuscations and tries to remain focused on the common future that she assumes he wants as much as she, Lovelace diverts her attention until Leman sounds the alarm; he begs, promises, expostulates, complains and proposes marriage.

Lovelace's proposal is important for two reasons. First, it telegraphs Clarissa's sincere intention of marrying him, although she insists that they must proceed decorously for the marriage to be socially unimpeachable. Second, the proposal demonstrates, by his insulting answer to Clarissa's acceptance, that Lovelace does not sincerely desire to marry her, for abduction is his real aim. "Fly with me," he tells her, hoping she will be attracted by the Romantic Escape motive, yet knowing her preference for propriety, he baits the hook: "if any imputations are cast upon you, give me the honour (*as I shall be found to deserve it*) to call you mine; and, when you are so, shall I not be able to protect both your person and character?" Clarissa accepts him, but as the Prudent Woman she sees that a Romantic Escape will have untoward effects, so she accepts his proposal but attaches procedural stipulations: "You yourself have given me a hint, which I will speak plainer to, than prudence, perhaps, on any other occasion, would allow." If, after the dreaded Wednesday has come, the Harlowes are still insistent that she marry Solmes, Clarissa will "contrive some way to meet [Lovelace] with Miss Howe" to get married; the reason she adds such stipulations surely is that she wishes her action to be more palatable to herself; thus she continues "when the Solemnity has passed, I shall think that step a duty, which *till* then will be criminal to take." Thus far, the proposal reveals Clarissa's sincerity in accepting him, but since Lovelace wishes to distract rather than to marry her, he ignores her answer. After she turns testy at his lack of enthusiasm for a "more favorable declaration than [she] had the thought of making" (II.326; 1.478–9), Lovelace provokes an argument by further insulting her, and she cooperates by being distracted and abandoning the subject of marriage. Thus one sees that he proposes marriage to Clarissa in essentially the same way that he proposed to Arabella, that is, fraudulently.

A second trick Lovelace uses to keep Clarissa occupied until Leman sounds the alarm is his pretense of manhandling her towards the waiting coach. Realizing that she will resist compulsion, he hustles and jostles her, angering her until she complains "Do not you, who blame my friends for endeavouring to compel me, *yourself* seek to compel me" (II.327; 1.479) ". . . I have no patience, sir, to be thus constrained. Must I never be at liberty to follow my own judgment? And then, freeing my hand . . ." (II.332; 1.483). By thus provoking her he raises opportunities to kneel and plead, always focusing attention on himself so she will be more shocked by Leman's alarm. This third device, startling Clarissa with an alarm that raises her fear for her family's safety, is effective because, although she has great moral courage, she is a physical coward who swoons as the Harlowes confront Lovelace during their previous altercation. Lovelace does not overtly abduct Clarissa, though he could carry her away under his strong arm and threaten to kill her family if she resists. But in that case she would go *in*voluntarily, and Lovelace wants her to go with him *vo*luntarily, although she intends *not* to. And after they have gone Leman will put the key in the lock "on the inside, that it may appear as if the door was opened by herself, with a key, which [the Harlowes] will suppose of my procuring (it being new) and left open by us. They *should* conclude that she is gone off by her own consent" (II.341; 1.490). And so they do.

Everyone believes Lovelace's false evidence that Clarissa is complicit with him in the flight. Everyone but Clarissa herself, for she knows perfectly well that she wanted *not* to leave Harlowe Place, since leaving with Lovelace would put difficulties in the way of their marriage, and she wishes to marry him. Nonetheless, she goes voluntarily. As a result one has to face the problem of interpreting the conflict between her willingness to do what she did and her declared intention of doing precisely the opposite. To interpret correctly, one has to distinguish between voluntary actions and intentional actions, since she left home voluntarily but not intentionally.

As Aquinas knows, something which is done because of fear is voluntary insofar as "it hinders a greater evil which was feared; thus the throwing of the cargo into the sea becomes voluntary during the storm, through fear of the danger." The danger which Clarissa faces beyond her family's garden door is similar: going with Lovelace because of fear for the safety of people she loves is "voluntary because the will is moved towards it," though what her will truly desires is not the thing it voluntarily does, but "something else," which, as one sees, is "to avoid an evil which is feared" (IaIIae, 6.6): having her relatives butchered as they struggle with Lovelace. But Clarissa's voluntary act of fleeing *cannot* be taken as the *enactment of her intention,* for her intent was to stay in Harlowe Place, not to leave. She cannot recognize the flight as her own act because it is the reverse of the action that she intended. As John Searle puts it, "If I am carrying out [an] intention, then the intention must play a causal role in the action." This causality is crucial since "if we break the causal connection between intention and action we no longer have a case of carrying out the intention" (86). That is Clarissa's situation. By leaving with him she is fulfilling Lovelace's intention rather than her own, for "Even in the case where a man is mistaken about what the results of his efforts are," Searle explains, "he still knows what he is *trying* to do" (90). Knowing very well what she was attempting to do, Clarissa feels the pain of remorse because she did exactly the opposite. In self-reflection after the fact, her grief and shame produce "a compunction that is more poignant methinks than if I had a dagger in my heart!" (II.334; 1.485). Lovelace has "stabbed [her] to the heart," as her dream knew, for he has corrupted her prudence and by doing that has defrauded her of herself.

Note

1   Paul Ricoeur's remarks on Descartes' *Treatise on the Passions* help to clarify
    the connections between Clarissa's intellect and emotion in the woodhouse
    meeting:

> in his *Treatise on the Passions*: [Descartes] does not draw emotion from a
> shock, but from a surprise; he describes it not as a crisis but as an incen-
> tive to act according to the lively representations which engender surprise.
> Only in this way is emotion intelligible: when it unhinges action by a spon-
> taneity perilous for self-mastery; but if the will ought always to guard its
> integrity against this spontaneity, it is also through emotion that it moves
> its body, according to the famous formula: "The will moves by desire."
> ("The Unity of the Voluntary and the Involuntary as a Limiting Idea" (1951),
> in Ricoeur 1978, 13)

Chapter 4

Lovelace Narcissist

Lovelace's conduct at Harlowe Place is strange, but after he has abducted Clarissa it becomes bizarre and even fantastic. Yet his actions are not inexplicable, and this chapter reveals why he acts as he does. Our first clue is Mrs. Howe's characterization of him as "a Narcissus." On March 25, Miss Howe relates how she says that the Harlowes are foolish to pick Solmes "to supplant in a Lady's affections one of the finest figures of a man, and one noted for his brilliant parts, and other accomplishments." Mrs. Howe emphatically disagrees with that assessment because, having benefited from broader experience of the world than her daughter, she realizes that "there hardly ever was a very handsome and very sprightly man who made a tender and affectionate Husband," their impediment being "that they were generally such Narcissus's, as to imagine every woman ought to think as highly of them, as they did of themselves" (II.81; 1.297). Though we know that Mrs. Howe is inclined to perceive people in terms of stereotypes, truth can be found in such types. While ill-informed about this particular narcissist, Mrs. Howe nonetheless recognizes that he is one.

The other identification of Lovelace as "a Narcissus" occurs in Miss Howe's April 18 letter, which is based on richer evidence of his conduct. Early in this letter she consoles Clarissa that Lovelace's change from "polite and obsequious" in Harlowe Place to his "turbulent" conduct since the flight—both "his readiness to offend" and "his equal readiness to humble himself"—suggests the good outcome that such variances "must keep a woman's passion alive" (III.170; 2.103). But in a passage which was added to the Third Edition, Miss Howe surrenders that early optimism because, having monitored his conduct in the week after the abduction, she perceives an ominous problem hidden behind his facade of engaging spontaneity:

- Your handsome Husbands, my dear, make a Wife's heart ake
- very often: And tho' you are as fine a person of a
- woman, at the least, as he is of a man; he will take too
- much delight in *himself* to think himself more indebted
- to your favour, than you are to his distinction and
- preference of you. But no man, take your finer mind
- with your very fine person, can deserve you. So you
- must be contented, should your merit be under-rated;
- since that must be so, marry whom you will. Perhaps
- you think I indulge these sort of reflections against
- your Narcissus's of men, to keep my Mother's choice
- for me of Hickman in countenance with myself—I don't
- know but there is something in it; at least, enough to
- have given birth to the reflection. (III.172–3; 2.105)

Miss Howe sees that Lovelace will make Clarissa's "heart ake very often," and it is some progress in psychological comprehension to see that Lovelace may keep her "passion alive" by tormenting her. But the most critical thing Miss Howe does here is put her finger on what provokes Lovelace's bizarre conduct—Clarissa's merit. Her merit first attracted Lovelace, but it also provokes his envy and his determination to be revenged because of her unwillingness to admire him.

If Miss Howe correctly apprehends his problem from outside, Lovelace himself tells the inside story of his relationship with Clarissa when he invents an analogy of a theft. In Lovelace's self-exculpatory exemplum one encounters a "have" figure, "*A,* a Miser, who hid a parcel of gold in a *secret place,*" opposed by a "have-not" character, "*B* [, who is] in such great want of this treasure, as to be unable to *live without it.*" Lovelace cannot distinguish the essence of his theft from the rape which is its enabling means:

> "guessing (being an arch, penetrating fellow) where the *sweet hoard* lies, he searches for it, when the Miser is in a *profound sleep,* finds it, and runs away with it." (VIII.144–5; 4.452)

The treasure is Clarissa's merit, not her hymen. Lovelace's story about the needy thief who stole the treasure invites us to explore its similarity to the theft-of-value story about Eros in Plato's *Symposium.* In Plato's story, Socrates recounts Diotima of Mantinea's fable about Eros, who, according to Diotima, is the son of Poros (Plenty) and Penia (Poverty). Though Penia came to Zeus's garden to beg food, while Poros slept she lay with him and conceived Love. In other words, her self-poverty caused her to steal self-substance from wealthy Poros. Eros resembles both of his parents. Like his father, Love is bold and enterprising, a mighty hunter, always pursuing the fair and the good. Like his mother, Love is resourceless, unhoused, ill-clothed, ill-fed and vulnerable. The two opposed characters found in Diotima's Love are found in Lovelace. The energetic, intelligent and masterful Lovelace who pursues the fair and the good is also the pitiful beggar who has no resources except a desire to become what he *is* not, because as Socrates has explained to Agathon, "every one who desires, desires that which . . . he has not, and is not, and of which he is in want" (162).

Ovid's story about Narcissus and Echo, overtly alluded to by Lovelace in describing Clarissa as his "adorable *Nemesis,*" also illuminates his condition. Lovelace's intention is that Clarissa will enact the part of Echo by loving him and suffering rejection and disappointment for her trouble. Instead, she appears to him to play the role of Nemesis, the goddess who condemns Narcissus always to love himself yet never to achieve fulfillment. Ovid's Narcissus pictures the inability to distinguish self from others; indeed, the mistaking of self-projections for persons external to oneself. In Ovid's narrative Narcissus, wearied by hunting, lies down in a glen where, "charmed by the quiet pool," he slakes his thirst. But as he ingests the water, a disturbing love-thirst grows within him:

> as he drank he saw before his eyes
> A form, a face, and loved with leaping heart
> A hope unreal and thought the shape was real.
> (63)

Ovid's Narcissus desires what he loves, but what he loves is his own reflection, which he cannot embrace. Because he has rejected Echo, and other lovers, Narcissus has earned the curse that falls upon him when Nemesis decides that he will have to bear the state of disappointed rejection that he has compelled others to endure. The curse of Nemesis falls upon Lovelace because the narcissist's fate is to love himself alone and to admire himself reflected in, for example, Clarissa. Here is the problem of mis-perception one finds Lovelace plagued by: when he looks at Clarissa what he *sees* is *himself,* yet he cannot take possession of that image. Clearly enough, one encounters the same psychic self-conflict whether one examines Lovelace's tale of the needy thief, Plato's story about Love's parentage, or Ovid's narrative of Narcissus's difficulty. In Richardson's novel one finds the same psychic problem that the classical narratives discuss. To become what he *is not*, Lovelace must attempt to steal Clarissa's merit and make it his own.

If classical myth is helpful in clarifying Lovelace's state of mind, contemporary psychoanalysis is further illuminating. As psychoanalyst Heinz Kohut says, there are "frequent instances of self pathology" in men where "the primary defect" in the self's structure "is covered over by promiscuous and sadistic *behavior* towards women," the "equally frequent" form being that "in which the defensive cover consists of *fantasies*" (1977, 193). If he only fantasized about abusing women, Lovelace's problem would be called "Narcissistic Personality Disorder," but since he enacts his fantasies, his problem is "Narcissistic Behavior Disorder."

Although Kohut had started his psychanalytic practice as an orthodox Freudian, he came to recognize by studying his patients that not all psychic difficulties are rooted in the Oedipal phase of development. He saw that narcissistic problems grow out of an earlier stage of self-formation, a stage when the young child is totally dependent on other people for the normal development of an effectively structured self. To articulate the psychological transaction between the young child and those who contribute to the formation of its self, Kohut invented the term "selfobject"; the concept that it names helps us to understand how Lovelace is attached to Belford and Clarissa. As Kohut says, selfobjects are people we experience as facets of our *selves* during our childhood development, and normal self-structure results from a successful interaction with the people "whom we experience as selfobjects" (1978, 414). Originally (1971), Kohut spelled the term "self-object," the hyphen marking those inadequate human relationships which cause narcissistic personality. Later (1978), he dropped the hyphen and widened the inclusiveness of the "selfobject" upon reflecting that everyone has and needs such people all life long.

Adults who act as selfobjects for the child perform several functions that help to structure the self. Some adults "respond to and confirm the child's innate sense of vigour, greatness and perfection" and thereby offer support for the child's "grandiose self." These are its "mirroring selfobjects." Other adults act as hero models "to whom the child can look up," and with whom the young child "can merge as an image of calmness, infallibility and omnipotence" (1978, 414); these act as "ideal selfobjects." Both the child's "mirroring" and "ideal" needs must be supplied during the time when it is groping towards a sense of personal identity, for what is at stake is whether it will feel whole and competent or fragmented and powerless. If the child does not have critical selfobject support, a damaged self-structure results, the common symptom of which is the compulsive anger that cripples the adult. Adults with narcissistic personalities have different manners of expressing their disability; they are vigorous and engaged if the rage they carry within them is enacted by promiscuous or sadistic conduct, but they are listless or supine should they suppress the rage they refuse to acknowledge. Lovelace, one finds, celebrates himself for not acting the hypocrite and suppressing the desires that other men entertain but timidly neglect to enact. Boldness like his, he brags, is the reason why "the Law-breakers have the advantage of the Law-keepers, all the world over" (III.64; 2.23).

Although Lovelace has no childhood because, of course, he is a fictional person, Richardson's text provides enough information to construct a plausible childhood in which the inadequacy of his selfobjects makes Kohut's analysis pertinent. Lovelace's father has long been dead, and one presumes that he did not help raise his son. It is also clear that his mother spoiled Robert; Lord M. regrets his sister's "indulgent folly to this favorite Boy of hers" (VI.220-1; 3.406). He grew up without parental control, as he himself later in the novel laments, blaming his mother because she failed to discipline him: "*Why, why did my Mother bring me up to bear no controul?*" (VIII.132; 4.442). Knowing that the child lacked adequate adult models, his uncle had hoped to function as an ideal selfobject for him, which is implied by Lord M's saying "do I not design to be better to you than your Father could be?" (IV.238; 2.409). But young Lovelace could not admire his uncle: "I was early suffocated with his *wisdom of nations,*" as he tells Belford, for "I had conceived of him [King Solomon] to be such another musty old fellow as my Uncle" (IV.128; 2.329). Thus the result seems to have been that Lovelace, whose childhood one can construct from the evidence of Richardson's novel, did not have adequate selfobjects, i.e., elders who might have compensated for his mother's deficiencies and his father's presumed absence.

If one suspects the origin of Lovelace's problems, one knows with certainty its effects. These are seen most obviously in his relations with Clarissa and Belford, because he presses them both into service as selfobjects. Some adult narcissists, Kohut says, are "mirror-hungry," others are "ideal-hungry," the difference in the two being their unsatisfied self-demands. Childhood neglect, unhappily, has made Lovelace *both* mirror-hungry and ideal-hungry. His self, his conception of who he is and what he can accomplish, has been imperfectly constructed and therefore is still formless, except for the form provided by rage and the desire for revenge. This is the Lovelace that Clarissa had never observed during the Harlowe Place action, the Son of Penia Lovelace who sets to work on her after the flight with such violent emotional fluctuations that she calls him "a perfect Proteus . . . a perfect chameleon" and complains that she can fathom his behavior only "according to the shape he assumes at the time" (III.141–2; 2.82). In truth, his self has no form except the shape he assumes "at the time."

As a mirror-hungry narcissist, Lovelace needs "selfobjects whose confirming and admiring responses" help to "nourish [his] famished self." He is "impelled" toward self-display to attract attention and thus "counteract, however fleetingly," his "sense of worthlessness and lack of self-esteem" (1978, 421). Belford is mainly responsible for providing Lovelace the mirroring praise he hungers for. Of course, Lovelace wants Clarissa's admiration, but since she finds nothing worthy in him, she refuses to admire him, and so Belford is left to carry the entire mirroring burden. But while Clarissa does not admire him, Lovelace admires her—or, more accurately, admires in her the admirable self she represents for him. Ideal-hungry narcissists, says Kohut, "are forever in search of others whom they can admire for their prestige, power, beauty, intelligence, or moral stature." Psychically empty, they "can experience themselves as worthwhile only so long as they can relate to" admirable selfobjects (1978, 421). Lovelace, starving for lack of the strong, admirable self which he does not possess, sees and admires such a self in Clarissa and wishes to "have" her self as his. That is the narcissistic root of his "love" of her. She can refuse him narcissistic mirroring, but she cannot prevent his utilizing her as an ideal. She has distinguished herself for her kindness and generosity, her prudence and moral stature, and so she has, indeed she IS, everything that Lovelace is not. What draws him is the opportunity to assume complete possession of the most valuable member of the community, against her family's will, even against her own will. "To secure her mine, in spite of them all;" as Lovelace tells Belford, "in spite of her own inflexible heart: Mine, without condition." (I.200; 1.148).

"Without condition," Lovelace says. Yet he does insist upon a condition of continuance that hints his psychic motives: "Until by MAT-

RIMONIAL, or EQUAL intimacies, I have found her *less than angel,* it is impossible to think of any other" (I.204; 1.150). The possibility that Clarissa will become "less than angel" holds the key to the psychic conflict which finally confounds Lovelace. Clarissa cannot permanently satisfy his psychic needs, for she is an ideal selfobject. He sees in her the mental image of an ideal self which he projects onto her and hungers to ingest, while she resists such "self appropriation" by acting independently of him. Her resistance makes her an alluring, inaccessible ideal; she can attract him only to disappoint him. The frustrated, ideal-hungry narcissist, needing to protect himself from envy and anger, looks for realistic flaws in the admirable one. According to Kohut the narcissist "inevitably finds" flaws (1978, 421). But Lovelace is not able to find in Clarissa the flaws that would dissolve her as an ideal, turn her into another fallen woman, and thereby let him renew his search for perfection elsewhere. As Lovelace says, "it is impossible to think of any other" woman until he can discover in Clarissa the flaws that will release him from his admiration. One realizes that the women who earlier functioned as Lovelace's ideal selfobjects showed their realistic defects by being "less than angel," which in Lovelace's code means "surrendering their virginity." When that happened, his "search for new idealizable selfobjects" was necessarily renewed, "always with the hope that the next [one would] not disappoint him" (Kohut 1978, 421). The women who "disappointed" him "satisfied" him by boosting his low self-esteem, for they cooperated in their seduction; but Clarissa remains unseduced, and, consequently, his admiration of her keeps pace with his wish to seduce and thus make her "less than angel." The unsolvable dilemma Lovelace is confounded by is that he needs Clarissa to be *without flaw,* so that she merits total admiration, at the same time that he needs to find her *flawed,* so that he can escape the self-reproaches which he experiences in her presence.

Because no point could be more crucial for our understanding of what goes on between Lovelace and Clarissa, Kohut's account of narcissistic motives will be seconded here by parallel testimony, but from literary critics rather than from other psychoanalysts. James Grantham Turner, reading Lovelace in light of "Libertinism" ("Lovelace and the Paradoxes of Libertinism"), says that Lovelace "fears, and craves, the function that he has himself imposed on Clarissa—that of mirroring him and solving the question of his own identity." The source of his complicated fears and cravings is his anxiety about his own identity, Turner explains; Lovelace must test Clarissa until she is ruined to quiet those anxieties: "He insists that Clarissa must fail his seduction-test . . . but he also longs intensely for her to pass it" (86–7). While Turner clarifies Lovelace in terms of Libertinism, Cynthia Griffin Wolff comes to much the same insight using simply her native competence in reading *Clarissa*. She says Lovelace's designs "are inevitably self-defeating. If [he] succeeds in his attempted conquest, then Clarissa's value will be reduced by the evidence of her moral weakness, and there will be no triumph for Lovelace . . . in defeating her. If on the other hand, she prevails against him, she will have proven her worth, but in doing so she will have rejected him. Neither of the possible results can possibly benefit Lovelace; yet he is unable to see the flaw in his fantastic plans" (123). Thus all three approaches arrive at the same critical insight. But what Kohut's commentary provides is a complete, cohesive investigative model of pathological narcissism which helps one to understand how Lovelace operates in the world.

The evidence of the text makes it clear that Richardson did portray Lovelace as a Narcissus, as both Miss Howe and her mother properly identify him. In fact, the more one compares Lovelace's traits to those contained in Kohut's descriptions of narcissistic personality the clearer it becomes that Richardson understood the "loveless" pathology. Kohut identifies the four typical marks of the narcissistic personality, and all four are found in Lovelace. He lacks compassion for others, he has attacks of uncontrollable rage, he is a pathological liar, and he cannot experience normal sexual desire (1971, 23). The first three characteristics can be discovered in his transactions with the people in Harlowe Place, and he will show more of his brutality and deception now that he has Clarissa in his power. But lack of interest in sex seems at first mention not applicable to Lovelace, whose "one fault," as he tells Belford, is an endless string of sexual seductions. His sexual potency is not in question, since we know he fathered Miss Betterton's child. What is at issue is the nature of his desire, the purpose which motivates him.

Lovelace's purpose in his sexual engagements is to enjoy not sexual pleasure, but the pleasure of domination of others. He is incapable of ordinary sexual arousal since his desire is focused on himself and his own narcissistic deficiencies. "The delicate negotiations whereby we coax each other into our bodies, so as to experience that intense excitement which transforms the sexual union into a union of persons," as Roger Scruton describes the process (32), cannot touch Lovelace. The "delicate negotiation" which interests him is falsely offering himself as a passionate lover to women, in order that when they give up their virginity in responsive affection he can feel the thrill of abandoning and disdaining them. Lovelace himself admits as much when he states that "*Preparation* and *Expectation* are in a manner every-thing," but "the *Fruition,* what is there in that? And yet That being the end, nature will not be satisfied without it" (I.234; 1.172–3). Focusing on the pleasures of "preparation" and "expectation," he expresses his psychological satisfaction in fantasies that he is enormously powerful and attractive to the women he seduces; "More truly delightful to me the seduction-progress than the crowning act: For that's a vapour, a bubble!" (IV.139; 2.337). Lovelace's intention is to protect himself from depletion and powerlessness, for, as Kohut says, "The need for the incessant, self-reassuring performance of sexual exploits by certain Don Juan types has the aim of counteracting a sense of self depletion" and forestalling the feeling of "self fragmentation" (1971, 119 note).

Yet Lovelace is fascinating because he conceals his defects so successfully. He appears to be normal and healthy since he is energetic, inventive, eloquent and elegant; he is everything that promises more than his conduct provides, for there are two facets to Lovelace, two complementary styles of self-presentation which collaborate in narcissistic harmony. One of them is Lovelace the Son of Poros, the handsome, delightful, engaging man who attracts and spellbinds women—in order to abuse them. Clarissa testifies to "that deceiving sweetness which appears in his smiles, in his accent, in his whole aspect and address, when he thinks it worth his while to oblige, or endeavour to attract." She perceives his deceit, yet his appearance is so persuasive that she supposes "he was not *naturally* the cruel" (III.337; 2.230) person that her own experience proves. Psychoanalyst Otto Kernberg, whose account of narcissism supplements that of Kohut, has addressed the "paradox of relatively good ego functioning and surface adaptation in the presence of a predominance of splitting mechanisms . . ." (216). Kernberg is describing in psychoanalytic language the distinction between the personable Lovelace—and the narcissistic psychopath. Comparing pathological narcissism to the normal narcissism of the young, Kernberg says "the coldness and aloofness of patients with pathological narcissism at times when their capacity for social charm is not in operation . . . are in striking contrast to the warm quality of the small child's self-centredness" (220). What shocks Clarissa is the "deceiving sweetness" which Lovelace shows "when he thinks it worth his while," but joined with cruelty too. That "paradox" is common in narcissists, says Kernberg, for they exhibit "excessive self-absorption" that only partly covers their "exploitativeness and ruthlessness." Their emotions oscillate between excitement and malaise: excitement fired by the "intense ambitiousness" and "grandiose fantasies" they engage in, malaise growing out of their "feelings of inferiority . . . boredom and emptiness." Chronically dissatisfied with themselves, they are overdependent on "external admiration and acclaim" (215).

As Kernberg leads one to expect, Lovelace's ambitiousness is evident in his desire to control Clarissa, and his dependence on external admiration in his appetite for Belford's approval of his grandiose narrative. However, his boredom and emptiness are kept hidden until Clarissa flees to Hamstead and triggers his psychic collapse. While he temporarily regains composure by repossessing her, Lovelace's dissatisfaction and boredom become visible again whenever he loses physical possession of her. Most illuminating is Kernberg's stress on the narcissist's "chronic, intense envy," along with compensatory "defenses against such envy." Lovelace's narcissistic need is for control over Clarissa; he is not "whole" unless he governs her; yet her declarations of independence raise his envy and anger, and these passions drive his "need to destroy the sources of love and gratification in order to eliminate the source of envy and projected rage." Lovelace must shield himself against his envy and rage, but also against "his deep convictions of unworthiness," as well as his "frightening image of the world as devoid of food and love" (221).

Lovelace seeks psychic health, but because his self was not properly developed he cannot act on his own behalf as do healthy people. Therefore, he presses Clarissa and Belford into service as psychic operators to perform for him the self-functions which he is unable to enact. Since they operate as parent surrogates, they are bound to him by the transference bond, the relationship that connects a psychoanalyst to his or her analysand. In fact, Lovelace's conduct with Clarissa and Belford mimics the acts and attitudes of narcissistic patients towards their analysts; in his letters to Belford, he imitates the typical narcissistic patient, who, as Kernberg puts it, "extends his own grandiosity to include the analyst." After accepting the analyst as his other self, the narcissist "really talks to himself . . . while apparently free associating in the presence of the analyst" (222). This psychic "extension" is the function Lovelace expects Belford to provide.

To his Belford self, Lovelace talks about his Clarissa self. He complains that Clarissa is an admirable, but an uncooperative, ideal. When

Kernberg says that the "self" a narcissistic patient talks about is a self "expanded into a grandiose 'self-observing' figure" to which the patient is connected as "an attachment or satellite" (222), he helps us to recognize what Lovelace does: he makes Clarissa into "a grandiose 'self-observing' figure" to whom he is attached like a "satellite." Because he perceives himself as the "remnant" portion of his real self (figured by Clarissa), and because he believes that his only hope for self-integrity is his "magical union" (Kernberg 216) with Clarissa, it is no wonder that he pretends to be her brother at St. Albans and her husband at Hamstead: brother/husband is "one flesh" with sister/wife in psychological figuration. Since Clarissa is the adorable object of his prayers for psychic health, he describes her in religious language: she is "this angel of a woman," "Goddess," "the divine Clarissa" and "the *Divinity*" (I.197-9; 1.145-7). Thus the love language common in the eighteenth century expresses pathological narcissism when Lovelace uses it to describe his idealization of Clarissa.

Like Clarissa, Belford is needed in Lovelace's narcissistic mental economy as the attentive audience to whom he can "extend his grandiosity" (Kernberg 222). His Belford mirror supplies the "confirming and admiring responses" he requires (Kohut 1978, 42). Abducting Clarissa to prove his power is not enough, for Lovelace needs Belford's admiration. Lovelace's expectation that Belford will mirror him is clear from his opening letter: "so as I do *but* write, thou sayest thou wilt be pleased. Be pleased then. I *command* thee to be pleased." To "command" Belford's pleasure is to treat him as an inferior, even an animal, as when he says "Lie thee down, oddity!" (IV.352; 1.490) as though silencing his dog. The humor conceals the importance of his mirror's being "pleased" with his actions, the theme reiterated at letter's end: "And so in the royal style (for am I not likely to be thy King and thy Emperor in the great affair before us?) I bid Thee very heartily *Farewell*" (I.206; 1.152). The "great affair" that Lovelace has undertaken in Harlowe Place does not lie "before" him alone, but "before *us*," because he extends "his own grandiosity to include" the Belford mirror whose admiration props his own deficient self.

Lovelace needs Belford's mirroring approval, certainly, not his moral censure. But when Clarissa is being brutalized beyond the limits of "*fair seduction*" (IV.26; 2.254), as he calls it, Belford insists that Lovelace treat her better, a response which changes Lovelace's monologue to a dialogue. But dialogue is not what a narcissist wants of his mirror. When Belford accuses him of lying about his motives ("If *Trial* only was thy end, as once was thy pretense, enough surely hast thou tried this paragon of virtue and vigilance" (IV.349; 2.488)) and contrasts a Clarissa "born to adorn the age she was given to" (IV.11; 2.243) with the Lovelace who "from thy Cradle . . . ever delightedst to sport with and torment the animal, whether bird or beast, that thou lovedst, and hadst a power over" (IV.342; 2.483), he violates the presumptive contract between himself and the narcissist he should mirror. Belford's role is to echo Lovelace's conviction that he is superior to Clarissa because he owns and governs her. So when Belford begins to charge him with moral turpitude, Lovelace finds that he must cope with both a stubbornly resistant Clarissa-ideal and an unexpectedly oppositional Belford-mirror.

How does Lovelace react to Belford's refusal to mirror him? He cannot fly into a rage because Belford is not the enemy; he is an essential aspect of the makeshift self Lovelace has fashioned out of the psychic materials available to him. His single option is to threaten and cajole Belford back to his mirroring function, for, in the absence of its approving audience, the narrative that is meant to protect his fragile self will collapse. So Lovelace invents the part Belford has to play: "I am not displeased that thou art so apprehensive of my resentment" (IV.126; 2.327). The man Belford is displaced by the fictional "Belford," the docile mirror who should follow his master's orders. Accusing Lovelace can have therapeutic value if it makes him "afraid of repeating" his error. But if he does not mend his ways he will be punished by Lovelace's silence, even though he takes "as much pleasure in writing" as Belford "canst have in reading" (IV.126–7; 2.327). When Belford continues his resistance by narrating the exemplum found in Belton's problems with his low-bred mistress Thomasine, Lovelace pretends that Belford likes the plot against Clarissa: "A blessing on thy heart, thou honest fellow! . . . Now will I proceed with courage in all my schemes" (IV.140; 2.337). Indeed, Lovelace has assigned the opinions that Belford can appropriately hold ("have I not, as I went along, made thee to say all that was necessary for thee to say?" (IV.352; 2.490)), his mirroring role being to protect the narcissist's tenuous and evanescent self.

The strongest evidence of the clarity with which Richardson understood his character's psychic fragmentation is the miniature psychomachia featuring "the affronted God of Love," the Lovelace who suffers on account of an inoperative self. Lovelace narrates the narcissistic drama on June 6th, just two days before the Fire Plot and less than a week before the rape. Here his agitation is near its peak because he confronts a double crisis: tiring of his abuse, Clarissa sends him packing, saying "Begone, Mr. Lovelace" (IV.202; 2.382), and Belford, knowing that he is lying, says "If *Trial* only was thy end . . . enough surely hast thou tried this paragon of virtue" (IV.349; 2.488). Lovelace's response to this double crisis is to appeal to Belford to keep functioning as his narcissistic mirror, and the "affronted God of Love" constitutes that appeal:

> I told thee, at my melancholy return, what were the contents of the Letter I wrote. And I shewed thee afterwards, her tyrannical Answer to it. Thou, then, Jack, lovedst thy friend; and pitiedst thy poor suffering Lovelace. Even the affronted God of Love approved then of my threatened vengeance against the fair promiser; tho' now with thee, in the Day of my power, forgetful of the Night of my sufferings, he is become an advocate for her.
>
> Nay, was it not he himself that brought to me my adorable *Nemesis;* and both together put me upon this very vow, "That I would never rest till I had drawn in this goddess daughter of the Harlowes to cohabit with me . . . ?"
>
> Nor canst thou forget this vow. (IV.356; 2.493–4)

The two key players in this psychomachia are "the affronted God of Love" and his "adorable *Nemesis.*" The "God of Love" is Lovelace's perception of himself as powerful, attractive and in control of his life—an experience of self which he can sustain only by the unending round of seductions of women who fall under his spell. This "god of Love" was formerly "dancing in my *eyes*" in Lovelace's oriental potentate fantasy (IV.21; 2.251) on May 3, in which Clarissa is utterly submissive to his will—the state of affairs he hungers for. But by June 6 his "God of Love" self has become "affronted" by Clarissa's refusals to admire and obey him, and in this psychomachia one finds the whining of an impoverished wretch who is indignant and revengeful because of her disrespect. He recollects the humiliation of "kneeling on the hoar moss," his "limbs absolutely numbed" by the March night air, waiting for her to come, while "Love and Rage kept my heart in motion." In other words, his self-division—into the strong hunter self who pursues the fair and the good, and the resourceless, weak self who pleads for help from the "tyrannical" woman—is being presented, for the first time, with insistence and clarity, in this psychomachia.

The other key actor, his "adorable *Nemesis,*" is not Clarissa but what psychoanalysts would technically call his "object-image" of her, which, like himself, is separated into two irreconcilable opposites: Clarissa represents the ideal self that Lovelace wants to possess, but she also represents the disdainful rejection that he cannot bear; she is adorable in the first sense, his "*Nemesis*" in the second—though not quite in the manner of Ovid's Nemesis. In Ovid's story of Narcissus, Nemesis *causes* his problem when she approves the curse that he share his victims' fate by falling in love—with what? Not with himself, but with his *image,* his self-representation. But Clarissa IS Lovelace's self-representation, because that is the self-enhancing role which he assigns to her. Clarissa herself—the woman—does not create Lovelace's problem, but her resistance to his seduction efforts *reveals* the existing narcissistic problem which he disavows, and in that sense she is his "*Nemesis.*" Lovelace is complaining that the woman Clarissa is undermining his preferred image of himself as the all-powerful grandiose God of Love, against whom no woman can stand, since all women kneel to the God. Clarissa will not kneel, and Lovelace is affronted by her blasphemy against his narcissistic self-worship.

Because Lovelace depends upon Clarissa and Belford for their selfobject support, he finds himself in perilous straits because of their defection, and he defends his sense of self-coherence by asking Belford to remember "the Night of my sufferings." Because earlier on, "both together"—his grandiose self become revengeful because of Clarissa's disdain, and Belford, who once mirrored him but now has started criticizing him—"put me upon this very vow," i.e., to be revenged upon her. Demanding his continuing sympathy and support, Lovelace describes for Belford his earlier mirroring of his narcissistic friend's painful suffering:

> At this instant I have thee before me, as then thou sorrowfully lookedst. Thy strong features glowing with compassion for me; thy lips twisted; thy forehead furrowed; thy whole face drawn out from the stupid round into the ghastly oval; every muscle contributing its power to complete the aspect-grievous; and not one word couldst thou utter, but *Amen* to my vow. (IV.357; 2.494)

Lovelace conjures up the "aspect grievous," the infuriated visage of the distressed child that figures his narcissistic disability, the helpless infant that Clarissa refuses to comfort and assist.

The truth about his narcissistic state is so dismaying that Lovelace cannot endure it, so he deceives himself, pretending to be psychically more healthy than he really is. How would someone who wants to deceive himself do so? Not just anyone, but someone like Lovelace, who must conceal his self-poverty if he intends to survive. Here, Herbert Fingarette is useful because he describes the process whereby one who wishes to be self-deceived can create and sustain a "self-covering policy" that can make self-deception feasible. A policy of this kind, Fingarette observes, "tends to generate a more or less elaborate 'cover-story,'" one which must, despite changing circumstances, be kept "as closely conforming as possible to the evident facts."

> Out of this protective tactic emerge the masks, disguises, rationalizations and superficialities of self-deception in all its forms. If the discrepancy increases, and in any case whenever new inconsistencies between actual engagements and cover-story arise, the individual is moved to ever continuing effort and ingenuity to elaborate his story and to protect its plausibility. (50)

The process which Fingarette describes here is the same activity in which Lovelace invests his considerable inventive energies all through the novel, creating cover-stories to conceal narcissistic actions and assign them a plausible semblance of human normality. The result is that Lovelace is engaged in telling three different stories: there is the narrative he conducts on the social stage, which is his deception of Clarissa and his pretense that he is a suitor; there is his narrative to Belford, which is a cover-story that he tells himself to disguise his narcissistic operations on Clarissa, a story featuring himself as her seducer; and there is an implicit, disguised narrative going on under the cover of his test/seduction plot. It is this third, most truthful, narrative which we have begun to identify and explore.

One problem to be faced in interpreting Lovelace is to find the truth about a character who disguises himself and practices to be other than he is. Thomas Beebee states that problem well when he says that, even though readers distrust Lovelace, "still all attempts at analyzing his character—including those that see him as a pathological liar—must be based upon his self-analyses, and hence must create truth out of his untruth" (7). The golden thread that leads through the maze of narcissistic self-deception into the truth of Lovelace's condition is his fantasies, because his fantasies dramatize the narcissistic compulsions he conceals with cover-stories. For instance, his fantasies of eating women express grandiose, revengeful compulsions. He describes himself as a "notorious woman-eater" (IV.359; 2.496), one who provides an essential service, since women want "to be eaten and drunk quite up by a voracious lover" (III.309; 2.209). In the same vein, he kisses to disguise narcissistic feeding, as when he "snatched her hand; and . . . was ready to devour it" (III.163; 2.98). This is a phenomenon that puzzles and astonishes Clarissa, whose parallel report on his eating/kissing is that he "would have devoured" her hand (III.140; 2.81), as on a similar occasion he "kissed my hand with such a savageness, that a redness remains upon it still" (IV.196; 2.377). These are essential clues to locating the truth that Lovelace attempts to hide from himself, for he tells himself that such kiss-eating is evidence of an inexhaustible fund of hot passion, when just the reverse is true. Cynthia Wolff penetrates that pretense when she says "The sexual act itself becomes almost identical to the notion of ingestion in his demented view, for it is the means by which woman is incorporated into [his] extended and unstructured notion of self . . . . Thus he speaks of wishing to "devour" Clarissa's hand when he kisses it . . . or refers to himself as "a notorious womaneater" (108–9). Lovelace's kiss-eating expresses both revengeful and grandiose compulsions since, before being eaten, women must be caught and caged, actions that symbolize the power and self-competence he lacks.[1]

Lovelace's favorite "catch-cage" fantasies feature women as birds. Though he once compares Clarissa to an "Eel," a "little wriggling rogue" who may "flip thro'" his fingers into "the muddy river her family, from which with so much difficulty I have taken her!" (III.322; 2.219), he mostly sees women as pretty songsters: captived, they offer delight by their plumage and sorrow equally. Lovelace's desire to trap and torture women is pictured in "the Simile of a Bird new-caught" (IV.14; 2.245) which slowly accepts imprisonment. He enjoys presiding over the "charming gradations by which the ensnared volatile" gradually accepts its captivity, growing calmer, singing plaintive songs. Clarissa has perfected "the Art of moving," Lovelace observes. "How charmingly," as he reflects, "must this divine creature warble forth" her "melodious Elegaics" (IV.23; 2.252) when she has been deflowered, humiliated and scornfully treated despite her aspirations to excellence.

Note

1 In "*Clarissa* and Ritual Cannibalism," Raymond F. Hillard rightly explains
that "It is cannibalism as a symbolic system" and not "the literal consumption
of human flesh" that clarifies *Clarissa*, because "The multiple kinds of oral-
verbal aggression in the novel coalesce in the most pervasive form of persecution, 'blame' or 'accusation,' which does far more than the rape to destroy
Clarissa" (1087–8). Regarding Lovelace's kiss/biting, Hillard says: "The source
and significance of [his] ambivalence about independence in his relationship
with Clarissa ("*love* and *revenge* taking turns" [3:244]) are aptly expressed in
his devouring urges." Hillard continues:

> To devour here is both to eat and to be eaten; it is both a denial of separa-
> tion and a revenge against the mother for frustrating the desire for
> reengulfment and for having 'a separate, uncontrollable subjective exist-
> ence' (Mahler et al. 60). . . . Lovelace shares with the other tyrannical
> misogynists in the novel—James and Mr. Harlowe, Uncle Antony, Solmes—
> a murderous, infantile rage at all signs of female intentionality, impulsivity,
> or 'independence' . . . . From the misogynists' vantage the story concerns
> an infuriating series of elopements or escapes by a 'rebellious' female cap-
> tive who must at all costs be 'controlled.' To Lovelace both seduction and
> rape are ways not of gratifying lust but of subduing the female will, his
> fantasy of raping Mrs. Howe, for example, being provoked by her display
> of independent judgment (2:419). (1090)

While I have adopted Kohut's self psychology as an investigative compass
because of its particularizing focus upon the individual in contrast to the gen-
eralizing impulse that yields sociological categories such as "tryannical mi-
sogynists," there is no conflict between Hillard's discussion and mine; "Mahler
et al" are just as helpful as "Kohut/Kernberg et al" in articulating what one
needs to understand about Lovelace's motives.

Chapter 5

The Amorous See-Saw

His success in abducting Clarissa on April 10 turns Lovelace ecstatic, for now he can extract narcissistic satisfactions from her at first hand. Unexpectedly, however, Clarissa is resentful and exasperated at his inexcusable conduct, and her disapproval ("I am ashamed to tell thee what a poor creature she made me look like!") turns his triumphal joy to brooding discontent; searching about for some device to lower her from her high moral ground, he invents an emotional torture machine for producing acute distress in Clarissa. He calls it the "amorous See-saw," for its function is to repeatedly raise her hopes, in order suddenly to dash them. The strategy which he develops to deal with her refusal to admire him is to lock Clarissa in Sinclair's, "where she cannot fly me," and then discover "what can be done by the *amorous See-saw*; now humble; now proud; now expecting, or demanding; now submitting, or acquiescing—till I have tired resistance" (III.75; 2.32). With the amorous See-saw, Lovelace will disguise his narcissistic actions, making them appear a plausible facsimile of normal human conduct. The emotional whipsawing Clarissa will be subjected to is not fortuitous, but purposeful. One purpose is to punish her for her rejections. Another is to remove the blame from himself by transferring blame to her. A third purpose is to acquire her personal merit for himself, and a fourth is to compel Clarissa to heal him. Self-deceived, Lovelace understands this only in part.

Interestingly, though, while Lovelace designs and intends to govern the various permutations of the amorous See-saw, one could argue that Clarissa, cast in the role of passive victim, has more control over the See-saw's outcome than he has. She governs the outcome by refusing the complementary roles of passive victim and approving selfobject. Whenever she rejects him on account of his bad conduct, she tears the fabric of illusions that he is weaving and compels him to confess that her disapproval is genuine. Each time that happens, Lovelace plummets into narcissistic bafflement (convinced, as he is, that she *cannot* disapprove of him) in which he invents another strategem that might extract her admiration or expose her defects. Moreover, the amorous See-saw's results are always the opposite of his expectations. Though he uses the See-saw to defend his narcissism and to protect his grandiosity, each of its permutations propels him towards deeper exploration of the defective self he keeps trying to disavow. Clarissa's refusal to endure his brutality without complaint drives that exploration.

The Test of Clarissa's Virtue

The test of Clarissa's virtue is designed at St. Albans by a Lovelace who is astonished to find her ungrateful for having been abducted from Harlowe Place. She resents having been tricked out of herself and her home, and Lovelace has lied to himself so well that he is really surprised. Denied the fruits of victory in the very ecstasy of his triumph, Lovelace's grandiosity shrivels when Clarissa states her realistic complaints. She is, she tells him, exasperated by "complimental flourishes" expressing his "visibly triumphing" (III.5; 1.495), she is angry about his pretense that they are brother and sister, her social reputation is ruined, she has few clothes, she has lost control over her personal will and actions, she has been "artfully" dealt with, and her heart bleeds for her parents' sorrow. Moreover, let him "protest and vow what he would," there is something "low and selfish" in a love that makes her sacrifice her duty and conscience. A gentleman acting out of "generous Love" would protect her honor and peace of mind (III.9–10; 1.498), she says; her intention is to encourage him to take whatever steps are necessary to correct her situation. But Lovelace's "love" is narcissistic admiration of his ideal self, her petulant complaints are unacceptable, and his answer to those complaints is to invent a plot to further his narcissistic aims.

Since Lovelace's pretense that he is rescuing Clarissa from her tyrannical parents is exploded by her accusations, he has to fashion another cover-story to provide his conduct the plausible appearance it needs if he is to explain that conduct to himself. This new story—Figure 1 represents its genesis schematically—is gradually emerging as Lovelace writes his eight "in continuation" letters composed at St. Albans, dated from April 11 to 13. These reveal Lovelace rising in

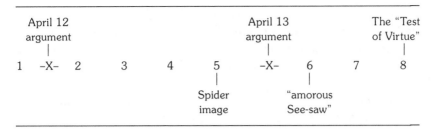

Fig. 1. The St. Alban's Letters: Genesis of the "amorous See-saw"

triumph because of his grandiose act of abduction, falling into despair because of Clarissa's opposition, and rising again into renewed hope because of his Test of Virtue Plot. The series of letters opens with Lovelace's assertion that he controls Clarissa. Yet the triumphant question "is she not IN MY POWER?" is answered by "Doubts, mistrusts, upbraidings, on her part: Humiliations the most abject, on mine" (III.31; 1.514); two arguments with Clarissa exacerbate his disquiet. Her "whole air throughout" their first argument shows her "believed superiority" over him, and her superiority is the reason why he both idealizes and envies her. After their first argument, Lovelace regains his grandiosity by recollecting, with "high satisfaction and heart's-ease," his victory over the Harlowe family. To celebrate his own power, he imagines himself as an "infectious Spider" who, having caught Clarissa in his web-trap, "winds round and round" her his "bowel-spun toils," after which he means to "suspend" her "as if for a spectacle to be exulted over." Thereafter, he, "sometimes advancing, sometimes retiring, preys at leisure upon [Clarissa's] vitals" (III.62–3; 2.23). Already in this fantasy, one finds the back-and-forth motion, the "advancing/retiring" oscillation which is articulated by the "amorous See-saw." The Spider is a version of Lovelace's favorite metafantasy of his attachment to Clarissa, the individual figural manifestations of which are legion.

In the infectious Spider fantasy, Lovelace tries to overcome by denial the astonishing reversal that has just been driven home to him: his power over Clarissa is illusory, while her power over him is strong. A second argument with her, on April 13, destroys his feeble peace of mind. When she tells him that she finds her "regrets [for leaving with him] increased, instead of diminished" (III.69; 2.28), Lovelace knows that she will "set up for herself, and dismiss me," for "the more she saw of *me,* and of *my ways,*" he says, "the less she liked of either" (III.73; 2.30). This crisis induces him to invent the test of virtue.

Clarissa's disapproval ("Why will she still wish to my face, that she had never left her Father's house?" (III.74; 2.31)) provokes his decision to put her "where she cannot fly me—And *then* to see how my will works, and what can be done by the *amorous See-saw*" (III.75; 2.32).

Although Lovelace convinces himself that sexual trial and if possible Clarissa's seduction is his aim, his self-reflections at St. Albans demonstrate that sexuality is not the point, and that the *real* purpose of his test of Clarissa's virtue is to right the imbalance of personal worth between himself and her. "If I could pull her down a little nearer to my own level," he tells Belford, "we should jog on much more equally" since the "remorse" would be "not all on one side" (III.124–5; 2.69). Self-deception will be necessary, for he must persuade himself that her condemnation of his conduct is simply a rationalization of her own. He does this by finding—actually, by inventing—hidden flaws in her that can justify his "test" of her veracity and virtue: "Am I not justified in my resolutions of trying her Virtue; who is resolved, as I may say, to try *mine*?" (III.88; 2.41).

Lovelace goes looking for "something wrong" in "this divine creature" because, as Kohut says, the narcissist needs his ideal to be flawless, yet at the same time needs to find imperfections to protect his vulnerable self-esteem. Because he knows Clarissa loves him, Lovelace can persuade himself that her "petulance and uneasiness" (III.76; 2.33) are the result not of his bad conduct, but of her wish to marry him. He tells himself that she is angry not at *him* but at not being *married* to him: this provides him the frame in which he can alternately raise and dash Clarissa's hopes by dangling proposals that never materialize. Determined to find her blameworthy, Lovelace convinces himself that Clarissa has two wrong motives. The first is her pride in giving a moral example, which he thinks is humbled. The second is the refusal to confess her love.

> ". . . has she had the candour, the openness, to *acknowledge* that Love?"
> She has not.

Lovelace is lying, for Clarissa *has* acknowledged her love. She has in person promised to marry him, although she knows that they must proceed with care since her family are angry and she has not been received by his. Yet because he is determined to find fault he lies again:

> "Well then, if Love it be at bottom, is there not another fault lurking beneath the shadow of that Love?—Has she not *Affectation*?—or is it *Pride of heart*?"
> (III.83; 2.38)

In truth, the only "love" Clarissa has withheld is her refusal to endorse Lovelace's vile conduct, but he needs to "pull her down a little nearer to [his] own level" for narcissistic reasons which have nothing to do with Clarissa the individual social person.

Whereas Lovelace activated and governed the Harlowes from a distance through anger, he attempts to control Clarissa in close proximity through the fallacious hopes which he generates. What is the same in both cases, however, is his parasitism. He raises emotions as much in order to feed upon them as to control others, and feeding on Clarissa's emotions is one of the main benefits of the amorous See-saw. Once she is safely locked up in Sinclair's, he raises an amazing amount of bustle, all of it meant to nourish his narcissistic appetite for the psychic vitality that he lacks, a deficit which he depends upon a succession of hosts to provide. He and Clarissa argue often, because the anger and disappointment he raises in others makes Lovelace feel fully engaged, competent.

But before he immobilizes Clarissa in Sinclair's, there is a space of time that is especially problematic for Lovelace because she is not yet situated "where she cannot fly" (III.75; 2.32), so he needs a device that can keep her with him during the dangerous interim: the marriage non-proposal. This trick turns on a number of artful dodges. Most frequently, he first angers Clarissa and then raises the subject of marriage. Or else he raises marriage and then turns angry to escape it. In either case, his intention is to demean, demoralize and humiliate her. Despite the variety of their working out, his non-proposals share the same structural traits. They divert Clarissa from topics that threaten to expose his criminal intentions, generally by introducing some trivially-flawed decoy persona. They always exploit the fluctuating states of uneasiness and anger, tearfulness and measured calm, that they evoke. And they are conducted in the manner that causes the most suffering. In his non-proposals, Lovelace the infectious Spider suspends her "as if for a spectacle to be exulted over" while he "preys at leisure upon [her] vitals" (III.63; 2.23).

Illustrative of the genre in its simplest, least elaborated form are the non-proposals of April 13 (III.70–1; 2.28–9) and April 15 (III.133–35; 2.75–80), both of which introduce marriage to shift Clarissa's attention away from an inadmissible subject. When for example she tells him she is competent to decide "whither to go" when he has left her, Lovelace, who would rather not discuss his promise to leave her, deflects her attention by raising marriage. By wishing "he were at liberty" without offending her "or being thought to intend to *infringe*

the articles [she] had stipulated and insisted upon to make one
humble proposal," he very smoothly pretends reverence toward her
long-withdrawn stipulations while, at the same time, implying that her
stubborn uncooperativeness is the one impediment to their marriage.
After he fumbles about for some while, thus pressing her to take up
the subject of marriage, she asks "in some confusion, what he would
say?" and lets herself be decoyed. He mumbles marriage with "great
diffidence, and many apologies" but, rather than make the proposal
she wishes to hear, he only proposes "speedy Solemnization: Which,
he said, would put all right; and make my first three or four months. . ."
(III.70; 2.28); he then describes post-marital visits to and from friends,
and reconciliation with the Harlowes, which Clarissa could enjoy if
only (he implies) she would stop obstructing their happiness. When
she realizes that he raises marriage to shift the topic, she tries—two
days later in his April 15 non-proposal—to make him stick to the point.
When he advises her to regain her estate by marrying him, Clarissa,
deflected from her decision to stay with Lady Betty, soon returns:
"Surely I am my own mistress; surely I need not ask your leave to
make what terms I please for myself." He cannot allow discussion of
this topic, however, so he deflects her once more by insulting her
family and feigning the persona of the vain Lovelace. This vain persona focuses her attention on an irritating but not a criminal trait. For
he tells Belford it is "more favorable" (III.51; 2.14) to be considered
vain than to be seen as the seducer he intends to be. When a tenacious
Clarissa returns to the topic of marriage once more by blaming him
for her family's anger and saying that "avowed despite" towards family
is not "proper courtship" (III.135; 2.77), Lovelace provokes another
angry argument, and thus the marriage topic is dropped.

The difficulty readers have with Lovelace's non-proposals is that,
though none of them is ever a genuine proposal of marriage, some of
them seem to be, and thus readers are fooled by plausible deceit. One
must realize that all of his non-proposals share the same generic traits,
the apparently sincere ones having the same form and purpose as the
others. Mark Kinkead-Weekes, who has the keenest reading eye of all,
thinks there are three scenes wherein Lovelace is "surprised into genuine proposals of marriage by the unexpected power of his own feelings" (190). Yet when we analyze these scenes we find that Lovelace's
purpose is to shift blame to Clarissa and to humiliate her, as in all his
other non-proposals. Not noticing that, Kinkead-Weekes is deceived
by Lovelace's cover story into blaming her for being "incapable of

adapting herself to her new situation" (187), for "calamitous misunderstanding" of Lovelace at crucial moments, and for "pride and disingenuousness" (191-2). "As soon as we read closely," he concludes, "there is no doubting Clarissa's integrity and responsibility," even though we are "made aware of the subtle ways in which these values are connected with her pride, and with a kind of emotional cowardice and dishonesty" (194).

This is serious misreading, and it stems from Lovelace's own self-deception: readers trust his narrative to Belford because he tells Belford the same story he tells himself. But although that makes him sincere, it does not make him trustworthy. Lovelace's self-story is not trustworthy. Clarissa's pride? Her emotional dishonesty? These are the faults Lovelace asserts: "Has she not *affectation*?—or is it *pride of heart*?" (III.83; 2.38). Lovelace transfers blame to her so very deftly that generations of readers have been deceived by his lies.[1] And yet Kinkead-Weekes is right to say "It is not merely . . . that [Clarissa] is incapable of any readiness to confess her feeling to Lovelace, but that every time it happens she is humiliated" (189). In the scenes where Lovelace seems to genuinely propose marriage, Clarissa is always humiliated by the non-proposal event sequence, especially in the rapid-fire persona shifting that Lovelace practices.

If one analyzes, for instance, the first of the three scenes in which Kinkead-Weekes believes that a sincere proposal is made, one sees that Lovelace's recriminating persona brings Clarissa to tears, his tender persona calms her, his angry persona distracts her the moment she regains her composure, and so the entire scene oscillates violently in a see-saw of high emotions; it works like all the other non-proposals except for its greater complexity and the broader range of emotions that are evoked, both of which help create its false impression of genuineness. Lovelace begins this non-proposal (III.215–6; 2.137–8) by asking in an argument, "Can you, Madam, consent to honour with your hand, a wretch whom you have never yet obliged with one *voluntary* favour?" In her anger, Clarissa does not expect marriage to be mentioned (any more than Arabella had expected it when she felt wrathful), and surely not in this "*recriminating*" and "*reproachful*" manner. She therefore is "thrown into . . . confusion." He responds by staring at her "confidently" and by feeding upon her confusion, gazing "as if he would have looked me through." Her reaction to Lovelace's stare is to "burst into tears." Predictably, Lovelace adopts another persona chosen to fit Clarissa's new mood: "At last I burst into tears," she

says, "and was going from him in high disgust: When, throwing his
arms about me, with an air . . . the most tenderly respectful, he gave
a *stupid* turn to the subject." However, such a "tenderly respectful"
persona is not a marriage proposal: "he came with his *half-sentences,*
apologizing for what he had not so much as *half-proposed.*" Crushed
because she understands that he is too socially penetrating to insult
her that egregiously unless he intends to, Clarissa breaks "into fresh
tears," for her "heart was fretted" by his evidently mocking half-sentences. Then, when Clarissa has "flung from him with indignation" at
this treatment, he proposes to her "in words the most clear and explicit," as she reports. Here, he is not "surprised into" the "genuine"
proposal that Kinkead-Weekes alleges; he is humiliating Clarissa by
making a proposal that will appear—she sees and tells Miss Howe—
rather "the effect of his compassion than of his love," for, instead of
"pressing his former question," he asks Clarissa whether she will forgive "*the humble suit he had made*" (III.215–6; 2.137–8).

If it be argued that this proposal must be authentic because its
impression of sincerity is compelling, the counterargument is that the
impression of sincerity is strong because of the manner of its telling;
Clarissa, who still believes Lovelace desires her as his wife, is the
narrator; her emotional authenticity provides the scene its sense of
truth. When Lovelace asks if she forgives "the humble suit he had
made," Clarissa interrogates Miss Howe, "What had I to do but to try
for a palliation of my confusion?," as Lovelace foresaw she would do.
Not understanding that she is being brutalized on the amorous See-
saw ("now humble; now proud; now expecting, or demanding" (III.75;
2.32)), Mark Kinkead-Weekes charges her with "disingenuousness"
and says "The moment is gone, and Lovelace bridles" (191). Lovelace
does "bridle," but that is because he sees that this is the right moment
to deflect Clarissa from the marriage track by throwing himself

> into a heat, rather than try to persuade; which any other man in his situ-
> ation, I should think, would have done: And this warmth obliged me to ad-
> here to my seeming negative. (III.216; 2.138)

"Any other man in his situation" would have persuaded her, but he is
not a suitor engaging in courtship; he is a narcissist feeding on Clarissa's
disappointment and transferring blame to her. Like the rest, this non-
proposal communicates cruelty, not affection.

The second non-proposal that Kinkead-Weekes takes as genuine
(III.274–7; 2.182–4) he sees as "the direct result of Clarissa's collapse" (192) on learning of her father's curse. He supposes that

Lovelace is so moved by compassion for the fatherless girl that he tenderly sustains her, and yet we should not forget that Lovelace is composing a cliffhanger narrative in which the hero, repeatedly threatened by external dangers as well as moments of inner weakness, could be "inevitably manacled" (III.274; 2.182) in marriage despite his slipperiness. His self-aggrandizing for Belford's admiration covers his fears of abandonment by Clarissa, who, on account of her collapse, is "soaring upward to her native Skies," so that "something extraordinary was to be done to keep her with us Sublunaries." Since Clarissa is the psychic divinity that he, the "Sublunary," depends on for his wellbeing, Lovelace can ill afford to lose her. In a related sense, he becomes "More than a Father to her" (III.277; 2.184) to assert the narcissistic bond that connects them—like pretending to be her brother at St. Albans and her husband at Hamstead. As one might predict, after Clarissa recovers from dejection she notices that the "*obsequious tenderness*" (III.290; 2.194) that Lovelace tells Belford was the motive of his "earnest" vow quickly vanishes, replaced by renewed demands for less standoffishness. Kinkead-Weekes says "One feels sorry for her" because "it is clearly no time for Lovelace to be pestering her for attentions" (192). But actually it is *just* the time to pester her, for his non-proposals are *designed* that way.

In a third allegedly sincere proposal (III.310–3; 2.209–12), Kinkead-Weekes thinks that Lovelace "convinces himself as he goes along and ends by pressing 'without reserve for Matrimony . . . , which state I little thought of urging upon her with so much strength and explicitness,'" while Clarissa herself "allows the moment to pass" because of a "complete failure of nerve" (193–4). One can make that argument only by completely ignoring the action context of April 28: by then Clarissa is locked up in Sinclair's, Lovelace has "*carried his two great points*" of making her pass as his wife and submit to his lodging in the house (III.307; 2.207), and is planning the dinner at which he will show off his captured prize to his rakish friends. No true marriage proposal can "fit" that action context because Lovelace's real intent is the reverse of what he "little thought of urging upon her." What happens is that he "declares" himself ["Why . . . will you not give the man, who has brought you into difficulties, and who so honourably wishes to extricate you from them, the happiness of doing so?" (III.310; 2.210)], then falls silent, and when Clarissa's "voice failed to second" her inclination "to say something not wholly discouraging to a point so warmly pressed," he begins describing the Fretchville frolic, the scam in which he will "instantly go out" and rent a "suitable house" for them to live in after their ("on some early day") marriage; but "here was no *Day* pressed for" and, the next day, "He now does nothing but talk of the *Ceremony;* but not indeed of the *Day*" (III.311,13; 2.210-1).

The instability of purpose that permits Lovelace to say what he "little thought of urging upon" Clarissa is partly feigned and partly the sober truth. He is, she says, "a perfect Proteus" who changes shape to fit situations, "a perfect chameleon" who colors in response to the emotions he provokes in her (III.141–2; 2.82). Though he persuades himself that his emotional abuse of Clarissa is skillful management of his amorous See-saw, the shadowy tribes of evanescent personae which feed upon her are ersatz imitations of normal emotional responsiveness and responsibility. He *cannot* fall in love because of the "excessive self-absorption" that lies behind his "exploitativeness and ruthlessness" (Kernberg 215).

Lovelace's test of Clarissa's virtue is the cover-story that he uses to explain his strange conduct to himself. Her seduction can be indefinitely postponed, however, so long as his wants are satisfied: he enjoys a state of narcissistic domesticity in which his grandiose need for control is gratified, as is his revengeful need to make her suffer—by suspending her as a "spectacle" to be gloated over. Defloration would end his contentment and make him start looking for another ideal woman to admire and destroy. His contentment, however, is dependent upon Clarissa's willingness to continue being emotionally abused. As she begins to withdraw her willingness, the specter of her withdrawal throws Lovelace into a terrible frenzy. It is this that makes Kinkead-Weekes right when he says Lovelace "is always liable to be surprised by the depths of his own emotion into actions that belie his strategy" (186). Threatened by Clarissa's abandonment, Lovelace erupts in strange self-abasing reactions that astonish him and terrify her.

During the test of virtue period Lovelace experiences four explosions of deepseated anxiety which suddenly reduce him to a state of supine admiration and abject begging. These eruptions of self-abasement are the evidences of narcissistic feelings that he cannot suppress, understand or convincingly disguise as sexual passion. Moreover, these fear-provoked self-abasement spasms are evidence that Lovelace harbors an unconscious desire to be healed by Clarissa. The first occurs on April 16, while the others are clustered during the third week of May when Clarissa is mentally readying herself to leave him. During their April 16 debate, in which she is comparing her actual to his pretended grievances, he becomes "so strangely wild and fervent, that [she] was perfectly frighted." He snatches Clarissa's hand,

> pressing it between both his, to his lips, in a strange wild way, Take me, take me to yourself: Mould me as you please: I am wax in your hands: Give me your own impression; and seal me for ever yours.—We were born for each other!—You to make me happy, and save a soul—I am all error, all crime. (III.139–40; 2.80–1)

When he babbles of being "wax" to bear her "impression" and her "seal," he is pleading with her to heal him by giving form to his inchoate self. He wishes to merge with his ideal. Devouring her ("I thought he would have devoured my hand") signifies the desire to internalize the admirable self she represents for him, so that she would no longer be *outside of* him, elusive and uncooperative. Lovelace has no language but the symbolic gesture of consuming to express his wish. At the same time, unable to admit that he has lost control, he pretends the "phrenzy" in his "manner" was fiery desire which "threw [Clarissa] into a panic, like that of Semele perhaps, when the Thunderer, in all his majesty, surrounded with ten thousand celestial burning-glasses, was about to scorch her into a cinder" (III.163; 2.98).

But the nature of his subsequent lapses belies him. There, too, his intentions are narcissistic, not sexual. On May 16, for example, during another argument, Clarissa once more compares her merits with his, to his disadvantage. While he justifies his bad conduct, she interrupts, "Would you evermore argue with me, as if you were a child?" The vast difference in their sentiments shows how "unpaired" they are, the inference being that they should not remain together. Hearing her remark, Lovelace turns so violently agitated that Clarissa is "a good deal terrified." His "Soul" is rising in "tumults" (IV.90; 2.301) for fear that she will abandon him. Like a naughty child arguing with its neglectful mother, he behaves better once he is threatened where it hurts. Soon after, he offers Clarissa marriage settlement papers as the token of his good behavior in the future.

Because Lovelace's authentic wish is to have Clarissa as his mother, not his wife[2]—because he wants her to cuddle and to feed him while he gazes into her eyes—disapproval is more than he can bear. Thus he is "vexed" into towering anger when, on May 21, he reads some of her letters and sees that she truly does disapprove of him. She secludes herself, he demands an audience. She comes forth as directed, but as she comes his "heart [is] dastardized" (IV.192; 2.375) and he begs instead of abusing her. Because her refusal of admiration strikes him as equivalent to hate, Lovelace accuses her of malevolent neglect, saying "You *hate* me, madam," to which she answers, "pray be not violent—*I have done you no hurt.*" Again his response is panicked.

> Sweet creature! And I clasped one arm about her, holding one hand in my other—*You have done me no hurt!* I could have devoured her—But restrained myself—You have done me the greatest hurt!—In what have I deserved the distance you keep me at?—I knew not what to say. She struggled to disengage herself. (IV.193; 2.376)

Customarily, he offers Belford a placebo explanation of his self-abasements, but this time, dumbfounded, he confesses "I knew not what to say." Terror at the thought that Clarissa will leave him causes Lovelace to suffer two more episodes of self-abasement in the same week. On May 22, realizing that his violent upbraiding of Dorcas expresses rage against *her,* Clarissa begins yet another argument. At length she tries to leave the room, but he blocks her exit; she throws herself into a chair, he kneels at her feet, but she refuses to listen. Rather, she rejects him in a decisive judgment: "Begone, Mr. Lovelace . . . My soul is above thee, man! with both her hands pushing [him] from her!" Hearing this, he is torn between admiration and despair:

> Forgive me, dearest creature! . . . Forgive my inadvertencies! Forgive my inequalities!—Pity my infirmities! . . . I trembled between Admiration and Love; and wrapt my arms about her knees, as she sat. She tried to rise at the moment; but my clasping round her thus ardently, drew her down again; and never was woman more affrighted. (IV.202; 2.383).

In this report to Belford, Lovelace has admitted to holding Clarissa's knees—lowering himself—declaring submission rather than risk losing her. And yet he lies, pretending that nothing extraordinary happened, claiming that her terror was "too great for the occasion." His litany of abject supplications that she "forgive" and "pity" him is too evidently real to be dismissed. Nonetheless, Lovelace pretends that he was engaging in sexual horseplay. "Did she never romp? Did she never from girlhood to now, hoyden?," he asks Belford, continuing, "The *innocent* kinds of freedom taken and allowed on these occasions, would have familiarized her to greater. Sacrilege but to touch the hem of her garment! Excess of delicacy!" (IV.203; 2.383). Lovelace's call for attention and care having been rejected, he suppresses the event and denies that it occurred. "Sacrilege to touch the hem of her garment," meant as deflating humor against Clarissa, continues the cover-story that he is seducing her. But even here he deceives himself, for the "hem of her garment" is an allusion to St. Matthew's story of the woman cured of chronic hemorrhage. In the scriptural account, the woman touches the hem of Jesus's garment, speaks inwardly her hope that he will heal her, and is suddenly cured by Jesus's words, "daughter, be of good comfort." By his wording, Lovelace involuntarily reveals his desire to be healed even as he suppresses that secret truth.

The Fire Plot

Lovelace's amorous See-saw test of Clarissa's sexual virtue has been the test not of her virginity, but of her prudence. To comprehend the transaction going on between these two characters, it is crucial to keep pace with her responses to his initiatives. During the Harlowe Place action, Clarissa took the false evidence of Lovelace's generosity and thought it a prudent course to marry him and help him reform, but the amorous See-saw has provided the evidence that belies his protestations of affection and persuades her to reverse that decision. Because she is alternately hopeful and fearful about being Lovelace's wife, one might think that her judgment would have become warped by vacillating emotions, but in fact her estimate of Lovelace is perfectly stable throughout.

The constancy of her negative assessment of Lovelace is seen if one examines the evaluative language she uses over hundreds of pages of text. The vocabulary describing her values derives from the system of virtue ethics which she has made her own: prudence, peace of mind, liberty, happiness, prospects, duty, conscience, heart, example, plain-dealing, delight, integrity and resolution. Her vocabulary describing Lovelace's actions includes words like artifice, cruel, design, tormentor, trifler, destroyer, specious, deluding, savage-hearted and encroaching. A third cluster shows that she understands his corruptive effects upon her: confusion, indiscretion, fault, grief, sacrifice, mistaken, evasion, shame, disgrace, affectation, frightened, prudery, devious, reserve and confused. Although Clarissa does not understand that the amorous See-saw is deliberate, her choice of language about its impact on her shows that it has had just the effect that Lovelace intended.

Though Lovelace has isolated Clarissa, two messages that are helpful in her reassessment reach her from the outside world: her father's curse, and her Cousin Morden's analysis of the character of a rake. Nothing could be more shattering to Clarissa than her father's curse, and nothing shadows its fulfilment more ominously than Morden's account of the anguish the rake's wife feels. The curse that she "meet [her] punishment, both *here* and *hereafter*" by means of the same scoundrel in whom she has "chosen to place" her "wicked confidence" (III.258; 2.170) is not just an explosion of Mr. Harlowe's personal disappointment and anger; rather, it is an official statement issued by the paternal authority, one which draws attention to her own responsibility. For having "chosen to place" her "confidence" in Lovelace (whatever her intention might have been), her future will be the condign punishment of enduring the results of her own wrong choice. Uncle Antony meant the same thing when he warned her "self-do, self-have" (I.222; 1.163).

The disastrous future predicted by the curse is endorsed by Morden's anatomy of the rake, which Clarissa realizes is accurate because it explains Lovelace's conduct with such precision. "Can you hope," asks Morden, "with such a man as This, to be *long* so good as you *now* are?" "How," Morden asks, "could you brook to go backward, instead of forward" on the road to personal excellence? "And how do you know, if you once give way, where you shall be suffered, where you shall be *able,* to stop?" (IV.31–2; 2.258–9). The Clarissa whose imagination had pictured Lovelace reformed by God's power and her help has been displaced by a better-informed Clarissa, one whose judgments are no longer infected by his false facts. Now, her imagination advances from her current experience of Lovelace's cruelty to her likely future as his wife. Morden's testimony allows her to foresee herself sharing her husband "with half the town, and that perhaps the dregs of it"; while she weeps and prays, he may bring "lewd companions" and "lewder women" home in order to view the "patient sufferings, and broken spirit" that he "boasts of to them" (IV.33; 2.260). Taken together, the curse and Morden's anatomy of the rake offer Clarissa an hypothesis for reevaluating the man she still supposes she will marry. Her own experience of the "amorous See-saw" matches that hypothesis like a template. Then the symbols of evil enter her self-reflections: she knows she is in error; she has lost her path; she who desired to be an example has become "a poor lost creature," without being aware of having entertained "one criminal or faulty inclination" (IV.37; 2.262).

After Clarissa recognizes that she loves a man who will ruin her, she does not deny her love; instead, she scrutinizes it with care and is terribly humiliated by what she discovers. Here is a model of prudence, the woman who lectured companions that a man's looks are unimportant when balanced against his moral character. She has just completed a reassessment of Lovelace that shows how morally deformed he is, yet she *continues* to be attracted by his handsome figure, his graceful appearance, and above all by

> that deceiving sweetness which appears in his smiles, in his accent, in his whole aspect and address, when he thinks it worth his while . . . he has, besides, an open, and, I think, an honest countenance. . . . On all these specious appearances, have I founded my hopes of seeing him a reformed man. (III.337; 2.230)

Prudence, obviously, will require that she change her mind. When the alternative to breaking with Lovelace is to be the wife whose "patient sufferings, and broken spirit" are put on show for "lewd companions" to marvel at, Clarissa must decide to make the break, and so she struggles to disentangle herself from an affection she cannot now reasonably continue. "You must not, my dear, suppose my heart to be still a confederate with my eye. That deluded eye now clearly sees its fault, and the misled heart despises it for it" (IV.58; 2.277). She is *shaming* herself out of her attraction to Lovelace, for it can continue only at the cost of her personal integrity. These strenuous self-accusations are her best defense against Lovelace's magnetic capacity to draw and hold women. She strengthens her resolve by rejecting any excuse that might defend attachment bonds that she knows must be severed. The process can succeed only in time, and even as late as Lovelace's ipecacuanha trick she is still working at breaking the bond: "If love, as it is called, is allowed to be an excuse for our most unreasonable follies, and to lay level all the fences that a careful education has surrounded us by," Clarissa questions herself, "what is meant by the doctrine of subduing our passions?" (IV.280; 2.437). She has no option but to reject Lovelace, for marrying him would ruin everything that she values. But breaking from him will be easier once analysis shows that he has neither generosity nor integrity.

While she continues to suffer emotional whipsawing, Clarissa moves toward a definitive break with Lovelace by returning to her first principles and stating her reasons for resenting his abuse. When, six days before her "Begone" rejection, Miss Howe charges that she has "*modesty'd away*" her chances to marry him, Clarissa says she has only lost a chance to be "the wife of a Libertine." The cause of her resentment is not "maidenly niceness" but rather her heart's "own judgment of the *Fit* and the *Unfit*." Because the innate principles that govern her actions are "implanted" by God, conscience requires that she "act up to them" (IV.96–7; 2.306). Having taken her stand on the foundation of an integrity that she believes is inalienable, Clarissa has already started to separate herself from Lovelace spiritually, even though she will need some appropriate occasion for rejecting him.

As she advances towards that rejection, Clarissa's religious anxieties have already been deeply moved even before their fuller activation in the Fire Plot. She infers that covert pride in her reputation as a moral example has caused her current humiliation, and she begins to ponder "how much truth there is in what Divines tell us, that we sin in our best performances" (IV.197; 2.378). She understands misfortune as the punishment of an "all-gracious Inflictor" to "mortify" her secret vanity, even though she is not conscious of "one criminal or faulty inclination" (IV.37; 2.262); this is the rock of scandal upon which she shall strike her foot and stumble after the rape, since she always intended to do good. Conscious that her earthly father's curse will soon be fulfilled, she prays to her heavenly Father: "Whom have I to raise me up, whom to comfort me, if I desert *myself?*—Thou, O Father who, I hope, hast not yet . . . cursed me!" (IV.197; 2.378). Thus after stiffening her resolution so that Lovelace will not frighten her into submission, she enacts their separation in this rejection:

> Begone, Mr. Lovelace, said she, with a rejecting motion, her fan in her hand . . . My soul is above thee, man! . . . Urge me not to tell thee, how sincerely I think my soul above thee! . . . Leave me, and leave me for ever! (IV.202; 2.382-3)

Having concluded her reassessment of Lovelace, she declares his unfitness to be her husband. Endowed with situational authority by his pretentions to marriage, she enacts her non-acceptance of his humiliating and fraudulent non-proposals in this declarative speech act, which pronounces them not-husband and not-wife.

But even though she dismisses him with violent indignation, there is reason to believe that Clarissa would accept his appeals if only he would behave better; her "Begone" repudiation needs to be understood as a final warning. The evidence is that after she endorses her rejection with similar energy the next day, Lovelace begins treating her better and she remains with him. This is not the action one would expect from Clarissa, who should immediately march out and have done with him—yet she remains. However, her previous spirit of cooperation has mostly evaporated, so that he cannot now establish fraudulent contexts for action and wait for her to destroy herself, as he had once expected. He has to find a more direct initiative with her.

The Fire Plot will be a more direct initiative, but Lovelace says he will not use force, for "There is no triumph in force—No conquest over the will—No prevailing, by gentle degrees, over the gentle passions!" (IV.223; 2.398). However, that disclaimer is hardly to be believed, for it misrepresents the situation that Lovelace *knows* he is going to bring about by the threat of fire. When the Fire Plot propels Clarissa out of bed in terror of being torched alive, she will be in a condition of absolute anxiety and not at all interested in those "gentle passions" that he pretends to hope will "prevail" over her. To the contrary, *terror is what he intends* to raise in Clarissa, and when she is tumbled from the terror of immediate incineration into an equivalent terror, which is that of defloration and the completion of Mr. Harlowe's curse, there is little reason even for the patient reader to believe the story that he is arousing her erotic passion "by gentle degrees." Even granting that Lovelace accepts his own cover-story, that his purpose is revenge and seduction his means, one ought to ask with not a little skepticism, why does it take him two weeks to invent the Fire Plot? and why is it so obviously designed to fail in its putative purpose of sexual seduction?

Unlike the Test of Virtue Plot invented during the three-day space from April 11 to 13, the Fire Plot emerges far more slowly, for Lovelace has no ideas in mind that could recover his purpose. Brooding upon what to do next, Lovelace engages in damage control with Clarissa while trying to discover another way of proceeding. He treats her more kindly, initiates the Tomlinson reconciliation scheme to make her more yielding and swallows ipecacuanha to make himself ill and remind her that she loves him. At the same time, in self-reflection he is often "soberized into awe and reverence" (IV.226; 2.400) by meditating on Clarissa's admirable traits, he writhes in pain at the thought that she "really does despise me" (IV.225; 2.399), he steels himself against her by "re-perusing some of Miss Howe's virulence" and recalling "the contempt they have both held me in" (IV.311; 2.460), he revels in past sexual exploits and his future rape of Miss and Mrs. Howe, he dismisses the "lurking varletess CONSCIENCE," which exits through an open window (IV.226; 2.400), and he counters with his "affronted God of Love" psychomachia Belford's plea that he be merciful to her. Until he can discover some design principle upon which to ground another plot, he lacks any purposeful strategy against Clarissa, and the result is that he vacillates between those contradictory impulses which compete within his narcissistic psyche.

The central reason for his vacillation is that the nature of Lovelace's psychic hunger has changed, and therefore the strategy towards Clarissa that he adopts ought to be different in order to be need-appropriate. Clarissa's "Begone" refusal drives Lovelace to compel her to forgive and heal him. Forgiveness and healing, the unacknowledged self-desire that stands revealed in Lovelace's self-abasements, has now been annexed to revenge and narcissistic feeding as another—and an increasingly more central—intention. Forgiveness and healing being his new motive, his design problem is to invent some device to extract Clarissa's forgiveness. How? What will evoke her forgiveness? The best procedure for gaining forgiveness might be to insult her, and thus provide the offense she can forgive. Lovelace needs half a month to figure that out, for he is unconscious of the alteration in his motives. He keeps searching about tentatively, then finally he grasps in his June 5 breast-kissing action the design principle he needs. Before that incident, Lovelace has not touched Clarissa in any erotic manner. There was always a possibility that she might cooperate were she approached directly, but the breast-kissing vignette demonstrates that she will not. That is the datum Lovelace must be assured of in order to design the Fire Plot. In this interlude, Clarissa is at peace, his cheek is upon her shoulder, while she is

> Apparently loath, and more loath, to quarrel with me; her downcast eye confessing more than her lips could utter. Now surely, thought I, is my time to try if she can forgive a still bolder freedom than I had ever yet taken. (IV.332-3; 2.476)

When Lovelace removes her bosom handkerchief and kisses a breast, she breaks free of his encircling arm "with indignation" and goes away, showing that she thinks him an insulting "encroacher." Her indignant response to his sexual fondling demonstrates that, were she insulted by "a *still bolder* freedom," she would not cooperate but strenuously resist. He has found the design principle of the Fire Plot—the "*still bolder* freedom"—the necessary insult which he hopes will evoke from Clarissa the forgiveness that he needs.

That Lovelace has a new motive in eliciting forgiveness does not mean that earlier motives of revenge and narcissistic feeding have been discontinued, for one can see clear evidence of them in his "Twin Lovelace" and Oriental Potentate fantasies. Lovelace imagines Clarissa with "a Twin Lovelace at each charming breast, drawing from it his first sustenance." But that fantasy does not signify the erotic wish to father her sons; instead, it signifies his desire to be fondled and nourished by Clarissa while he feeds parasitically on her distressed emotion; he imagines her as "full of wishes, for the sake of the pretty varlets, and for her own sake, that I would deign to legitimate" (IV.334; 2.477) to remove the shame of illegitimacy. Like the "Twin Lovelace" fantasy, the Oriental Potentate shows sadistic brutality as sexual domination:

> thou seest me sitting supinely cross-kneed, reclining on my soffa, the god of Love dancing in my eyes . . . the sweet rogue, late such a proud rogue, wholly in my power . . . She tenders her purple mouth . . . Once more bend to my ardent lips the swanny glossiness of a neck lately so stately. (IV.21-2; 2.251)

For Lovelace, sexuality encodes, enacts and enforces narcissistic desire, as shown by the fantasied Clarissa pleading with a lordly Lovelace to "legitimate" their children, as she lifts her "purple mouth [Her coral lips will be purple then, Jack!]" to this sadist master who holds her in thrall.

Examining his conduct during the Fire Plot, one finds strong evidence that defloration is not what Lovelace genuinely intends. When Clarissa flees her room in terror of incineration, she meets a narcissist who devours her emotions while she pleads "I conjure you not to make me abhor myself!" (IV.369; 2.503). But he fails to enact the sexual violation which he had protested he intended. He does not physically subdue Clarissa to test whether she would show "*consent in struggle*" and "*yielding in resistance*" (IV.13-4; 2.245). Instead, he is content to press his person against hers: her "sweet bosom . . . heaved and panted" so that Lovelace could "distinguish her dear heart flutter, flutter, flutter against" his own and he "feared she would go into fits" (IV.366-7; 2.501). Why is he delinquent? Why does he not finish his work? Because the job to be done is not essentially sexual. His purpose really is narcissistic and not erotic. If in sexual arousal one becomes "acquainted with the pulsing of the spirit in the flesh, which fills the body with a pervasive 'I'" and turns it into "something strange, precious and possessible" (Roger Scruton 30), then what one sees in the Fire Plot is not sexual response, not in Clarissa and not in him. Clarissa's strong physical reaction is provoked by the twin terrors of bodily violation and religious defilement. And one sees that when Lovelace tells Belford to "reflect" on his suffering on account of Clarissa's neglect, he is enjoying having gotten omnipotent control over his maternal selfobject.

Irritation because of maternal neglect is always Lovelace's complaint. In the April 12 argument at St. Albans, for instance, he complained that his "chearfulness and ardor" (III.13; 1.500) had been returned by Clarissa's neglect. Immediately before his "affronted God of Love" psychomachia on June 6, Lovelace re-lives his sufferings outside Harlowe Place in the cold night, "Kneeling on the hoar moss on one knee, writing on the other," waiting for Clarissa to come, knowing he will be disappointed—his heart kept in motion by "Love and Rage" (IV.356; 2.493). The same complaint is expressed in the Fire Plot, the only difference being that he now intends to *force* her to provide her attention and acceptance:

> And now, Belford, reflect upon the distance at which the watchful Charmer had hitherto kept me: Reflect upon my Love, and upon my Sufferings for her: Reflect upon her Vigilance, and how long I had lain in wait to elude it; the awe I had stood in, because of her frozen virtue and over-niceness; and that I never before was so happy with her; and then think how ungovernable must be my transports in those happy moments!—And yet . . . I was both decent and generous. (IV.367; 2.501–2)

These are not the reflections of a sexually aroused male bent on the advancement, enhancement and appropriate conclusion of erotic engagements with a woman. They are the complaints of a neglected child trying to wrest maternal warmth from its neglectful mother.

The innovation which happens midway through the Fire Plot is that Lovelace's feeding on Clarissa's emotion is displaced by his irritation at the accusations she brings against him, which wound his heart and refocus his attention on the desire to be forgiven. When she calls him a "villain," he does not deflower her but asks *"Am* I then a villain, Madam?—" *"Am* I then a villain, say you?" (IV.370; 1.503) and begs her to retract. The triumph he relishes in the "Twin Lovelace" and Oriental Potentate fantasies is again disappointed, for his heart is "dastardized" precisely as it had been during his May 21 self-abasement. Again Clarissa's control overmasters Lovelace's, for he pleads where he intended to force, insisting that she forgive him "heartily" and "freely" and "look upon" him tomorrow "as if nothing has passed." Clarissa promises because she must, but she sounds insincere, which exasperates him enormously because eliciting her forgiveness was his real motive. She promises to forgive, but her "peevish affirmatives" sound too much like "intentional negatives" (IV.373; 2.505). Thus the Fire Plot does not conclude with the forced seduction Lovelace said he intended. Instead, it ends with the inconclusive continuation of the unhappy narcissistic transaction that is concealed behind his seduction cover-story, which is a narcissistic "stalking-horse."

The psychic collapse that could be foretold from Lovelace's earlier self-abasements occurs when Clarissa abandons him after the Fire Plot. To demand that she look upon him "as if nothing had passed" shows that he does not feel responsible for his acts, but Clarissa does consider him responsible, and flees Sinclair's. Her unexpected abandonment causes Lovelace's palpable expressions of that "sense of worthless and lack of self-esteem" (Kohut 1978, 421) which his grandiose pretenses had masked, and he undergoes a complete psychic collapse. She has, he says, stolen "the dearest property I had *ever* purchased" (V.17; 2.518), the ideal self that he cannot live without. Lovelace endures a triple sorrow because he cannot see Clarissa, or hear her, or experience her comforting physical presence. Compelling evidence of his psychic implosion can be found in his description of her empty room:

> I have been traversing her room, meditating, or taking up every-thing she but touched or used: The glass she dressed at, I was ready to break, for not giving me the personal image it was wont to reflect, of *her*, whose idea is for ever present with me. I call for her, now in the tenderest, now in the most reproachful terms, as if within hearing: Wanting *her*, I want my own soul, at least every-thing dear to it. What a void in my heart! What a chilliness in my blood, as if its circulation were arrested! . . . (V.25–6; 2.524).

Wanting to break her mirror shows the anguish of a self no longer validated by Clarissa, with the result that his psychic stability collapses. As to the "void" and "chilliness" in his blood, Kohut points out that the vascular systems of narcissistic persons often are psychosomatically weakened. In narcissists "the self has not been solidly established," with the result that its "cohesion and firmness" have to be effected by "the presence of a self-object." Losing Clarissa causes "simple enfeeblement, various regressions, and fragmentation" (Kohut 1977, 137).

> when, in my first fury, at my return, I went up two pair of stairs . . . and beheld the vainly-burnt windowboard, and recollected my baffled contrivances, baffled by my own weak folly, I thought my distraction completed; and down I ran as one frighted at a spectre, ready to howl for vexation; my head and my temples shooting with a violence I had never felt before; and my back aching as if the vertebrae were disjointed, and falling in pieces. (V.26; 2.524)

Lovelace truly is "falling in pieces" as the result of Clarissa's abandonment.

Notes

1   William Beatty Warner improves Lovelace's allegedly "sincere" proposals into evidence of Clarissa's general mendacity. Thus he says: "Clarissa arranges to have a book edited that will tell her story. But, in order to make her past appear as an inevitable-looking cause-and-effect sequence that sweeps her toward death, Clarissa must repress and conceal the contingent moments of the past, the chancy moments in the genuine proposal scenes where the story of Clarissa and Lovelace suddenly opens out to comedy and love" (x). Warner is reading Richardson's novel through the eyes of harlequin romance, for Lovelace's proposals are never sincere, and nothing ever "suddenly opens out to comedy and love."

2   I am not alone in this perception, for Paul Coates says about Lovelace that his "helpless submission to her pull [can] be seen as an attempt to recover the intensity of the mother's love for the young child" (37).

Chapter 6

The Rising Blow

Once the Fire Plot has revealed Lovelace's malevolence and prompted Clarissa to withdraw the last vestiges of her belief in his veracity, the rape becomes inevitable. Though Lovelace says that he will avoid force since it provides "no conquest over the will" (IV.223; 2.398), physical force has always been imminent, for when Belford cautions him "it would be a million of pities to ruin a woman . . . who is in your protection, and has suffered so much for you" (IV.11–2; 2.244), Lovelace replies that cruelty may be needed in Clarissa's test: "there may be *consent in struggle*; there may be *yielding in resistance*" (IV.13-4; 2.245). In fact, though, he uses force because he cannot achieve a "conquest over" her will any other way. The "rising blow" (V.224; 3.147) of rape is designed to overmaster Clarissa by annihilating her ability to resist. "Consent" and "yielding" are irrelevant in any case, the opiate having deadened her consciousness. Lovelace's pretense of "testing" her virtue has always had the function of rationalizing his subconscious narcissistic intention: Clarissa's extinction in revenge for a murder attempt upon him, as her nightmare had seen.

But though in retrospect Clarissa will recognize Lovelace's intention as having been murderous, in the period leading to the Fire Plot his malevolence is by no means that clear. She remains with him because, though she would not be happy as his wife, she desires to be reconciled with her relatives. Lovelace's pretense of promoting that reconciliation keeps her with him, even though she finds him less attractive as a potential husband now than she once did. To Miss Howe, Clarissa says:

> I, who have now but one only friend, shall . . . have as many new ones as there are persons in Mr. Lovelace's family; and this whether Mr. Lovelace treat me kindly or not. And who knows, but that by degrees, those new friends,

by their rank and merit, may have weight enough to get me restored to the favour of my relations. (IV.251; 2.418)

Given what she knows (Lovelace's conduct is "very unaccountable," but whether owing to "the want of a clear head, or a sound heart" she "cannot determine" (IV.213; 2.391)), the hope of securing new friends and recovering her relatives by marrying Lovelace despite his demerits is a reasonable hope—though a bleak one. It is the snare which Lovelace is setting when he informs Captain Tomlinson in Clarissa's hearing, "I will not only co-operate with Mr. John Harlowe, as you ask; but I will meet Mr. James Harlowe senior, and his Lady, *all the way*" (IV.309–10; 2.459–60). She embraces that hope saying, "Oh, Mr. Lovelace, how happy shall I be . . . When I shall again have Uncles and Aunts, and a Brother and Sister, all striving who shall show most kindness and favour to the poor outcast, then no more an outcast" (IV.311–2; 2.461).

After this period of reasonable hope of reconciliation ends with the Fire Plot, nothing tempts Clarissa to marry the man who, she now understands, means to destroy her. Her comprehension of Lovelace's deceit needs both time and reflection, for, unlike her readers, she is unaware of the enormous scope of his plot against her. By reflection, she gains hindsight and comes to understand her deceiver. Immediately following the Fire Plot, she tells him "The more I reflect upon your vileness, your ingrateful, your barbarous vileness, the more I am exasperated against you" (V.9; 2.512). And as her exasperation deepens with further reflection, she informs Lovelace at Hamstead, "At once my mind takes in the whole of thy crooked behaviour; and if thou thinkest of Clarissa Harlowe as her proud heart tells her thou oughtest to . . . seek thy fortunes elsewhere" (V.130; 3.76). Knowing that he is unable to accept the truth, Clarissa bypasses Lovelace and addresses his creature, Captain Tomlinson, fervently explaining that "It is now *wickedness*" for Lovelace to tell the lie "that his last cruel and ungrateful insult [the Fire Plot] was not a *premeditated* one." The Fire Plot has expunged her "byas in his favour, and made me chuse to forego all the inviting prospects he talks of [family reconciliation], and to run all hazards, to free myself from his power" (V.185; 3.117).

But the unshakable decisiveness of her rejection of Lovelace is most clear in the letter she writes Miss Howe from Hamstead in which she recognizes Lovelace's intent as Satanic. She no longer has any other concern, she says, than to flee the "great fiend of all" who is now "unchained" on her (I.53; 3.18). *Unchained* is the clue that Clarissa understands Lovelace's deceptions in light of *Revelation,* chapters 12 and 20, with its great dragon named Devil and Satan, the fiend who "deceiveth the whole world" and persecutes the woman who "brought forth the man child." Clarissa in her *Revelation* allusion and Lovelace in his "Twin Lovelace" fantasy both realize that the woman is being attacked for having angered the dragon. *Revelation's* Satan is defeated because the faithful "overcame him by the blood of the Lamb, and by the word of their testimony." That is, the price of telling the truth in Satan's face is the victorious defeat of the martyrs, who "loved not their lives unto the death."

In *Revelation,* the dragon's attack causes death by immersion in fiendish falsehoods: "The serpent cast out of his mouth water as a flood after the woman, that he might cause her to be carried away of the flood" (12:15). After Clarissa has been raped, Miss Howe will compare her to a traveller whose path is "overcome" by flood waters: "If you can, without impeding your progress, be the means of asswaging the inundation, of bounding the waters within their natural chanel, and thereby of recovering the overwhelmed path for the sake of future passengers who travel the same way," counsels Miss Howe, "what a merit will yours be" (VI.235; 3.416). However, she is too sanguine, for Clarissa will be "carried away" by the rape, of which the Fire Plot has already been a frightful portent. Clarissa herself does not expect that, for she intends to escape from this "specious form" who has been sneaking toward her, concealing his "feet and talons" until, as her nightmare had foreseen, he can strike at her heart and "trample upon" her honor (V.53; 3.18).

If Clarissa's reconciliation hopes are dashed by her terror of destruction by the "great fiend," Lovelace's hopes and fears are feverishly aroused by her escape. He has wanted to continue punishing her for revenge and feeding on the distress he creates, but above all he has wanted to be forgiven and healed; healing is now the preeminent motive in his melange of pathological desires. Foreshadowed in his selfabasements and articulated in the Fire Plot, his expectation of being healed by Clarissa is powerfully presented when he first sees her at Hamstead. "Thou canst not imagine," he tells Belford, "how my heart danced to my mouth at the very glimpse of her; so that I was afraid the thump, thump, thumping villain would have choked me" (V.77; 3.36). When her apartment door opens, Clarissa blazes upon Lovelace "in a flood of light, like what one might imagine a man, who, born blind, had by some propitious power been blessed with his sight, all at once, in a meridian Sun. Upon my Soul, I never was so strangely affected before" (V.83; 3.40–1). He anticipates the ecstacy of self-completion when admiring the room that symbolizes Clarissa: "There is room," he says, "for my wife's Cabinet" with its "many jewels" of "high price." Even without Lovelace's comparison of Clarissa's virginity to miser's gold hidden in a secret spot, one knows that the imagery is sexual, but it is crucial to grasp that this sexual imagery symbolizes Lovelace's hope for union with the admirable self Clarissa represents. His repossession of her can, he thinks, heal his psychic disability. That is why he presents himself to her as a gift and expects her to be happy to have him. When she "started, and looked at me with terror," Lovelace knows

> it was impossible to conceal myself longer from her, any more than (from the violent impulses of my passion) to forbear manifesting myself. I unbuttoned therefore my cape, I pulled off my flapt slouched hat; I threw open my great coat, and, like the Devil in Milton . . .
> *I started up in my own form divine,*
> *Touch'd by the beam of her celestial eye,*
> *More potent than Ithuriel's spear!* (V.83; 3.41)

The "excited hypervitality" of this self-presentation to Clarissa masks the "deep sense of uncared-for worthlessness and rejection" which Lovelace feels, the "incessant hunger for response" and the "yearning for reassurance" that are typical manifestations of the narcissistic personality (Kohut 1977, 5); as the gouty old fellow is transformed into a vibrant youth, so Lovelace wants to be made whole by the curative power of Clarissa's "celestial eye." He is anticipating a "sexualized merger with the rejecting features" of the "omnipotent parental imago" (Kohut 1977, 127) who demanded of him, "Would you evermore argue with me, as if you were a child?" (IV.90; 2.301). Because his narcissistic self does not "provide him with [the] enriching ideals" (127) she embodies, he has tried to heal himself by taking Clarissa from her home and imprisoning her in Sinclair's, and her escape to Hamstead is the "rejecting feature" that he hopes to overcome by their "sexualized merger." Thus Lovelace's complicated Hamstead fabrication, featuring the disappointed husband whose reluctant wife refuses to consummate and thereby brings rape upon herself, makes narcissistic sense.

Lovelace's desire to be forgiven and healed by Clarissa is not fortuitous; it is a hope which holds at bay the corresponding fear that he may succumb to a desire for self-annihilation, since rejection by an ideal self is tantamount to self-rejection. Thus one arrives at the best hidden motive in his narcissistic psyche: Lovelace's fear of self-annihilation and his decision to protect himself by sacrificing Clarissa. Because his fantasies are the key to his unconsciously narcissistic self, it is not surprising that this deep motive has already been darkly articulated in the "poor hungry fox" fantasy. When Belford warns that deflowering Clarissa would be disappointing because "a Partington, a Horton, a Martin, would make a Sensualist a thousand time happier than she either will or can" (IV.12; 2.244), the wildly misunderstood Lovelace corrects Belford's misconceptions by telling fantasies which articulate the narcissistic motives that he himself cannot understand. One of them, the "poor hungry fox" fantasy, begins to explore questions of fault, guilt, punishment and justice that lie at the heart of Lovelace's defective self.

When the fantasy opens, the fox, "watching his opportunity" as Lovelace watched near Harlowe Place, "had seized by the neck, and shouldered, a sleek-feathered goose" to feed on later at his leisure. As is evident from other self-descriptions, Lovelace sees himself as both the controller of others and their helpless victim. The same contradiction is seen in the "poor hungry fox" fantasy, for no sooner has it pictured his grandiose self as the daring thief than it refocuses upon his helpless victim self, an endangered vermin being chased by

> the whole vicinage of boys and girls, old men, and old women, all the furrows and wrinkles of the latter filled up with malice for the time; the old men armed with prongs, pitchforks, clubs, and catsticks; the old women with mops, brooms, fire-shovels, tongs, and pokers; and the younger fry with dirt, stones, and brickbats, gathering as they ran like a snowball, in pursuit of the wind-outstripping prowler; all the mongrel curs of the *circumjacencies* yelp, yelp, yelp, at their heels, completing the horrid chorus. (IV.16–7; 2.247)

Though Lovelace tells the story as if the malice that the fantasy dramatizes were some external threat, in truth the "old men armed with prongs" and the "old women with mops" running "in pursuit of the wind-outstripping prowler" are neither society in general nor the Harlowes in particular. The malicious pursuers represent the unconscious desire for self-annihilation which Lovelace projects onto the social world.

The "poor hungry fox" fantasy is not required to demonstrate that Lovelace shifts blame to Clarissa and feeds on her distress, for that has already become evident. But the fox fantasy reveals that Lovelace's most deeply hidden motive is the desire to shield himself from self-annihilation, and that discovery is achieved by following a series of sequential steps. The first step is to see that the "malice" directed at the Lovelace-fox in the fantasy has been tranferred to Clarissa. One realizes for instance that when Lovelace displays her at the party for his friends, he wants them to view her "Before her beamy eyes have lost their lustre: While yet her charming face is surrounded with all its virgin glories; and before the plough of disappointment has thrown up furrows of distress upon every lovely feature" (III.316; 2.214). Violating her, as Lovelace plans to do, will destroy that majestic beauty, and her loss of beauty will be his gain in grandiose self-esteem. What most deserves attention is the phrase "furrows of distress," which echoes the "furrows and wrinkles" filled with "malice" that the "poor hungry fox" fantasy attributes to the vicious villagers in pursuit; both of his descriptions of malice-furrowed faces are other versions of the scowling face of the angry infant mirrored upon Belford's face in the "affronted God of Love" psychomachia.

Thus far we have been traversing familiar ground, Lovelace's transfer of guilt to Clarissa, but we are now entering unexplored territory in pursuit of his most secret and elusive motives. The "poor hungry fox" fantasy appears not by itself but gathered into a sheaf with other fantasies that are focused on Lovelace's anger towards women (like the "Bird new-caught"). Personal animus does not enter into his wish to brutalize Clarissa, for she is a woman and all women deserve to be punished. On the heels of the "poor hungry fox" comes a fantasy of punishing cruel women because they enjoy preparing food from the bodies of living, suffering beasts. He sees himself as a vigilante magistrate, dispensing justice and punishing cruelty by seducing women; thus he seduced the girl who enjoyed watching her cat torture its mouse before eating it, and so too he seduced the girl who whipped pigs and roasted lobsters while yet alive and scraped fish "the contrary way of the scales" to make them "leap in the stew-pan"—all this for luxury, raising an appetite, while his appetite is ravenous "without stimulation" (IV.17; 2.248). These fantasies all reveal that his transference of blame to women and his punishment of their alleged cruelty are generic to his narcissistic self—but what makes the "poor hungry fox" fantasy so uniquely valuable as an interpretive tool is that it brings Lovelace towards the figural reversal that most clearly reveals the psychic threat he most carefully masks from himself.

Lovelace's hidden motive stands revealed: when Belford warns him that raping Clarissa will make her unhappy all her life while it cannot make the ravisher himself "happy for a single moment," Lovelace replies, "Does not the keen foxhunter endanger his neck and his bones in pursuit of a vermin, which, when killed, is neither fit food for men nor dogs?" (IV.19; 2.244). Here the fox is no longer an heroic emblem of Lovelace's grandiose self, for, in a surprising reversal, it has been transformed to an emblem of the worthless self that is vigorously hunted and destroyed by his foxhunter self. The Lovelace-hunter pursuing the Lovelace-fox in sport is figurally identical with those villagers who, armed with "prongs, pitchforks, clubs, and catsticks," come after him intent on his total destruction. That the foxhunter endangers "his neck and his bones" pursuing an animal unfit to eat figures Lovelace's unconscious recognition that he is without value. The villagers chasing Reynard, like the Lovelace-foxhunter, are, in Kernberg's vocabulary, "devalued shadowy images" of the fragmented self that actively (though covertly) desires its own extinction.

Thus Clarissa is doomed, because, although she is incapable of healing Lovelace's disfunctional self, she is quite capable of suffering the violence he would otherwise direct against himself. Because rejection by her is equivalent to self-rejection, he must defend himself against self-annihilation by annihilating her, and rape is that annihilating action. So Clarissa unwittingly seals her own fate when, at Hamstead, she adamantly repulses Lovelace's effort to extract some minimal token of her forgiveness, approval and acceptance. Readers often have the impression that Clarissa wavers here, for Lovelace controls the narrative from his arrival at Hamstead until her second escape from Mrs. Sinclair's brothel. He creates the impression that Clarissa is leaning in his favor, despite her clear declarations to the contrary, for we follow the action only as he projects it onto the screen of his narcissism. Tom Keymer warns us about this part of the novel that Lovelace's control over the narrative means his "particular view of events" governs our responses, and he draws attention to "the oppressive dominance of Lovelace's viewpoint before the rape" (1992, 46). If Clarissa were vacillating, Lovelace could hope for acceptance, and he would postpone force until it became absolutely necessary. Clarissa's stout rejection means that rape becomes necessary now: "would I not have avoided it [force], if I could?—Have I not tried every other method? Have I any other recourse left me?" (V.283; 3.190).

At Hamstead, the "foreign aid" Lovelace calls in, Captain Tomlinson and the Lady Betty impersonators, provide him a final hold on Clarissa, though that hold is weak because she suspects "a confederacy of his creatures" (V.198; 3.127). "Mr. Lovelace has the art to make himself many" (V.190; 3.121), Clarissa tells Tomlinson, who does her no harm because she refuses to take his bait, but the women impersonating Lady Betty and Cousin Charlotte gain more ground, and Clarissa's response to them can be mistaken as evidence that she wavers in her rejection of Lovelace. She is reluctant to meet them, for she knows that when they press her to forgive and marry Lovelace she will be unable to be frank: "I was sorry that I had given way to this visit. For I knew not how, in tenderness to relatives (as I thought them) so worthy, to treat so freely as he deserved, a man nearly allied to them: So that my arguments, and my resolutions, were deprived of their greatest force." Nevertheless, her social reluctance to give particulars of Lovelace's bad conduct for his aunt and cousin does not weaken her decision to refuse him: "as to the success of their requests in behalf of their Kinsman . . . *that*, I begged their pardon, was out of the question" (VI.152–3; 3.355–6).

Beseiged as she is, Clarissa agrees to "consider the matter" further, but in such narrow boundaries that it is equivalent to a socially tactful denial of the impersonators' pleas.[1] She agrees to rethink her plans if the "measures" she has already "resolved upon" do not work out, but this is her habitual prudence at work. Furthermore, after the rape Clarissa says that *had* they persuaded her to marry him, her "principal inducement" would have been to bring "an unsullied honour in dowry, to a wretch destitute of all honour," in order to earn "the gratulations of a family to which thy life has been one continued disgrace" (V.338; 3.232). That she is attracted by the bait the pretended noble ladies offer her testifies to the firmness of Clarissa's refusal of Lovelace: the subsidiary goods offered are inadequate to effect her compliance.

But although Clarissa wants to be polite to the prostitutes whom she thinks noble ladies, she is unwilling to marry Lovelace to please them. It is true that she "had not been so indulgently treated a great while by a person of character and distinction" (VI.152; 3.355), and it is also true that she is very interested in their express wish to further "general Reconciliation between the two families" (VI.154; 3.357), but it is not accurate to say that she would seek reconciliation at the price of marrying him. That had been her position *before* the Fire Plot, but now that she recognizes his essential fraudulence, she will not agree to marry the "great fiend," knowing he wants to ruin her. Nonetheless, if Lady Betty and Cousin Charlotte are the good people that Clarissa supposes them, it is reasonable for her to believe that they would agree to work toward reconciliation without expecting her to marry Lovelace as the *quid pro quo*. Lovelace himself understands that she is not wavering in her refusals, for he does not introduce the impersonators until *after* he concludes that rape will be needed, and he relishes the certainty that she cannot escape being raped. He had intended the flight to show that she loves him *better* than her family, and he is angry, Clarissa tells Miss Howe, because he recognizes that "any favor I was to confer upon him was to be the result of—There he stopt—And not of my choice" (VI.154; 3.356).

That is exactly the rub. Lovelace cannot be satisfied with anything less than Clarissa's "own choice," and still she refuses him, so rape becomes necessary to destroy her *capacity* to refuse. Because she functions as his self, her rejection is equivalent to *self*-rejection; he demands that she do for him what he cannot do for himself, which is to condone his vile conduct. The moment of crisis arrives in the midnight rumination at the midpoint of his unsuccessful four-day Hamstead campaign to extract her approval. The rape, he first tells Belford, can "make a greater fault serve as a sponge to wipe out the less." But the addendum "Wafer'd on" (V.221–2; 3.144–5) to his original letter presents still another psychomachia. In this psychomachia, Clarissa (as conscience) has "stolen my pen" and "in a hand exactly like my own" pictured the "happiness" of one who "moves regularly to some laudable end, and has nothing to reproach himself with in his progress to it!" If he lived morally he would not be "*compelled* to be the wretch my choice has made me," nor would he be "a machine at last" instead of "a free agent" (V.223–4; 3.146). Knowing that the rape/murder of Clarissa would render him "a machine at last," he nevertheless decides to murder his Clarissa-conscience:

> I seized her by the throat . . . Take *that*, for a rising blow!—And now will *thy* pain, and *my* pain from *thee*, soon be over.—Lie there! Welter on!—Had I not given thee thy death's wound, thou wouldst have robbed me of all my joys. Thou couldest not have mended me, 'tis plain. Thou couldest only have thrown me into despair. (V.224; 3.147)

Clarissa's murder in narcissistic self-reflection is the climax of the novel for Lovelace because it is here that he endorses the pathological compulsions she challenges in him. Trying to become an ethical adult would have "thrown him into despair." And self-defense, nature's first law, demands that he silence her.

Once Lovelace has protected himself from Clarissa's refusals by killing the conscience she represents, he sounds variations on the theme of death. "It would be hard, if I could not overlay a young Conscience"

(V.236; 3.155), he tells Belford, as neglectful mothers "overlay" and smother their infants. The alternative to killing her would be suicide—the hanging, drowning, or shooting that he says Clarissa's departure letter is meant to drive him to (V.238; 3.157). Her denunciations of his chicanery are dangerous because in his heart Lovelace realizes that Clarissa's judgments are true. That is why he proceeds with the murder of conscience; he shields himself from the truth about himself by silencing her:

> the haughty Beauty will not refuse me, when her pride of being corporally inviolate is brought down; when she can tell no tales . . . ; and when that Modesty, which may fill her bosom with resentment, will lock up her speech. (V.283; 3.190)

Rather than reform himself and earn her praise, he will "lock up her speech" by an insult which is unforgivable—and unspeakable.

Stanley Rosenman's interpretation of Ovid's Narcissus myth, in which the river god Cephisus rapes and nearly drowns the water nymph Liriope, Narcissus's mother, confirms our understanding of Lovelace's behavior. Liriope's son spends his whole life trying to escape "mortifying captivity by another person who violates his very being" (530). He does so by mirroring the violence he himself endures. He victimizes others to assure himself "that he is godly and special." Like Kohut, Rosenman describes a process that raises the fragile narcissist above his "needy, depreciated victim" (529). Rosenman's reading of Narcissus also provides a clearer understanding of Lovelace's dependence upon Clarissa for self-approval. As Narcissus gazes into his pool, Lovelace gazes at Clarissa and "whimpers for the image to tell him whether he is a lovable or a naughty child. He surrenders power to the other to be his judge [and] decide whether he deserves to live" (538). Clarissa's rejection signifies that Lovelace does not deserve to live, which is why he reads her last letter as intended to make him kill himself. Rosenman also illuminates Lovelace's psychic identification with Clarissa during the rape, which is an act of suicide along with a murder: "Narcissus also undergoes Liriope's terror, being prostrate in the hands of the homicidal god" (540).

Lovelace's psychological identification with Clarissa, the surrogate self whose destruction will ward off self-destruction, is further suggested in his narration of her final hours before the rape. Just before the defloration, Lovelace dramatizes her terror at the violence she will suffer. He narrates Clarissa's anguish with empathy, observing it but also experiencing it. By entering her emotional state, he shares her waning consciousness and monitors her intense feeling of disorientation:

> "Once more she urges—To Mrs. Leeson's let me go, Lovelace! Good Lovelace, let me go to Mrs. Leeson's. What is Miss Montague's illness to my terror?— For the Almighty's sake, Mr. Lovelace!—her hands clasped. O my angel! What a wildness is this! (V.289; 3.195).

In this way his "sexualized merger" with the "rejecting features" of the omnipotent parent (Kohut 1977, 127) is imaged and enacted.

Though Lovelace's murder of conscience is verbally rendered, Clarissa's rape is not narrated. Although convention may forbid telling it, the absence of the rape narrative helps to compound our sense that Lovelace is as much the victim as the victimizer. Symbolically enacting his own self-obliteration obliterates his self-awareness. Given the transference bond that connects him to Clarissa, Lovelace is the co-victim of the violence which he aims at her. This explains why he becomes passive during the rape and transfers to Mrs. Sinclair and her women the brute physical force of the act. Though he is the rapist in the sense that his sexual organ violates Clarissa, it is the prostitutes who enact the rape as a social reality, using him as their instrument. His empathy with Clarissa's agony—which is not sympathy or compassion, to be sure—is a function of his denial of responsibility for the rape, which the narcissist perceives as being done *to* him, not *by* him.[2]

Lovelace's expectation of the rape's outcome is disappointed in every way. He expects that Clarissa will forgive him and that forgiveness will amount to tacit approval, he being "the only man on earth, whom she could forgive on the like occasion" (V.297; 3.200). But she does not forgive, and expectation of a grandiose triumph is likewise disappointed, for instead of meeting him with "face averted: Speech lost in sighs—Abashed" and with "downcast countenance" (V.320; 3.218) after being raped, she advances with dignity: "her eyes neither fierce nor mild, but very earnest; and a fixed sedateness in her whole aspect, which seemed to be the effect of deep contemplation" (V.322; 3.218–9). His narcissistic situation is more untenable after the rape than before. As ever, he vacillates between admiration and revenge, for while he feeds upon her moral achievement ("My very crime is your glory" (V.339; 3.232)), he concurrently transfers his guilt onto her; he intends to punish her for his own guilt; should she "carry her rejection into violence," she will provoke "fresh violence" (V.335; 3.229) which (in his mind) will justify the original violence of rape.

In fact, all the narcissistic symptoms seen before the rape still operate, more intensely, following it. Lovelace's fear of being abandoned—
activated by his supposition that when Clarissa bumps her nose upon
a chair (blood "running in a stream down her bosom") she has killed
herself—causes him to draw his sword in a "wild agony" (V.349; 3.240)
to kill himself. The self-abasements which used to be infrequent have
become his predictable responses towards her. Two days after her
nosebleed, while insisting that her indignation cannot exceed his regret for the rape, Lovelace takes hold of her clothing and, as she
struggles to leave, pleads "I will not permit you to withdraw [still holding her gown] till you tell me you will *consider*." When Clarissa scorns
him, he in craven admiration answers her "Your scorn but augments
my love" (VI.26–7; 3.260–1).

Not only are Lovelace's narcissistic symptoms worsened after the
rape, some of them lose any plausibility and simply go wild. For instance, he begins a feeding frenzy that makes grotesquely clear his
wish to eat Clarissa; he "snatched her hand," he says, pressing it to his
lips in such "wild disorder" that she "might have felt [his heart] ready
to burst its bars" (VI.40; 3.271) as it did during his Hamstead repossession of her. Such feeding on her is no longer disguised as erotic
kiss-biting. It is an open, palpable effort to force an emotional indebt-
edness or attachment. Even Clarissa's furious indignation encourages
his more vigorous efforts: "I hung over her throbbing bosom," he
says, "and putting my other arm round her waist—And you say, you
hate me, Madam—And you say, you despise me—And you say, you
promised me nothing"—(VI.41; 3.272).

The rape thus demonstrates both the complete exhaustion of
Lovelace's power over Clarissa and the failure of his narrative to prop
up his deficient self-esteem. The low point of that dual humiliation is
the Penknife Scene, in which Clarissa, the "fair briberess" about to be
tried for corrupting a servant, repudiates the "contemptible and abandoned" wretch who has designed such a "poor villainous plot" (VI.60–
1; 3.287). The compulsion to make himself magnificent in the eyes of
his admiring mirror cannot be controlled and stopped just because his
grandeur has evaporated. Ironically, the compulsion to dramatize his
own failure replaces his earlier need to celebrate his omnipotent control. He cannot help narrating his own abject defeat. "Thou shalt have
it all," he tells Belford, "Thou canst not despise me more than I despise myself" (VI.59; 3.286–7). Clarissa's conclusive demonstration
of her power over him is the scene in which, by holding the penknife

with its "point to her own bosom, grasping resolutely the whole handle" (VI.61), she composes her own ending to Lovelace's play:

> What an admirable contriver did I think myself till now! . . . Scratch out, erase, never to be read, every part of my preceding Letters, where I have boastingly mentioned it. . . What a cursed hand have I made of this plot!" (VI.66–7; 3.292)

The upshot of the rape is to leave Lovelace confused, beaten and demoralized. This is not a bad outcome—if the narcissist's loss is the man's gain in self-knowledge. But self-knowledge is more than Lovelace can bear. For the time being, however, he is suspended between his guiltless grandiosity and a newly acquired uneasiness in which he simultaneously blames and defends himself. He would prefer to believe that Clarissa's rape was an accident, but he believes in villains, not accidents: "Have I nobody whose throat, either for carelessness or treachery, I ought to cut in order to pacify my vengeance?" (VI.102; 3.318). Having in effect cut his own throat by giving her the "rising blow," he now wishes to kill her murderer.

Lovelace's post-rape condition is pictured in two fantasies found in his June 30 letter, which responds to Clarissa's June 28 escape from Sinclair's. The first, his "chevalier in armour," is Lovelace's figurative admission that, by ruining Clarissa, he has destroyed his own life's hope. Imagining his life if he reformed and married her, he pictures their family in church together, the fruitful spouses attended by their many offspring, the chevalier advancing with his wife to the altar, "marching with her thither, at the head of their boys and girls, processionally as it were." But then the whole entourage are transported to the land of the dead and transfixed into monumental stone:

> And then, what a comely sight, all kneeling down together in one pew, according to eldership, as we have seen in effigie, a whole family upon some old monument, where the honest chevalier in armour is presented kneeling, with uplifted hands . . . Facing his pious dame . . . Over their heads semilunary rays darting from gilded clouds. (VI.100; 3.316)

Ostensibly, the fantasy pictures Lovelace's rejection of ordinary domesticity, for when he imagines himself a husband and a father he imagines a state of death, a funeral past which is distanced by the woman's old-fashioned ruff and the chevalier's carapace of armor. The marmoreal stiffness of the actors, the regimentation of their positioning ("in one pew, according to eldership"), well expresses Lovelace's aversion to marriage "according to the old Patriarchal system" (VI.99–100; 3.316). Observed in this light, Lovelace is dramatizing his distaste for "shackles." But behind this cover-story one sees the actual import of this fantasy, its narcissistic content. The clue is in his midnight psychomachia, where Lovelace "enacted" the rape: "Thou couldst not have mended me, 'tis plain. Thou couldst only have thrown me into despair" (V.224; 3.147). Behind his insuperable aversion to marriage lies his inability to engage with Clarissa in an adult manner. While the "chevalier in armour" figures the future with Clarissa which he declines to have, the fact that he pictures that future as an inaccessible funereal past expresses unconscious despair: despair that the rape has failed to ameliorate, despair that Lovelace can neither escape nor conceal.

The same letter contains Lovelace's other post-rape fantasy, the "*laced-hat orator*" with his "picture-of-the-world vehicle." The "orator" fantasy pictures the narcissistic envy and revenge that the rape enacted, but it also shows the alteration in self-projection that the transaction with Clarissa has brought about. To see the change, one need only compare his self-congratulatory grandiosity after the flight with his Clarissa-accusatory stance after the rape. At St. Albans after the flight, Lovelace crows:

> I am taller by half a yard in my imagination than I was. I look *down* upon everybody now. Last night . . . I took off my hat, as I walked, to see if the Lace were not scorched, supposing it had brushed down a star; and, before I put it on again, in mere wantonness, and heart's-ease, I was for buffeting the moon. (II.32; 1.515)

But after the rape, the "laced-hat orator" no longer insists upon the star-brushing levitation of his earlier naive narcissism; now he assumes the more defensive stance of accusing Clarissa instead of congratulating himself; his prior grandiosity is reassigned to a "pretty little Miss" walking through the "great Fair" the world

> Till at last, taken with the invitation of the *laced-hat orator,* and seeing several pretty little bib-wearers stuck together in the flying-coaches, cutting safely the yielding air, in the One-go-up the Other-go-down picture-of-the-world vehicle, and with as little fear as wit, is tempted to ride next. (VI.101; 3.317)

Here Lovelace shields himself from accusation by transferring the fault to the Clarissa-child who destroys herself by following her own reckless, hubristic impulse to reform a rake ("She had formed pretty no-

tions how charming it would look to have a penitent of her own making dangling at her side to church" (VI.100; 3.316)), and thus she has
only herself to blame when the "amorous See-saw" finishes its work:
"after two or three ups and downs, her pretty head turns giddy, and
she throws herself out of the coach when at its elevation, and so dashes
out her pretty little brains" (VI.101; 3.317). In this fantasy Lovelace
stands upon the ground while his hubristic surrogate-self Clarissa plummets like Icarus. Though that ought to have solved the problem,
Lovelace continues seething with envy and anger against this "pretty
little miss," this Clarissa-child who does everything well and is admired and beloved by everyone—which, of course, is the reason why
he went to Harlowe Place to take possession of her.

As the "chevalier in armour" figure dramatizes the happiness
Lovelace will never find with her, the "laced-hat orator" fantasy shows
him ruining Clarissa's prospects without enhancing his own. His destruction of the ideal self he loves but cannot achieve has resulted only
in self-pity: "would not the losing of any ordinary child . . . of less
shining or amiable qualities" have been as upsetting "to that family, as
the losing this pretty little miss could be to hers?" (VI.102; 3.317).
Again, the "ordinary child," the enraged, the disappointed infant that
Belford's scowling face had mirrored, intrudes its self. Lovelace's fantasies reveal the sad truth that, behind his facade of grandiose
posturings, he has no "shining or amiable qualities."

Notes

1 Clarissa tells Miss Howe: "In short, my dear, I was so hard set, that I was obliged to come to a more favourable compromise with them, than I had intended. I would wait for your Answer to my Letter, I said: And if that made doubtful or difficult the change of measures I had resolved upon, and the scheme of life I had formed, I would then consider of the matter; and, if they would permit me, lay all before them, and take their advice upon it, in conjunction with yours, as if the one were my own Aunt, and the other were my own Cousin" (VI.153; 3.356).

2 Judith Wilt and Raymond Hillard have illuminated this point. Wilt's "perhaps outrageous hypothesis" that the rape either was incomplete or "was carried out by the man's female 'accomplices'" (19–32) is an engaging device for drawing attention to Lovelace's passivity during the rape. Wilt's observations corroborate those of Rosenman, expecially in seeing Sinclair as disdainful mother. Wilt observes that Sinclair "counted on and used the 'woman' in [Lovelace] to bring him to the verge of rape," which makes sense if one sees the events not as Lovelace narrates them, but as Mrs. Sinclair would do. Wilt's observation that "Lovelace is shocked" to find in Clarissa's detention for debt "evidence of Sinclair's independent malicious agency" is correct, but Lovelace has always disavowed his own guilt by being "shocked" when accomplices carry out his own intentions. Once he goes into his not-guilty stance, Lovelace is happy to step aside and be scandalized by the women's "natural crescendo of duplicity, malice, and violence," in which he becomes "more openly to his own intelligence their tool" until at last they proceed "without him" (27).

Hillard's comments are closer to Rosenman's than are Wilt's because he employs psychoanalytic concepts to explicate the rape. Echoing Wilt by noting the rape's "peculiarities," Hillard says

> The oft-noted peculiarities of the episode—Lovelace's hesitation, the text's reticence about the actual violation—are best understood in relation to the preponderant role taken by the sinister matrons, 'Lady Betty' and Sinclair herself, whose significance is underscored by the unfailing marks of orality. The physical violence actually described is exclusively oral, Sinclair 'blubbering and exclaiming' at Clarissa with 'mouth . . . distorted' and Lovelace looking on with 'shut teeth' as the women force her to drink stupefying potions by which she is 'almost choked.'

As Hillard points out, Lovelace is not a "free agent" during the rape episode. He is "the machine of an introjected cannibalistic mother." Hilliard is right, for the prostitutes are carriers of the destructive half of his divided object image of woman as both admirable and horrible. Hillard continues, the various episodes surrounding the rape reveal him as torn between an idealized Clarissa and the wicked Mother Sinclair, who ridicules and prods him toward violation each time the 'divine' Clarissa overawes him. He hopes by the rape . . . to assert total autonomy and omnipotence, to reduce Clarissa to 'absolute dependence' on him. (1090–1)

Chapter 7

Clarissa Agonistes

The problem that the rape poses for Clarissa is, above all, a problem of intelligibility. How does Clarissa understand the moral world before the rape? The answer is, of course, that she knows what she has been taught by her family, which can be found in the Harlowes' favorite biblical text, Ecclesiasticus. There, she has learned about duties towards parents, charity towards the poor, humility and self-possession, distrust of the wicked, the certainty of retribution, the importance of foresight, prudence and vigilance, all of it presented in Uncle Antony's plain talk. When Clarissa approaches the Harlowes to request a last blessing, Uncle Antony accuses her by quoting from Ecclesiasticus ("Your poor Father but yesterday shewed me this text: With bitter grief he shewed it me . . . 'A Father waketh for his Daughter, when no man knoweth; and the care of her taketh away his sleep . . . lest she make thee a laughing-stock to thine enemies' [*as you have made us all to this cursed Lovelace*] *Ecclus.* xlii. 9, 10, &c.")," adding a further stinging admonition, "Would to the Lord you had acted up but to one half of what you know!" (VII.105–6; 4.104). Uncle Antony still views the moral world in the simplistic terms that Clarissa formerly shared but no longer does, baffled as she is by her inexplicable personal experience.

The vision of human wisdom that Clarissa has been taught by Ecclesiasticus is based on the concept of merit. As Paul Ricoeur says, "being pleasing to God does not remain external" to a man's essential self: "it adds something to his personality, his inmost existence," and that something is merit, "the imprint of the just act [which is] a modification of the good will . . . an increase in the worth of a man, issuing from the worth of his acts." This self-enhancing notion of merit connects it to the idea of reward, because "to have merit is to merit something; it is to merit a reward." On the contrary, failing to act justly merits condign punishment, and punishment is essentially a personal loss, since "what is lost is what is subtracted from existence, as merit is an increase in life" (Ricoeur 1967, 129–30). Clarissa's life is unintelligible after she is raped because she has received what Ecclesiasticus would call the Evil Man's reward, even though she intended her actions to demonstrate that she is the Just Woman.

What is at stake here is Clarissa's foundational ambition in life, for she hopes to live the life of excellence. Her personal temperament and character formation have made her the embodiment of what Ricoeur calls "the subtle and delicate conscience." The problem is that that character structure, while admirable in many ways, is vulnerable to a flaw caused by its own ethical strength. What can happen is that "merit, by which conscience gains worth, becomes an advantage, a possession, on which [one's] conscience presumes" (139). Clarissa's ethical vision of the world is what Ricoeur calls Pharisaism, which is centered on the conception of "a liberty entirely responsible and always at its own disposal" (130). As those essential words "entirely" and "always" testify, the Pharisaic vision assumes that one's will and capacity to act are strong enough for every moral test; that is why Ricoeur says "The ethical universe of Pharisaism is already that of Pelagius" (131). As Reinhold Niebuhr points out, when Pelagianism tries to increase "the sense of responsibility for individual sinful acts by emphasizing the freedom in which they are committed," the end result is "to make every sinful act appear as a conscious choice of evil in defiance of a known good" (247)—a paradoxical outcome which only worsens the problem Pelagianism wished to solve. What Saint Paul advocates in opposition to the Pharisaic and Pelagian conception of morality is an entirely different conception of sin in which evil is based not on the breaking of divine commands but on "the will to save oneself by satisfying the law." Saint Paul calls this "boasting in the law," in which, in place of a radical "confession of sins as affecting the person as a whole" (Ricoeur 1967, 145), one substitutes scrupulous examination of the purity of one's intentions. This is what Clarissa does when asking for Miss Howe's help as a "looking-glass" to reflect "imperfections" (I.65; 1.48) in her conduct which—having seen—she can correct.

Clarissa's *de facto* theological position is Pelagianism, for as Carol Houlihan Flynn explains, "She labors to perfect herself, showing a Pelagian faith in the power of good works." The rape, however, assaults Clarissa's "latitudinarian optimism," forcing her to reconsider "her notion of herself and her salvation" (26). Clarissa's earlier conception of herself and her salvation was an unstable mixture of the theological doctrines she had learned and the intuitive experience of herself as capable of doing good and avoiding evil by her deliberate choice. She had been *taught* that "ORIGINAL Sin standeth not in the following of *Adam* (as the *Pelagians* do vainly talk;) but it is the fault and corruption of the Nature of every man" (Art. of Religion No. IX, Book of Common Prayer). Yet she *lives* as though sin consisted in "the following of *Adam,*" in the sense of choosing evil instead of good. If that is Clarissa's belief earlier in the action, on May 21 humiliation by Lovelace already makes her hold her optimism suspect—"I had not given myself leisure to reflect . . . how much truth there is in what Divines tell us, that we sin in our best performances" (IV.197; 2.378).

Clarissa's theological vocation after the rape is the effort to reinvent the doctrine of original sin based upon the evidence of her own experience. Original sin, as Ricoeur describes it, is a "dogmatic mythology," but one in which Saint Augustine captures "something that Pelagius completely misunderstood," the something which Clarissa too failed to understand ("'Original Sin': A Study in Meaning" 1974, 281). With symbols like wandering, revolt, the missed target, the tortuous path, and captivity, biblical writers found and drew attention to "certain obscure and obsessive traits of the human experience of evil" that cannot be expressed by "the purely negative concept of fault" (1974, 282). The indication of sin is not consciousness of sin, nor is sinfulness reducible to a conception of individual guilt, because sin is a power that holds captive—not a "swerving" but a "fundamental impotence" (282-3).

To find intelligibility in her experience of evil, Clarissa asks *how else*—other than as punishment—can her awful experience be plausibly described? In the penitential experience of Israel, concepts such as judgment, condemnation and punishment provide "a schema of representations." But the realities that such concepts express are "ontological relations," or relations between God and his human creatures. Though the relationships between humans and the divine can be represented by juridical ideas like punishment, they can also be represented using an analogy of person-to-person interchanges. In fact, God's Covenant with Israel has never been limited to expression in juridical figures, for the Covenant with Israel is also represented as a mutuality in love. God's "wrath" and the "conjugal" bond tying God to

Israel constitute the tragic and the lyric images for expressing their love-pact. God's wrath and the conjugal union are complementary metaphors which, working together, represent the relations of human beings and God without any need for "the ethical framework of law" as a representational figure ("Interpretation of the Myth of Punishment" 1974, 368–70). This is the fresh understanding that Clarissa gradually acquires, one that makes possible her reading of her disaster as the divine application of cleansing wrath in preparation for union with God.

Clarissa interprets the rape as the wrath of God. The rape is a physical action which has profound implications because its intrapsychic and social fruit is defilement, that is, Clarissa's experience of being symbolically soiled by contact with a quasi-physical source of evil, in this case the man Lovelace. When he decides to deflower her, Lovelace's conscious intent is to "lock up her speech," but Clarissa announces her defloration publicly, and by doing so she "enacts" her defilement into social reality: it is only "in the sight of other people who excite the feeling of shame" that a stain becomes defilement, for to be defiled one has to be "regarded as defiled" (1967, 36,40–1). The confession enacting her defilement begins when Clarissa challenges Lovelace, "thinkest thou, that I will give a Harlot-niece to thy honourable Uncle, and to thy *real* Aunts; and a Cousin to thy Cousins from a Brothel?" (V.338; 3.232).

If enactment of her defilement comes naturally to a woman in the habit of speaking the truth who *knows* she has been soiled and transformed into a social pariah, it is difficult for Clarissa to answer the question that defilement raises, i.e., what sin have I committed? Presuming that disaster is God's punishment for sin, and presuming further that sin is willful transgression of divine law, Clarissa is baffled, for she has not intended to do evil and is not conscious of having committed any. The whole point of her prudence has been to *avoid evil* by foresight, self-discipline and rational choice. Yet somehow it is her prudence which has itself brought her to her post-rape impasse. What is this but the same paradox which Saint Paul states by saying, "when I would do good, evil is present with me" (Rom. 7:21))—the same insight echoed by the Book of Common Prayer's contrast of "original guilt" and "all actual sins of men." The Clarissa who once ignored the evidences of "original guilt," who once believed sin voluntary and intended to avoid evil by scrupulous oversight of her own motives, has set foot upon unfamiliar territory. She has no other alternative but to explore the experiential darkness of her defiled self, hoping to find an explanation for what seems inexplicable.

The trauma of being raped, which undermines Clarissa's sense of who she is, discloses itself in three stages: defilement, sin and guilt. The first stage, defilement, feels like a stain; the the second stage, sin, is like deviation from her true path; the final stage, guilt, feels like accusation of wrongdoing (Ricoeur 1967, 18). In her post-rape papers and elsewhere, one recognizes that Clarissa is trying to understand the changes within her self in terms of defilement, sin and guilt. It is critical to realize that her sin is neither the ethical fault of violating the taboo against intercourse outside marriage, nor the "juridical offense" of disobeying a father's will. Her sin, as Ricoeur expresses it, is the alienation that makes her "incomprehensible to [her]self," the outcome being that "God is hidden" and "the course of things no longer has meaning" (1967, 8). Clarissa's sin is, then, that puzzling experience of self-alienation which lies behind the myth of Adam's fall and the doctrine of original sin that derives from the myth. The experience of rape is incomprehensible to Clarissa until she can find a language to articulate what has happened to her, and in her post-rape papers she begins that work of semantic discovery.

Clarissa's defilement by rape marks her with the symbolic stain she anticipates in the Fire Plot, fear of which triggers the physical, ethical and religious terror of being made filthy by the contagious source of evil: "I conjure you not to make me abhor myself!—Not to make me vile in my own eyes! . . . Let not my Father's curse thus dreadfully operate" (IV.369–71; 2.503). Her terror includes fear of punishment anticipated for violating the taboo upon intercourse before marriage, the most distressing dimension of which one might call "loss of the personal core" of her existence (Ricoeur 1967, 41). Clarissa's fear of defilement raises the related fears of being pursued by demons and abandoned by God, who, she surmises to Lovelace, "will not wholly abandon me when I am out of your power—But while in it, I cannot expect a gleam of Divine grace or favour to reach me" (V.127; 3.73). All her anxieties have been realized in the rape, which makes her abhorrent to herself, fulfills her father's curse and draws God's punishment upon her.

Clarissa's defilement reveals not that she *intended* to sin, but that she has entered the *condition* of sin, meaning that she has strayed from the right path.[1] "Ever since I knew you," she tells Lovelace, "I have been in a wilderness of doubt and error" (I.92; 3.47–8). The

rape reveals that Clarissa is separated from God, for what differenti-
ates sin from defilement is "the personal relation to a god" (1967,
48). That separation from God provokes her penitential effort of searching backward from the known facts to the obscure background that
can explain her being lost.

Clarissa's Penitential Mourning

Clarissa progresses in her post-rape papers from defilement, to the
recognition that she has deviated, to the self-accusation which constitutes guilt. If sin reveals "the real situation of man before God," thereby
condemning the complacency of one's self consciousness, guilt is the
accusation that transforms the sinner into a penitent. Guilt, or awareness of one's faults as they are "represented by the tribunal of conscience" (Ricoeur 1967, 104), is the interior act by which Clarissa
assumes responsibility for her deeds. When she said "Let me wrap
myself about in the mantle of my own Integrity, and take comfort in
my unfaulty intention!" (III.256; 2.168), she had been sincere but short-
sighted, for she could neither foresee her future nor apprehend the
extent of her own unintended culpability; once she has recognized
that, she rejects the comfort of good intentions and assumes responsibility for her condition by accusing herself of bad judgment. Her guilt
is the willingness of ethical adults to assume responsibility for the
unintended results of their action. By taking responsibility for her situation, Clarissa demonstrates that she is prepared to atone for her mistakes through her sufferings. At that juncture, she begins to see that
she is engaged in dialogue with God, whose censure she experiences
as absence and silence, and she begins to overcome their separation
in her post-rape papers.

The ten fragmentary papers that Clarissa writes and discards in
distress under her table as she slowly recovers sanity make up a sequence of internal dialogues that examine the damage her self has
sustained, predict its effects and assign blame. In these papers, as
Kinkead-Weekes says, the Clarissa readers have come to think of as
"an analytic mind, collected, firm, penetrating" suddenly drops away
and one sees "a lost and bewildered teenage girl, confused and grief-
stricken . . . seeking desperately for reassurance and love . . . and
failing to find any" (233). But though she is deranged rather than
collected and firm, her mind continues analytic and penetrating. Paper 1, which seems spoken to Miss Howe, is in fact spoken to Clarissa's
intra-psychic idea of their friendly relationship. It begins the fact-find-

ing with the observation that "I am no longer what I was in any one thing" (V.303; 3.205). Thus when she begins to write "I am still, and I ever will be, *Your true——*", she is unable to write "friend," because the self who was Miss Howe's friend is gone. Neither can she conclude with her personal signature, since that token of her identity is not accurate either. No longer what she was "in any one thing," Clarissa cannot recognize her self.

Paper 2, addressed to a mental conception which combines her loving father and that father who has cursed her, is also focused upon the question of personal identity: she is the unworthy child of a father who cannot "resolve for ever to reprobate [his] poor child." Out of this intuitive trust she calls upon him for help. She calls universally ("will nobody plead for your poor suffering girl?"), and then she calls specifically on her father, and, like Job calling on the Lord to defend him against the Lord, she asks what he cannot deny: "Why, then, dearest Sir, let it be an act of your own innate goodness, which I have so much experienced, and so much abused." Dismissing the paternal curse as the temporary interruption of their continuing relationship, Clarissa declares herself her father's daughter: "I *will* call you Papa, and help yourself as you can—for you are my own dear Papa, whether you will or not—And tho' I am an unworthy child—yet I *am* your child—" (V.304; 3.206). After this declarative speech act, the executive "I" of Clarissa's personality can reassume its personal authority, for she is no longer hovering on the brink of madness.

Her identity being assured, Clarissa in Paper 3 searches for the cause of her disaster by inventing a beast fable about a lady who tried to tame a lion or a bear cub. This fable personalizes the figures of the prophets Amos and Hosea to her own case. Amos insists that the "Day of the Lord" will be a day of carnage, "As if a man did flee from a lion, and a bear met him; or went into the house, and leaned his hand on the wall, and a serpent bit him." Hosea prophecies that the Lord, "as a bear," will "rend the [membrane] of [the Israelites'] heart" and "devour them like a lion." Beginning to interpret the violence she has suffered, Clarissa sees Lovelace as the instrument of the Lord's Wrath, in the same way that Assyria and Babylon were instruments of God's punishment of the delinquent Israelites. Hence Clarissa's beast fable about the lady who "took a great fancy to a young Lion, or a Bear" and "fed it with her own hand," until having neglected to "satisfy its hungry maw, it resumed its nature; and on a sudden fell upon her, and tore her in pieces" (V.304; 3.206).

There is strong cohesion between Paper 2, which emphasizes Clarissa's father's "innate goodness" and continuing love despite his curse, and Paper 3, which insists on God's paternal anger in preparation for his forgiveness. Once her parabolic beast fable helps her to see that she is being punished by the wrath of God, Clarissa is able to take the next step, which is to embrace that wrath by assuming responsibility and declaring herself culpable. Paper 4 speaks with the prophetic voice established by the Amos and Hosea allusions in Paper 3. The voice is that of Clarissa's own heart, which finds the cause of her defilement in the sin of pride: "How art thou now humbled in the dust, thou proud Clarissa Harlowe!" Searching for some plausible reason for her fall from God's pleasure, she charges herself with being complacent towards the "expected applauses of all that beheld" her; that is, she was proud in her being "*satisfied* with the adulations paid" to her. By self-accusal, Clarissa increases her awareness of her formerly unrealized fault. Undressing before bed each night, she had "put off every-thing but [her] Vanity!" (V.305; 3.206). This insight metamorphoses the "mantle of integrity," which she once wore with confidence, into a symbol of culpable blindness. Self-accusation is continued in Paper 5, where her "mantle of Integrity" becomes the "thin veil of humility" that formerly concealed her "foolish heart." By Paper 5 Clarissa sees that the specious innocence of good intentions is self-righteousness, of which she now accuses herself. She had been, she admits, "too secure in the knowledge I thought I had of my own heart," for "My fall had not else been permitted." Interpreting being raped as the wrath of God permits Clarissa to repudiate presumptuous self-approval and to recognize that her "supposed advantages became a snare" to her. Given that fact, "what now is the end of all?" (V.305; 3.207).

Paper 6 answers by mourning the "prospects of a happy life" which once opened before her. She mourns the loss of a husband and children, and also her ruined reputation: "No elevation now for conscious merit, and applauded purity, to look down from on a prostrate adorer, and an admiring world, and up to pleased and rejoicing parents and relations!" Her lament shifts attention to the parasite who has spoiled "the laborious toil . . . of the painful Husbandman," and Paper 7, her Ode to Evil, indicts that ruinous pest: "Thou pernicious Caterpiller, that preyest upon the fair leaf of Virgin Fame, and poisonest those leaves which thou canst not devour!" Again, the prophetic images Clarissa uses are reminiscent of Amos's language when he sees God's wrath as forces of nature: "I have smitten you with blasting and mildew . . . yet have ye not returned unto me, saith the LORD" (4:9). Hosea, too, prophecies that "Though he be fruitful among his brethren, an east wind shall come, the wind of the LORD shall come up from the wilderness . . . [and] spoil the treasure of all pleasant vessels" (13:15). Clarissa adopts the same natural figures when she pictures Lovelace as the "fell Blight," the "Eastern Blast," the "overspreading Mildew, that destroyeth the early promises of the shining year," the "fretting Moth" that ruined her hopes, and the "eating cankerworm" (I.306; 3.207); like Amos and Hosea, her purpose is to dramatize Lovelace's function, the wrath of God.

But the wrath of God always summons a potential penitent to repentence. It is true that both Amos and Hosea use figures of natural defilement ("spoiling" by worm or mildew) to image God's intention of punishing a prodigal child. But sin, "the rupture of a relation," is difficult to express in terms of defilement, which is caused by contagious contact with some impersonal source of infecting impurity. Nevertheless, because the metaphors which Amos and Hosea use imply a connection between natural defilement and divine wrath, Clarissa can use them to advance from her sense of having been defiled by Lovelace, to a recognition that she has fallen into the condition of sin, to the consequent insight that her own flawed relationship with God constitutes that sinfulness. Thus she can trace her defilement to a rupture-creating attitude. And because the confession of sin is a figurative cleansing, with the symbolic effects "of spitting out, of burying, of banishment" (Ricoeur 1967, 70,41), when Clarissa announces her defilement in terms of the wrath of God she is beginning her own purification.

Continuing to probe the damage for its roots, Clarissa moves from Lovelace as instrument of the wrath of God to Lovelace as a hypocritical, deceitful man—"Vice itself." Written in prose far quieter than the tremulous plangency of Paper 7, Paper 8 uncovers the self-deception of Clarissa's belief that Lovelace would make a suitable husband. He had seemed "frank, as well as generous," she did not know except by hearsay of "any flagrant instances of" his bad conduct, yet she was guilty of self-deception: "Whatever qualities [she] wished to find" in him she was "ready to find; and, when found . . . believed them to be natives of the soil" (V.307; 3.208). But even when she admits her own self-deception, candor demands that Clarissa find Lovelace more at fault than she is. Paper 9 contrasts her benevolent wish to do good against his criminality, and her cruelest realization is that he never could have ruined her had she not generously tried to help him reform. The just woman has received the reward of the wicked man, and at the hands of the wicked man himself, operating not simply on his own initiative but as the instrument of the paternal curse which Clarissa takes as willed by God.

Clarissa's only recourse after concluding her damage report with the rending pain of betrayal by the man she loved and tried to help is to collapse in dejection and despair, a collapse that is intimated by Paper 10's anguished heap of recollected verses. Most of these show death as a "friend," the "brink of peace" and her one "retreat from infamy." That Clarissa's misfortunes have come tumbling "like waves" incessantly "renew'd" (V.308; 3.209) extends the water imagery of the "great fiend" in Revelation who cast water out of his mouth "after the woman, that he might cause her to be carried away of the flood" (12:15). Clarissa uses this language when she tells Lady Betty that, while trying to "save a drowning wretch," she was "not accidentally, but premeditatedly, and of set purpose, drawn in after him" (VI.125; 3.335).

Unlike Papers 1 through 9, Paper 10 is not addressed to a single psychic audience but breaks in pieces aimed at Clarissa's various personal attachments. Some of the verses she remembers ask Miss Howe to speak "words of peace" to her "divided Soul," others are directed by Clarissa to herself, and yet others speak in a distanced voice of impersonal suffering that broods over the human condition as the grieving woman hesitates between vigorous engagement and escape in death. Her wish to escape pain by going into her grave corresponds exactly to Job's outcry: "Let the day perish wherein I was born" (3:1–3). The most revealing of these verse fragments probes Clarissa's psyche and finds an implication of incest. In the quotation in which Hamlet indicts Gertrude for incest and for complicity in parricide, Clarissa's memory tailors the quote for her own situation, omitting the words "Calls virtue hypocrite," and altering "blurs the grace" to the more definitive obliteration "blots the face":

> —Oh! you have done an act
> That blots the face and blush of modesty;
>   Takes off the rose
> From the fair forehead of an innocent Love,
> And makes a blister there!—

The passage reverberates in several directions, to Lovelace, and to her family, especially her father. In the main, it denounces Lovelace, who, by sullying her "conscious merit" (Paper 6), puts on her forehead the "blister" of self-recognition as his harlot. As Hamlet makes Gertrude reflect upon the difference between her noble first husband and the swinish Claudius, Clarissa contrasts the honorable man she hoped Lovelace would become and the wretch he is. She also reflects upon the process by which she succumbed to the poisonous flattery of her corrupter, and we find once more the images of her Ode to Evil in the words Hamlet directs to his mother, words that we can take Clarissa to be applying to her own situation: "Here is your husband, like a mildewed ear,/ Blasting his wholesome brother."

But the quotation also implicates the Harlowes, especially her father. Clarissa has been defiled by Lovelace, it is true, but we understand him to be the instrument of her brother James sacrificing her with her father's authorization. Her defilement having been prophecied by her father's curse, the accusation of incestuous rape casts its shadow. What does rape of a daughter by a father signify—not in terms of Freudian archaeology, but in the domain of ethics? It signifies the betrayal of respect and piety, the ultimate corruption of "duty." The quote from *Hamlet* is memorable for the outrage and indignation caused by the shame and guilt of incest. But while Hamlet has been contaminated by incest at one remove, his mother having been physically involved rather than himself, Clarissa is defiled in her own person by the man who is her family's tool. She understands perfectly well the *vengeance* which the sexual assault enacted on her; ten days after the rape she apostrophizes Lovelace "O thou *cruel implement of my Brother's causeless vengeance,*" to which Lovelace reacts with the shock appropriate to hearing himself described as James Harlowe's penis. "Her *Brother's* implement! . . . Zounds, Jack! what words were these!" (VI.35; 3.267). The incest here is symbolic, beyond doubt, but defilement is in essence a symbolic stain. In Harlowe Place Clarissa's male relatives had sensed Lovelace's dishonoring of them. Now Clarissa, too, feels the sexual insult—to herself, and to her family from Lovelace, and to her father because of the impiety of her deeds. Like Hamlet, she feels the terrible shame of familial betrayal, for incest violates the bonds of attachment that guarantee the stability and the identity of the self—which is the problem she confronts when she returns to consciousness.

In her post-rape fragments Clarissa begins withdrawing what John Bowlby would call her "emotional investment" in her earlier self, which is a crucial step towards forming another self based on her present condition of irrecoverable loss ("I shall never be myself again" (V.311; 3.212)). This is the function of mourning, which Bowlby describes as a four-stage process in which a mourner recovers the "capacity to maintain love relationships" (1980, 25, 40). In her papers Clarissa begins Bowlby's initial, or numbing, stage. She is stunned, incredulous, hungers for consolation from friends and undergoes sudden bursts of panic and rage followed by periods of unusual calm (85). As Lovelace writes Belford on June 16, Clarissa is sometimes so "stupefied" as to seem "destitute of will," while at other times she is "as much too lively, as before she was too stupid" (V.298,301; 3.201,3). The letter she writes the same day to Lovelace expresses her two contrary impulses, to disappear from sight and to fight against his violence; she wants on the one hand to be put into a private madhouse with only "ink, and paper, allowed me," though her mad letters should not be sent and thus "trouble" her friends, while on the other hand she hopes to expose Lovelace, for she warns him "I shall find out all your villainies in time—Indeed I shall" (V.312-13; 3.213).

Clarissa's vacillations between the impulse to flee and the impulse to stand and fight extend from the numbing phase into the second phase of her mourning, the "yearning and searching" stage, which continues from her June 28 escape from Sinclair's until she finishes writing her rape narrative on July 8. During this time, Clarissa writes Lady Betty and Mrs. Hodges to collect information about the full reach of Lovelace's deception, and she writes Miss Howe and Mrs. Norton hoping to get their support and consolation. Struggling to recover the lost self that she cannot yet surrender but will never regain, Clarissa is attacked by "pangs of intense pining," "spasms of distress and tearful sobbing," restlessness, insomnia, and preoccupation with the admirable Clarissa who once held up her head and looked forward to happy prospects. Scanning the environment for signs of her former self (Bowlby 86–8), she writes Miss Howe on June 28, thinking that renewed communication with her only friend might help to recover her ruined self. "Let me, at awful distance, revere my beloved Anna Howe, and in *her* reflect upon what her Clarissa Harlowe once was!" The defiled woman gazes with anguish and admiration at this virginal friend, "Whose mind, all robed in spotless white, charms and irradiates" while it reflects the self that Clarissa has irrecoverably lost (VI.106–7; 3.321).

When Clarissa writes Lady Betty asking whether there was any basis to Lovelace's fraud, she is continuing to announce publicly the private defilement which her defloration has effected. That she tolerates the truth about herself and speaks it to others is evidence that the yearning and searching phase of her mourning is going well, since the truth must be faced. "Why," she asks Lady Betty rhetorically, "should I seek to conceal that disgrace from others which I cannot hide from myself?" (VI.126; 3.336), which makes it transparently clear that she is no longer the admirable young woman who once might have restored honor to the dishonored Lovelace family. Instead of clinging to the memory of her former self and shrinking in embarrassment from indecorously introducing herself to Lady Betty as her nephew's whore, Clarissa endures the shame involved and announces her disaster to pertinent other, for defilement is a serious business to be treated seriously.

Similarly, in writing to her Uncle Harlowe's housekeeper and paramour, Mrs. Hodges, Clarissa is gathering information that can help her understand how the tragedy she wished to avoid happened. In this, she resembles relatives of the dead person who gather to examine the accident scene, standing as close to the deceased one as permanent separation will allow while they try to accept their loss. As she writes Mrs. Hodges, Clarissa must be acutely aware that she cannot now "look down" from her former position of moral superiority upon this family embarrassment, an uncle's mistress, since she has herself become a greater embarrassment. She writes Mrs. Hodges to learn whether the family gathered for her uncle's birthday, for she is too ashamed to write them directly and risk a violent rejection which she could not endure at this time.

Clarissa's letter appealing to Miss Howe for her compassion, written the day of her June 28 escape from Sinclair's, finds its way into Mrs. Howe's hands, and her sharp reply ("the whole *Sex* is indeed wounded by you") draws "fresh streams of blood from a bleeding heart" (VI.108–9; 3.323), until Miss Howe herself writes on July 5 to point out that Clarissa's "errors" must "weaken" her positive opinion of her, thereby laying "a foundation for future distance, and perhaps disgust" (VI.144; 3.350); this abrasiveness is Lovelace's fault, of course, whose interceptions and forgeries are the cause of Miss Howe's catty accusation. By contrast, Mrs. Norton gives Clarissa real support, and her "grateful" acceptance of the condolences her spiritual mentor extends is another signal that she is "working through" her mourning (Bowlby

93). Clarissa gets needed consolation from her second mother, who suffered like sorrows and not only prevailed over hopelessness but learned from her tragedy to rely on divine providence with faith and courage; while Mrs. Norton was left pregnant and indigent when her husband died, her misfortune was "the happy means" of her being hiring as wet-nurse for Clarissa. Speaking out of personal experience, she reminds her suffering protege that "you know not what God has in store for you" (VI.117–8; 3.329–30), so "Chear up . . . your dear heart, and do not despair" (VI.136; 3.344).

Mrs. Norton's July 3 "Chear up" is timely, since Clarissa is turning increasingly pessimistic, as her July 2 resentment at the Harlowes reveals. Because her family have not located and helped her she thinks they may have found her to be a bastard and turned from her with an "indignation that such a discovery will warrant" (VI.127; 3.337). Bitterness and pessimism are usual phenomena in the yearning and searching phase since desire for recovery of the lost loved one coexists with the "deep and pervasive sadness" of knowing that recovery "is at best improbable" (Bowlby 92). Great sadness also pervades the rape narrative which she writes between July 6 and 8 (VI.154–78; 3.358–74), since she must re-live events that she was too drugged and fearful to fully experience earlier. Her "heart sinks under the thoughts of a recollection so painful" (VI.148; 3.352), yet mourning will succeed only when the bereaved person faces the worst news and endures. A better informed Miss Howe may, after perusing the rape narrative, beg forgiveness for the "harsh things" she wrote four days earlier and celebrate the "sweet meekness and superior greatness of soul" (VI.182; 3.337) that makes Clarissa remarkable, but the two companions have been forced apart by events. Miss Howe is more inclined to pity than admire Clarissa, who, by being raped, has become damaged goods.

The intense grief provoked by Clarissa's recollection of the rape triggers the third or "disintegration and despair" stage of mourning when the agitated hopes kept alive during yearning and searching give way to dejected collapse, and Clarissa surrenders to sorrow. Having forfeited her future, she wishes to die, even though she is still concerned about others. She hopes that her father will revoke his curse rather than "hereafter be grieved" (VI.195; 3.387), and she wonders what will happen to the "false and perjured" Lovelace. Her only personal wish, however, is to "slide quietly" into her grave (VI.177–8; 3.374).

Clarissa's wish is contravened by Mrs. Sinclair's desire to recover her for the brothel, to labor as a prostitute along with her "sisters"

Sally and Polly. When Clarissa is seized for debt and detained at Officer Rowland's house in mid-July, her capacity to reject despair during the "disintegration and despair" phase—which lasts from July 8 until July 20 when she is again with the Smiths—is severely tested. Because she knows that detention in Rowland's is simply a ruse meant to recover her for the brothel, Clarissa realizes that everything depends on her ability not to give way under the double burden of this fresh insult heaped upon former injuries. Her violent hysterics, physical collapse, and a spiritual inwardness so tightly sealed that when Belford comes to release her she "would not, or could not" open her eyes or talk (VI.272; 3.444) show that she is stressed to her limit. Yet she proves in detention that she can bear the "buffeting of emotion" required of her. During detention Clarissa recovers her future, because only a mourner who can endure the grief comes "gradually to recognize and accept" the fact that the loss is permanent and to understand that his or her life will have to be "shaped anew" (Bowlby 93).

While in Rowland's, Clarissa prays fervently to generate the strength she needs. She disappears into her prayer, which occurs not in the social but in the religious register of meaning; while she can transcribe, she can hardly narrate her prayer, because it is not addressed to any earthly audience. Richardson circumvents prayer's essential privacy of address by having Sally, who visits to recruit for the brothel, note that Clarissa has "doubled down the *useful places*" in her bible, such as "*The Book of Job! . . . Ecclesiasticus* too!" (VI.265-6; 3.439). Sally's mockery helps to dramatize the nature of the decision that Clarissa is faced with: either to surrender to circumstances and embrace the gentleman's kind offer to pay her debt and release her from Rowland's, or to remain strong against the tacit despair of expedience. It is the Book of Job that gives Clarissa the figurative language she needs to express desolation and to articulate the suspicion that God is unjust. Job provides the hypothesis she tentatively accepts ("*if they be bound in fetters, and holden in cords of affliction, then He sheweth them their work and their transgressions*" (36:8–9)) as justifying God's conduct while she awaits growth in understanding.

Freed from detention, Clarissa advances to the last stage of mourning, that in which she redefines her self and her situation, actively taking charge of her life once again. Such redefinition is "no mere release of affect," says Bowlby, "but a cognitive act on which all else turns" (94). Her mind begins to "strengthen" and she occasionally finds herself "superior to [her] calamities" (VI.319; 3.479), as happens in mourning's fourth stage, in which disintegration alternates with restoration. When Clarissa finds "her spirits free, and her mind tolerably easy," she gets to work and is once more "a good housewife of her hours" (VI.247; 3.499). Apart from her recovered calm and sense of purpose, another sign of her redefined self is the self-story she tells at the Smiths', in which she narrates her life as the history of an "undutiful" daughter of her very "indulgent" parents. "What some people call cruelty in them, is owing but to the excess of their Love, and to their disappointment; having had reason to expect better from me" (VI.354; 3.504). Her present state, itself a facet of mourning, is one of "humiliation and penitence for the rash step which has been followed by so much evil." She looks forward gratefully to death— "Rest to the most wearied traveller that ever reached his journey's end" (VI.357–8; 3.506–7)—but she conceives of death as the completion of a journey, and she is determined to travel the right path to her journey's end.

That Clarissa begins to prepare for death is so surprising a turn that she is sometimes accused of suicide. However, the text says that she dies of her broken heart. Her reasons for thinking she will soon die, one sees, are based on ruptured relationships, to herself, the Harlowes, Lovelace, and friends she disappointed. One can argue that she could construct her new self on the belief that several decades of life remain, but the novel postulates her intuition that death will come soon. The reasonable thing to do is to accept the postulate and ask, not "why does Clarissa die?," but "what other self can Clarissa fashion in the time remaining?" In the letter wherein she intuits her early death, she states her determination to "possess" her soul "with tolerable patience" in "humble imitation of the sublimest Exemplar" (VI.379; 3.522). She always aimed to imitate Christ ("who *became all things to all men, that he might gain some*" (I Cor. 9:23), as Miss Howe tells us (VIII.221; 4.509)). It is evident that Clarissa, who suffered Lovelace's violence because of her wish to assist him, is forming a new self on the basis of what Heinz Kohut calls her "core self" and "nuclear ambitions,"[2] by bearing unjust suffering in "humble imitation of the sublimest Exemplar."

Though it is true that Clarissa goes through the four stages of mourning described by John Bowlby, it is equally true that her mourning is complicated by the incremental, overlapping nature of her losses, which begin with the loss of tranquillity and love in Harlowe Place and continue increasing their intensity without any relief until shortly before she dies. Once Clarissa has regained time for her own use she becomes "a good housewife of her hours," matriculating in "the School of Affliction," which teaches us to "know ourselves," to "compassionate and bear with one another," and "look up to a better hope" (VI.386; 4.2). While she has put Lovelace behind her, she feels herself obliged to "compassionate and bear with" the Harlowes. She wants to express her penitence, needs their forgiveness, and yearns to have their final blessing. Clarissa's anguish remains intense, but it no longer prevents her from getting on with her life, and reconciliation with her family is the last major task she attempts. While the effort fails, the benign result of its failure is to release Clarissa from anxiety by forcing her to "look up to a better hope," that is, to the God who would not let her rely on anybody but Himself.

The Harlowes are easily, indeed inevitably, misunderstood by readers because their point of view is not presented in the novel except as it is interpreted by Clarissa's and Lovelace's letters. Clarissa, however, has reevaluated her life and realizes how much she has offended them by her apparent defection (VII.43–5; 4.59). Readers who desire to comprehend her conciliatory attitude to the Harlowes have to empathize with her penitential intentions toward her family and make the effort that is required to see the events from *their* viewpoint. In late July they remain in the same state of belief as in early April, when Clarissa insulted them by going with Lovelace. Since then they have fumed and moped, cultivating their anger and suffering pangs of separation from this deceiver, whom they want, of course, to readmit when Lovelace tires of her. Being, as they are, the Harlowes, they look forward to corrective punishment which her trespass deserves. They cannot believe that she will die because it is literally unthinkable: she must return to them, be punished, and be readmitted to their family where she belongs. That is why her death comes as lightning, illuminating their darkness when they realize what they have done: "Now indeed they have it—" (VIII.80; 4.403) says Colonel Morden when he sees them crushed. Clarissa foresees their sorrow crushing them, and because the School of Affliction tells us to "compassionate and bear with" one another, she is solicitous to reduce their sorrow by receiving their last blessing in time for it to console them.

When Clarissa writes them to express penitence and request their forgiveness, the Harlowes answer with furious indignation. One needs to see that the family are beginning the reconciliation procedure with a preliminary refusal to forgive. Since she seems "working about" to be forgiven, they will hear nothing favorable about her, though her father revokes his curse and will, in time, be her "faithful Steward" (VII.32,5; 4.53). Having thus taken an initial step, they move ahead to articulation of their grievances (the sorrow she caused them (VII.39–40; 4.56–7)), exploration of a potential reunion (her Uncle's question about the complication raised by a possible pregnancy), formulation of requirements for readmission, finding a common cause that can reunite her with the family (ideally, bringing Lovelace "to the gallows" for his wound to the "whole injured family" (VII.217; 4.188)), and finally, the joyful reunion which Mrs. Norton calls for ("Let all be forgotten now on this jubilee change" (VIII.11; 4.351)) when it is too late for it to happen.

Disappointed in her hope of a blessing, Clarissa must learn not to succumb to despair. She must "look up to a better hope." The passion of hope is a movement toward a future good, something that is difficult, but possible, to obtain, says Aquinas (IaIIae, 23.1), like the expectation that her family will give a blessing. When they will not, Clarissa must stop hoping for what she cannot have, and that disappointment can cause despair, hope's opposite, the negative recoil from the unattainable object (IaIIae, 40.1). Yet the hope that is disappointed here is what Aquinas would call a natural hope, and the "better hope" which Clarissa needs cannot be achieved until all natural hope is disappointed. This "better hope" emerges within a framework of trial, says Gabriel Marcel, a captivity in which one is "deprived for an indefinite period of a certain light" (30) that one longs for. The trial brings sorrow without any foreseeable end and raises the temptation to despair, which is to "go to pieces," to "disarm before the inevitable" and abandon "the idea of remaining oneself" (37). But patience helps one "keep a firm hold on oneself" and "safeguard one's integrity" (38). Patience is the flexible attitude towards time that allows Clarissa to endure an extended period of anguish, holding on with no hope, yet embracing her pain as "destined to be absorbed and transmuted by the inner workings of a certain creative process" (39). The sorrow of being disappointed by the Harlowes' dilatory neglect is not mortal to Clarissa, for the hope that she creates by strong endurance "tends inevitably to transcend the particular object to which it at first seems to be attached" (32). Marcel's phenomenological hope, i.e., a "response of the creature to the infinite Being to whom it is conscious of owing everything that it has and upon whom it cannot impose any condition whatsoever" (47), is in fact the theological virtue, because it is situated in one's relationship with God.

To avoid despair, Clarissa cultivates a patient resignation, but she also continues to interpret her misfortunes. For if her history is proceeding under the aegis of divine providence as she believes, all things are working towards the good. Therefore she will expect to discover tokens of significance, signs of a wisdom that only disappointment can teach. Among these is a sign we can call "the blessing refused," since Clarissa expects the Harlowes' refusal to be an intelligible contribution to her life's meaning. From the "sign" of "the blessing refused" she learns resignation, the unmistakable accent of which is first heard in her August 19 letter to Dr. Lewen. Interrupting the litany of misfortunes she has been reciting, she breaks into resignation, asking "Why these unavailing retrospections now?—I *was* to be unhappy—In order to *be* happy; that is my hope!" (VII.212; 4.184). Here, Clarissa is announcing the radical change in outlook which she reiterates two days later, by asking Mrs. Norton's prayers that she be "blessed with patience and due resignation" (VII.228; 4.195), resignation meaning having "got above all human dependence" (VII.241; 4.204). After internalizing that resigned condition, Clarissa understands her tragedy as an intelligible fatality; as she tells Mr. Wyerley on August 26, when tactfully rejecting his marriage proposal and reflecting on the configuration of her history, "There was a kind of fatality by which our whole family was impelled, as I may say; and which none of us were permitted to avoid" (VII.240; 4.204).

From that point on, Clarissa is no longer driven by anxiety. Thus on August 31, after having read Brand's inflammatory letter falsely accusing her of promiscuous behavior, she reflects that, though "There was a time . . . when such a Letter as this would have greatly pained" her, she is now indifferent to his calumny:

> There is a good and a bad light in which every-thing that befalls us may be taken. If the human mind will busy itself to make the worst of every disagreeable occurrence, it will never want woe. (VII.297; 4.246)

Following her own sound advice, she accepts the letter in a "good light," reflecting that, had the Harlowes not been "prepossessed" by Brand's lies, they would not have been "immovably determined" to refuse their blessing. How could she expect their pardon and blessing, she reflects, when her penitence seemed to them a mask worn by a "vile hypocrite" to disguise "profligate courses?" Her natural hope is fading before the "better hope" she has acquired, but because that hope is rooted in her relationship with God, she can reach it only by resolving that most difficult of theological problems, the issue of God's injustice.

Clarissa's Meditations

As Clarissa becomes patiently silent in the latter part of the novel, readers can lose touch with her, mistaking Belford's Clarissa or Miss Howe's Clarissa for the woman herself. Because he intends to make his friend penitent, Belford describes her as the pitiful victim of Lovelace's brutality, narrating the "heart-moving" tableau picturing Clarissa with "One faded cheek" resting upon Mrs. Lovick's, "whose tears bedew'd the sweet face which her motherly bosom supported" (VII.412;4.332–3). Belford's Clarissa is a rhetorically exaggerated porcelain saint, not the angry and despondent woman attempting to discover intelligible meaning in her inexplicable disaster. Emphasizing the picture of the white-clad saint in her cell, "kneeling in a corner of the room" with the "fore-finger of her right hand in her bible" (VI.273–4; 3.445), he fails to inquire what she is *doing* in that posture.

Miss Howe's Clarissa is even more pernicious than Belford's. She has urged her friend to marry Lovelace and insisted that she take her advice; when she does not, Miss Howe shifts her position and, writing to Lovelace's relatives, attributes to Clarissa the motives of recrimination and revenge that Clarissa—a disobedient and penitent daughter— is attempting to master. When Clarissa is adamant in refusing to marry Lovelace, Miss Howe alters her story and claims that her friend is dying because "she thinks her first and *only* fault cannot be expiated but by death." Thus, when she trivializes the fault, and then says Clarissa will die to expiate the very fault she has trivialized, Miss Howe is doubly in error. Ignorant of Clarissa's genuine intentions, Miss Howe continues to compare the virtuous woman with the vicious man. Wishing him to be adequately punished, Miss Howe demands that he be "excluded by his crimes from the benefit even of christian forgiveness," which is why she asks that Lovelace's relatives "join with me to admire her and execrate him" (VII.27–8; 4:48). Miss Howe's Clarissa is a pernicious travesty of the sorrowing woman working to overcome the natural instinct to recriminate against those who have harmed her.

So Miss Howe and Belford both misinterpret Clarissa. To get a reading more accurate than theirs, one must attend to what she herself reveals in virtually the only place she reveals it, i.e., in her Meditations upon biblical texts. "On every extraordinary provocation," Belford says, she tries "to regulate her vehemence by sacred precedents"

(VII.126; 4.120). In her Meditations, she answers the question Mowbray asked on her escape from Sinclair's, "Where will she mend herself" (VI.87; 3.307). The "mending" that Clarissa must accomplish to arrive at the state of "blessed hope" which we have seen her express in her late-August letters goes on by means of her Meditations, which because of their importance in her post-rape self-recovery deserve our focal attention.[3]

Clarissa's Meditations are her most important speech actions because they are the essential means by which she regains for her own purposes the time that Lovelace has taken from her. In them, she gradually overcomes debilitating memories of her disaster and makes the turn towards the possibility of recovered expectations. Ricoeur says that expectation is properly called "the analogue to memory" because it presents "the event that does not yet exist" (1984, Vol. I, 11). The expectation that Clarissa's Meditations partially present is the outcome of the developmental process St. Paul summarizes, saying, "we glory in tribulations . . . knowing that tribulation worketh patience; And patience, experience; and experience, hope: And hope maketh not ashamed" (Rom. 5:3–5). Her version of the sentiment "hope maketh not ashamed" is located in Meditation 4: "There is a shame which bringeth glory and grace." Clarissa meditates in order to make the journey from the slough of despond to the country of hope— which is foretold, predicted, proclaimed (says Ricoeur) by expectation.

The struggle is intense because Clarissa finds it virtually impossible to ponder her experience except in the unintelligible terms of "merit" and "reward." Though she tries, as Girard says about Job, "to separate the divine from the human persecutors" accusing her, her efforts are clumsy since her language "remains in the system of violence and the sacred" (1987, 131). And yet, Clarissa gradually learns to discover fresh significance in the familiar words. Job is useful for her developing understanding because it contains the "exemplary history of guilt" which helps Clarissa interpret her experience of evil. Learning to read her disaster "according to the figures of [Job's] exemplary history" helps her to arrive at "adult guilt" and to stop blaming herself for breaking divine law. "The contrary of sin is not morality but faith" (Ricoeur 1974, 347–8). That is the lesson Clarissa learns by adopting "the faith of Job" while she surrenders "the religion of his friends" (351).

Clarissa's Meditations, the texts wherein she engages in her internal Joban dialogue, are provoked by "extraordinary" events such as her detention for debt, being denied a last blessing, and being relentlessly pursued by Lovelace. The "sacred precedents" she uses to "regulate her vehemence" are from the wisdom books in the bible; these contain the semantic paradigms that can help her interpret her experience. To facilitate this spiritual work, she produces five collage texts, selections of verses taken from Job, Psalms and Ecclesiasticus chosen for their pertinence to her own history. Their significance lies less in the individual verses which she adopts than in the contour of the entire text; the form of each Meditation, sometimes balanced and sometimes unbalanced, represents the mental state it helps express. An analogy might be the contrast between the Italian sonnet, which is balanced between octave and sestet, and the English sonnet, unbalanced by three quattrains against a closing couplet. In a similar manner, Clarissa's Meditations are sometimes "in balance," which suggests a placid or at least controlled and stable mental state, at other times "out of balance," imitating the condition of severe mental distress and violent agitation, accompanied by loss of stability and mental control. It is in that sense that each of Clarissa's Meditations represents the mental state that she is "enacting" in prayer, and which Belford (by later incorporating them within his narrative) "enacts" on the social stage of his epistolary prose.

In Meditation 1 (VI.392; 4.6–7), Clarissa's prison-induced awareness of her total ruin is expressed by the imbalance in the stanzaic structure: the first ten verses, which express grinding sorrow, all but overwhelm the final two verses, which attempt to hold off her incipient despair. Her feeling of absolute futility is tempered in this Meditation by the intuition that, because God "*despiseth not any,*" those who are bound "*in cords of affliction*" can trust God's intention, though they cannot understand it. One remembers that when in detention in Rowland's Clarissa is working through the disintegration and despair stage of mourning, so that one is not startled by the anguish her meditation expresses. Her later Meditations image her continued suffering of disintegration and incipient dispair, melding gradually towards the fourth stage of mourning, redefinition of self and situation, with expectation of her eventual triumph over hopelessness and despair.

Clarissa's Meditation 2 (VII.93–4; 4.96) is also bipartite, but its more equitably balanced halves show her growing stability and mental focus after she has departed Rowland's. Its first six verses, all from Ecclesiasticus, are followed by five verses from Psalms. As post-rape Paper 3 had spoken in the admonishing voice of Wisdom ("how art thou humbled in the dust, thou proud Clarissa Harlowe"), so in Meditation 2 that same admonishing voice intones the first six verses: "*Say not thou it is through the Lord that I fell away.*" In the remainder of this Meditation, Clarissa's question at the "turn" from the sestave to the pentet—"*And now, Lord, what is my hope?*"—is answered by the good counsel Wisdom provides and meditation is meant to internalize. In Meditation 2 Clarissa is divided into a sorrowing self in need of wisdom and a prophetic self who points the way. Because she adopts Wisdom's lessons, the verses of the second part are all from Psalms, which offer the hopeful language appropriate to her state of mind.

Meditation 2's persistent prayer that Clarissa be delivered from "*offences*" does not specify particular faults but refers to anything that may have caused her sinful condition. It further expresses her relinquishing the demand that her merit be rewarded by good fortune. In its second part, Clarissa vacillates between two opposed versions of the deliverance prayer, one that is based on fault, one that is not. "*Deliver me from all my offenses*" is fault-based, but "*Turn thee unto me, and have mercy upon me; for I am desolate and afflicted*" is not attentive to fault. It asks only the relief from desolation that mercy grants. Meditation 2 also shows Clarissa's altered attitude to time. In the loss of her beauty "*as it were a moth fretting a garment,*" she reads the message of mortality. If having her beauty "*consume away*" can be interpreted as a "*rebuke*" with which the Lord "*dost chasten man for sin,*" then in figural terms sin resembles the inevitability of natural processes. Although in Meditation 1 Clarissa lamented that her days, passing by "*swifter than a weaver's shuttle,*" are "*spent without hope,*" she has become more patiently resigned to watching her body being slowly "*consumed away.*" She is gradually accepting physical decline as not only inevitable, but as perhaps spiritually fruitful, whether or not that is intelligible to her.

Meditation 3 (VII.100–1; 4.101), stitched with black silk to the bottom of Uncle Harlowe's letter asking if she is pregnant, is also bipartite, and, as in Meditation 1, one observes a gross imbalance between the two sections. Twelve verses of anguished complaint from Job are followed by a two-verse conclusion which attempts to ward off despair. "*My purposes are broken off,*" she laments, for the Harlowes refuse their forgiveness and blessing. Her soul has chosen "*strangling, and death rather than life.*" However, one sees that even though she expresses the extremity of suffering which typifies Meditation 1, it no longer disables her. The prayers that began in Meditation 2 continue vigorously. God, the "*Preserver of men*," has made her his enemy; God has set her "*as a mark against*" Him, and therefore she has become a "*burden*" to herself. She cannot understand the paradox, nor does she try to. Clarissa's developing capacity to bear inexplicable failure is articulated in the structure of Meditation 3, for at the turn which moves from the complaint to the two concluding verses, the affective weight of twelve verses of anguish crushes down on the half-line question, "*And where now is my hope?—*" (Job 17:15). To this, like the turn at a sonnet's couplet, Clarissa replies,

> *Yet all the days of my appointed time will I wait, till my change come* (Job 14:14).

The wisdom which Clarissa achieves in Meditation 3 instructs her to stop making conditions and to trust in the covenant with God. Presuming that patience shall triumph over despair, Meditation 3 foresees an alteration in "*appointed time*" that does not require prior understanding. Clarissa is now prepared to wait "*all the days of*" that time, because she sees waiting as something she is expected to do. Earlier, she measured time by sleepless tossing, and even now she sleeps uneasily ("*thou scarest me with dreams, and terrifiest me through visions*" (Med 3, v. 6)). But now her anguish is no longer the *measure* of her time, as it had been in Meditation I: "*When I lie down, I say, When shall I arise? When will the night be gone? And I am full of tossings to and fro, unto the dawning of the day.*" (v. 4). Meditation 3 does not take her continuing spiritual anguish as the decisive proof that time has broken off her purposes.

Meditation 4 (nine verses from Job, two from Ecclesiasticus (VII.126–7; 4.120–1)) addresses her family. It is not bipartite, for Clarissa is no longer a fragmented self who requires mending. Instead, Meditation 4 speaks with the voice of the reintegrated woman who insists to her family—more accurately, to her psychic conception of her relationship with them—that they must become reconciled to her. As the verses from Ecclesiasticus say, "*there is a shame which bringeth glory and grace*" (4:21), and "*Mercy is seasonable in the time of affliction*" (35:24). It is instructive to note that Clarissa does *not* use Chapter 35's humble man who is "inconsolable" until his prayer "pierces the clouds" (35:17), for she no longer insists on knowing the reasons for her bad fortune. Similarly, she ignores the brutal God who "crushes" the loins of the merciless and exacts vengeance on the nations (35:20) because she adopts Ecclesiasticus's alternative wisdom. Since she is a penitent, hers is a shame "*which bringeth glory and grace.*" She expects the Harlowes to understand that "*mercy is seasonable in the time of affliction*" because it is so needed, "*as clouds of rain in the time of drought*" (35:24).

Meditation 5 (VII.152–3; 4.140), which is addressed to God, is the prayer of the fully coherent self that Clarissa has again become. Because she is "*hunted after by the Enemy of my Soul,*" the Meditation is framed by a prayer for deliverance. The first verse implores God, "*DELIVER me, O Lord, from the evil man,*" and the last verse implores that He "*Grant not . . . the desires of the wicked: further not his devices, lest he exalt himself.*" The sixteen verses in between articulate, in metaphoric language, her need for deliverance. Meditation 5 shows that she has untangled the confusion between God and Lovelace. In Meditation 1 she says "*the arrows of the Almighty are within me; the poison whereof drinketh up my spirit,*" and again, "*The terrors of God do set themselves in array against me.*" God's "arrows" and "poison" expressed Clarissa's anguish at having been raped, as well as the guilt of incestuous defilement. All of her earlier Meditations had conflated God with the instrumental, the Satanic, Lovelace, whose "arrows" and "poison" belonged to God as punisher. With no burden of paradox, Meditation 5 now distinguishes between God and Lovelace, who is the "*enemy of [her] Soul*" for the reason that he continues to pursue her. God as a "hunter" had been inextricably linked with Lovelace as predator, but that link has been severed. Lovelace's "design" on her is not identical with God's plot.

By the time she composes Meditation 5, Clarissa is close to perceiving another crucial distinction, the one between Lovelace the defective man and Lovelace the Satan of her religious anxiety who is the "enemy of [her] Soul." By the time she is dying, she knows Lovelace is not beyond all hope of reform, or she would not write a posthumous letter urging him to try. Here, when Clarissa prays that God deliver her from "*the evil man*" and "*the violent man*" and "*the desires of the wicked,*" she prays to be released from Lovelace's criminal compulsions, from which she will soon be able to hope that he may be delivered.

Meditation 5 also demonstrates that Clarissa's purification is under way, because her death-longing here expresses a wish to be cleansed and made spotless. When she says "*Hide not thy face from me,*" she is asking God to give her light, since Lovelace has made her "*dwell in darkness as those that have been long dead,*" those "half-dissolved carcasses" of her nightmare of being killed and buried (II.264; 1.433). Meditation 5 continues the process which began in Meditation 2: her *"days are consumed like smoke,"* her *"bones are burnt as the hearth,"* she has eaten *"ashes like bread,"* she has *"mingled [her] drink with weeping."* Clarissa is clearly expressing her desire to be purified.[4] Her Meditations are finished when the wrath of God has dissipated and she awaits with patience an appointed time when "the symbolic figure of God" will retain "from the theology of anger only what can be assumed into the theology of love" (Ricoeur 1974, 351).

Notes

1   Florian Stuber has observed that what Paul Ricoeur calls the "symbolism of evil" (lost in the dark, captive, strayed from the right path) first occurs when Clarissa, "Determined not to leave her family," waits in the garden for Lovelace "the day he tricks her into going off with him through that back door, a door which 'leads to a place so *pathless* and *lonesome*' (2.282). The words pathless and lonesome reverberate symbolically" since "What began as natural description becomes a metaphor" whose "pathos" derives from its being "literally grounded" (1995, 106–7).

2   Contrasting his own "self psychology" with the psychoanalytic work of, for example, Hartmann and Erikson, Heinz Kohut says

> It is psychoanalytic self psychology which has hypothesized the existence of a core self consisting of nuclear ambitions, nuclear skills and talents, and nuclear idealized goals and has thus explained the fact that the human self is poised toward the future. The dynamic tension of the program laid down in our nuclear self strives toward realization and thus gives to each of us a specific destiny that we either fulfill, partially fulfill, or fail to fulfill in the course of our lives. It is this hypothesis of a central program that makes up the core of each person's self. (Kohut, 1980, 544)

By being again a "good housewife of her hours," Clarissa recovers what Kohut calls the "program laid down in [her] nuclear self."

3   Tom Keymer's article "Richardson's *Meditations*: Clarissa's *Clarissa*" (in S. R.: Tercentenary Essays 1989), a commentary on "*Meditations Collected from the Sacred Books; And Adapted* . . ." (1749), informs us that Meditations VIII, XII, XIII, XVII and XVIII in *Meditations Collected from* . . . appear in Richardson's novel in that order. I discuss them as Meditations 1 through 5.

4   Regarding the purification theme which one finds expressed in Clarissa's prayerful effort toward self-restoration, Keymer says, "In Meditation XXI, she quotes Psalm 51 for a precise answer to the snow-water image in Meditation V: 'Thou shalt purge me with hyssop, and I shall be clean: Thou shalt wash me, and I shall be whiter than snow' (p. 47)." The cleansing process continues until Clarissa is "purified, healed, and saved" (1989, 99–100).

Chapter 8

Clarissa's Enlargement

The day before she dies Clarissa requests Miss Howe's help one last time: "hope for my enlargement before to-morrow sun-set" (VII.408; 4.329). Clarissa's enlargement is her release from the spiritual dejection which would blight any social future she can imagine, as she says in the July 23 self-assessment written after she regains enough mental tranquillity to contemplate her future. Because she has forfeited "that *noble confidence,* which arises from a mind unconscious of having deserved reproach," Clarissa if married would "*creep to*" her violator and be a prisoner of shame and regret within her own house:

> Do you not see me creep about mine own house, preferring all my honest maidens to myself—as if afraid, too, to open my lips, either by way of reproof or admonition, lest their bolder eyes should bid me look inward, and not expect perfection from them? (VI.375; 3.520)

Unmarried, her situation would be equally unsatisfactory, for she would "*now* sit brooding over my past afflictions . . . And would not my conscious eye confess my fault, whether the eyes of others accused me or not?" (VI.377; 3.521). Getting even with Lovelace does not interest Clarissa; she will not press charges in a court of law for the reasons she specifies to Dr. Lewen, and she is not seeking revenge by dying, though Lovelace believes that to be her intent ("her desire of revenge insensibly became stronger in her than the desire of life: And now she is willing to die . . . [to] cut my heart-strings asunder. And still the more to be revenged, puts on the Christian, and forgives me" (VII.403-4; 4.326)). Her danger is not in answering Lovelace's violence by taking revenge, but in letting resentment towards him turn into self-repudiation. Doing so would endorse Lovelace's violence by tacitly accepting his valuation of her and render Clarissa his permanent victim. Only marriage to him, which as she says would sanctify his abuse, could be worse.

Because she is determined not to endorse by tacit acceptance the violence done her, Clarissa sets out to reconstruct her self, a complex effort which requires that she push forward on several projects simultaneously. While she works through her Meditations to learn resignation, she also tries to recover her lost home and to purify her defiled body. Aside from having defined herself as a daughter, a niece, a sister and a friend, Clarissa has defined who she is in relation to Harlowe Place, the house and grounds of which had been her home; there she received visitors and returned after visits; her portrait in the Van Dyke manner once hung there in a place of honor to celebrate her presence, her belongingness. Using Kohut's term selfobject, one can say that Clarissa has lost her Home Selfobject, that is, her habitual personal experience of her father's house as the "place" in the world where she is fully herself and most truly at home. Similarly, reconstructive effort will be needed to restore her Body Selfobject, since the rape has so corrupted her immediate experience of her body that she cannot now make present within it the mind which she experienced before defilement: the mind "robed in spotless white" which charmed and irradiated (VI.106–7; 3.321) all who knew her. "Dig a hole deep enough to cram in and conceal this unhappy body" (V.343; 3.235), she tells Lovelace, the "unhappy" condition of her body being its scrofulous and putrid symbolic reality. Finding herself homeless and sullied, Clarissa must regain a new home and recover her body from the symbolic condition of rotting enfleshedness that Mildew, Blight and the crawling Caterpillar had expressed in Paper 7.

Her Father's House

As Clarissa's field of action becomes less the ethical and more the religious register of meaning, her audience also changes because she increasingly addresses God rather than Miss Howe and others. And her language becomes increasingly more metaphorical. In terms of verbal inventiveness, Lovelace is without peer in the novel because whenever he dips his pen in ink the fresh metaphors come boiling from him. Clarissa's relationship with language is very different, for she is not an innovator. When she feels the need to articulate her turbulent emotions, she avails herself of biblical texts which contain conventional figures of speech that cultural familiarity has made into dead metaphors. Nonetheless, when Clarissa employs them they become powerful because they are wholly appropriate for the pain she suffers and needs to express. As Tom Keymer puts it, she finds in biblical wisdom the "luminous and cogent symbolism" which enables her "not only to endure, but also to articulate, her experience." It is crucial that Clarissa find reliable language, since, as Keymer says, after the rape she is "less sure . . . of the reliability of self as an organizing principle" and therefore needs "purer and less vulnerable forms of discourse" (1989, 92–4). Clearly, Clarissa's turn towards God requires the shift to new language.

If one must understand Lovelace's narcissistic images as the expressions of meanings that are otherwise inaccessible, one must likewise attend closely to the deeply lived quality of Clarissa's traditional metaphors. During mourning, she pictures the future she expects, and by the act of expecting it produces a memory of that future. After expressing her injury and grief in the images of bondage, exile, failed purpose and darkness which characterize her Meditations, Clarissa begins using figures of "recollection, living fullness, being at home, and light," figures which express her recovery (Ricoeur 1984, Vol I, 28).

Clarissa's history is the story of her relationship with her father, summarized in three phases: father's will, father's curse, father's house. Each phase represents the theology which matches her concurrent religious understanding. In her initial account, she is being punished for violating a divine law expressed by her father's will. But because her reaction to being defiled is too personal for the legalistic metaphor to satisfy her, she proceeds to her second theology, which focuses upon her father's curse and the wrath of God. Thus Paper 2 juxtaposes her unworthiness with his "innate goodness," which she has "so much experienced, and so much abused." Likewise, Paper 3 sees in her defilement the wrath God. As her theological reflection advances, Clarissa surrenders the metaphor of punishment in favor of the theology of love. The analogy of God's love as conjugal love promises that her contrite return will transform God's wrath into its contrary, her marriage to the Heavenly Bridegroom.[1]

Clarissa's return to her Father's House begins at the moment of greatest distance from her father: her consciousness after the rape that her father's curse is fulfilled and that violating his will has made her a spiritual pariah. Paper 2, addressed to Mr. Harlowe, is equally addressed to God the Father. As Lois Bueler shows, her situation, language, and prayers for mercy in spite of her unworthiness constitute an allusion to the prayer before Holy Communion in the Anglican rite (a prayer which requests "that our sinful bodies may be made clean by [Christ's] body . . . and that we may evermore dwell in him, and he in us"). Bueler points out that Clarissa's appeal to Mr. Harlowe is "the first text in which the paternal identity is explicitly ambiguous," since "the cry of the abandoned child to the absent father" alludes not only to the relationship between Clarissa and her biological father but "that between all Christians and their God." The prayer to which paper 2 alludes is the "Prayer of Humble Access," which consists of two parts: first, the statement of relationship, in which petitioners declare their unworthiness, and second, the request:

> We do not presume to come to this thy Table, O merciful Lord, trusting in our own righteousness, but in thy manifold and great mercies. We are not worthy so much as to gather up the crumbs under thy Table. But thou art the same Lord, whose property is always to have mercy:
> Grant us therefore . . . ,

after which the text considers "the acts and the significance of the Eucharist." Regarding the significance of this allusion for Clarissa's post-rape situation, Bueler says

> The statement portion of this prayer not only does what Clarissa is attempting to do, but does it in much the same language. The difference lies in the degree of sureness with which the statement is unfolded: Clarissa is forced to try to establish the foundation for each of her points, to assert her filial right to use this language and perform this act, whereas the prayer assumes that right. (92–3)

Thus at the very time when she faces her condition of defilement and exile, Clarissa trusts herself to God's "manifold and great mercies" and anticipates being received into her Father's House as a prodigal but forgiven daughter.

Initially an expression of the irretrievable losses she has suffered, her Father's House comes to represent the relationship with God that survives Clarissa's feeling of alienation from Him, and eventually it becomes the main image of her recovered future. During the third week of July, the metaphor stands for everything that she has lost. When on July 21 she narrates her story at the Smiths, she publicly recollects a happy childhood in her father's and her uncles' homes: "I was the joy of their hearts; and, with theirs and my Father's, I had three houses to call my own . . . I was beloved by every-body" (VI.356–

7; 3.506). In the same vein, her July 23 lament employs Job's vocabulary of alienation (29:2-5) to express her feelings of exile: "O! That I were . . . as in the the days when God preserved me! . . . When *I was in my Father's house*; When I washed my steps with butter" (VI.372–3; 3.518). But by August 22 the father's house figures her recovered future: "I am setting out with all diligence for my Father's House," she tells Lovelace, where she is assured of "thorough Reconciliation, thro' the interposition of a dear blessed friend whom I always loved and honoured." Busy with "preparation for this joyful and long-wished-for journey," she "cannot spare one moment" (VII.175; 4.157) for Lovelace's meddling interference.

Using the Father's House figure, Clarissa turns her personal recollections into metaphoric thinking to discover things she had not realized before. By metaphor, the mind discovers connections that advance beyond one's conscious thought. Meditating upon her father's and uncles' houses, tokens of an irrecoverable paradisal past, Clarissa repositions those houses in time and significance until they become the beckoning symbols of the desirable time of her "enlargement" into God's own Home. Of course she supplements the materials supplied by personal memory with the Father's House figures in the New Testament, the textual origin of the extended analogy she uses. When Jesus drives the money lenders out of the temple, he refers to it as his father's house, a house of prayer that should not become a den of thieves; when Jesus says that in his father's house there are many mansions, he is continuing and widening the meaning that "house of prayer" already established. Clarissa's thought accepts the invitation of these New Testament father's house texts, as in the letter telling Lovelace that she "cannot spare" time for him because she is preoccupied by travel preparations. Whether or not she recalls Jesus's "I am the door: by me if any man enter in, he shall be saved" (John 10:9), she is happy over her expectation of being received through the advocacy of the "dear, blessed friend" Jesus who calls himself "the door."

In Clarissa's psychic economy, the "Father's House" performs the idealizing work that James Grotstein calls the *selfobject of destiny*: Father's House represents the "repository" of her self's agenda, the "house of its ideals," the "guarantor" of her self's "ambition" (189). The joy of knowing she will be received there is what enables Clarissa to complete her spiritual obligations to the Harlowes and Lovelace. Once her future is thus restored, she can address her father "With exulting confidence" and her mother no longer with "the conscious-

ness of a self-convicted criminal" (VIII.22–3; 4.360). In her Meditations, she develops confidence which makes possible her posthumous
letters and her Will. This experience of "living" inside the "house of
her ideals" provides her the sense of achievement of a difficult bit of
work finished competently and on schedule that Belford observes when
she hands him the key to the drawer that holds her papers after "all is
in order" (VII.355; 4.289–90).

To undertake the journey to her Father's House Clarissa must leave
this world and Richardson's text. Both of these departures occur gradually, the first by means of her religious Meditations, the second by
means of Belford's increasing prominence within and control over the
novel's text. Richardson uses Belford's textual intervention to remove
her from deep engagement in the narrative texture of the novel without removing her from its thematic core. Belford's ordinariness is the
foil Richardson uses to highlight the extraordinary nature of Clarissa's
actions while she prepares for death. As Clarissa is "taken up" by the
rising energy of her continuing prayers for deliverance, her inner spiritual struggle is presented indirectly, through Belford's mundane point
of view. The longer she lives, the farther she moves beyond his empirical monitoring. Positioning Belford in the field of worldly concern
that she is abandoning allows Richardson to gradually "fade out" the
chief character without weakening the force of her spiritual admonitions. Fading Clarissa out meets the difficulty of ending the novel without her; using Belford seems natural because he is her successor as
narrator and ethical exemplar. So when Belford describes Clarissa
meditating on her Father's House—"What . . . must be the State itself
. . ." (VII.248; 4.210)—he orchestrates the drama that fascinates her
public, at the same time that, like them, he fails to understand fully.
The narrative thus presents Clarissa privately exploring her hopeful
future while we remain, with Belford, within temporality.

The use of Belford to enrich our responses to Clarissa's way of
thinking is most intricately developed in the coffin sequence. On the
border between life and death, Clarissa is possessing her soul in patience and finishing her life by disposing of what she owns. She links
these efforts by purchasing a "house" (VII.207; 4.180), her coffin,
and using it to meditate on death. Belford dramatizes how disturbing
the coffin's presence is for ordinary human feelings by narrating
Morden's rumination, "What must her reflections have been, all the
time she was thinking of [buying it] . . . and what must they be, every
time she turns her head towards it?" (VII.413; 4.333). The novel is

not content merely to offer Belford's and Morden's ethically norma-
tive shock or to provide only Clarissa's contemplative motive. It insists
on the collision—the disparity—between their emotions and Clarissa's.
Belford's shock invites Clarissa to explain how she has overcome her
distress by the analogy of leading "a starting Steed" back to an object
that worries it "to familiarize him to it, and cure his starting." Similarly, she asks "Why may we not be as reasonably shocked" to see
funeral monuments that remind us of the ancestors "with whose dust
we even *hope* our dust shall be one day mingled" (VII.309–10; 4.255).
Belford is fascinated but repelled, for the natural man clings to life, but
Clarissa is overcoming her natural desires, overcoming them so totally
that she says, "I dwell on, I indulge (and, strictly speaking, I enjoy) the
thought of death."

    Without Belford's narrative to focus our attention upon the coffin
and to elicit Clarissa's reason for so bizarre an activity as finding en-
joyment in contemplating her death, the Intentional state she experiences mentally would lack occasion to be enacted into social reality by
speech; we need Belford's incomprehension as a foil for drawing forth
Clarissa's explanation that thinking of death "does what nothing else
can do" for her:

> It teaches me, by strengthening in me the force of the Divinest Example, to
> forgive the injuries I have received; and shuts out the remembrance of past
> evils from my soul. (VII.313–4; 4.258).

The counterforce that is activated through her coffin meditations helps
her overcome her natural resentment and desire for revenge. Shutting
out "remembrance of past evils" requires the suppression of accusatory emotions, which she achieves by "inviting" death to take her. In
such reflections she "takes up" death before it can take her; she strengthens her determination not to "disarm before the inevitable," as Gabriel
Marcel puts it.

    The coffin helps Clarissa to continue standing in the breach and
struggling to overcome "black clouds of despondency" that she suffers. Then, surprisingly, one week before she dies meditation begins
to produce intimations of eternity and the conviction that her prayers
are answered. In this realistic novel Richardson, of course, cannot
bring God on stage to reply directly to Clarissa's continuing supplications, but the novel form does permit personal testimonials, such as
hers on August 28, that she is occasionally "blessed with bright hours"
and with such "joyful assurances" of the divine acceptance that she

can "hardly contain herself." At this threshold of her "enlargement," she reaches confidently into an unknown but expected future by wondering, to Mrs. Lovick, what must be "the State itself, the very aspirations after which have often cast a beamy light thro' the thickest darkness, and . . . dispelled the black clouds of despondency?" (VII.248; 4.210). Whether she is its origin or whether the light issues from the "State itself" towards which she aspires is not a distinction her syntax insists on, yet Clarissa's intent clearly is to state that her reaching-towards is being responded to with the "beamy light" of God's answer.

The metaphorical language Clarissa uses ("black clouds" and "beamy light") is, to repeat the point made earlier, conventional enough, but the stark power and immediacy of her experience gives it fresh currency. She increasingly sees metaphoric significance in the ordinary workaday language which she has always preferred. Again a week later on September 5 she testifies to her experience that thinking about death "before the dark hours" when it arrives has generated in memory the mediating "reflections" which "let in upon my departing soul a ray of Divine Mercy; to illuminate my passage into an awful eternity" (VII.369; 4.300). Her experience of light is accompanied by the reversal of her desponding emotion into its hopeful opposite. Thus, she feels "charming forebodings of happiness already," along with "prospects and assurances" that increase her confidence (VII.379; 4.301), as well as "*foretastes* and *assurances*" (VIII.5; 4.346) that comfort her as she expires. The word "assurances" suggests that she is trusting the promises God has made, which—unlike Lovelace's—are reliable, dependable. Permitting Clarissa to infer from her experiences of "foretastes" and "charming forebodings" God's approving, beckoning response to her continuing prayer is as much as novelistic realism can allow.

Clarissa's response to the inflooding of light and portents of joy is expressed in clothes imagery: the "mantle of integrity" she lost in the rape is replaced by the bridal gown she will wear in her marriage to the Heavenly Bridegroom. As if recovering her unselfconscious pleasure in the common usages of ordinary living, she is delighted to find that dying is as easy and "familiar" to her as "dressing and undressing" (VII.254; 4.215). If "familiar" and easy, it is as memorable and happy an experience as marrying: "never Bride was so ready as I am," she tells Mrs. Norton, since her burial clothes are "wedding garments" that provide "security" against "anxieties, pains, and perturbations"

(VII.373; 4.303) or the precariousness of temporality. As if she were undressing for her bridegroom, Clarissa aspires to be "divested of these *rags of mortality*" (VII.376; 4.305). The "disrobing" figure is repeated when she foresees eventual heavenly reunion with Miss Howe: then, after they have been "divested of the shades of body," they shall be transformed into post-temporal existence and become "all light and all mind" (VII.407; 4.328).

When Clarissa, "all light and all mind," enters her Father's House, the "shades of body" which have been putrified by Lovelace will be put off. Here we find the completion of the purification procedure which began in her Meditations. Her defilement is the symbolic dirtying that grieves her until the "shades" and "rags" of her "unhappy" body are removed. Hope of purification explains Clarissa's complex attitude toward her corpse; her coffin's satin lining will soon "be tarnished by viler earth than any it could be covered by" (VII.313; 4.257), for her dead flesh will corrupt to "vile worms" (VII.368; 4.299), yet her diligent preparations for the funeral and burial reveal that she respects her corpse. "This vile body ought not so much to engage my cares," Clarissa says, yet she defends that concern: "let it be called a *natural* weakness, and I shall be excused; especially when a reverential gratitude shall be known to be the foundation of it" (VII.370; 4.301). Reverence towards the family demands respect toward her body, her "remains," which will be buried in Harlowe Place. And so one sees that by continual meditation Clarissa compensates for her loss of Harlowe Place by appropriating her Father's House as symbol of an assured future, while at the same time she purifies her defilement by divesting herself of "the shades of body"—not out of Gnostic contempt of the flesh but to repair her wholeness and to regain her "prospects."

While Clarissa's coffin focuses her private meditations, the decorations on the coffin-lid themselves constitute her final Meditation upon her experience, this one addressed to the public. Meditation 6, as one could call it, summarizes her tragic history and represents it as exemplary of the human condition in general. Our first task is to describe the coffin-lid and to visualize it accurately as the symbolic configuration which Clarissa intends. The coffin is wooden, it has been "covered with fine black cloth" (VII.313; 4.258), and it needs to be around 5 feet long by 2 feet broad to accommodate her corpse. The entire flat surface of the coffin-lid is used as a ground for Clarissa's design. Belford's account reveals that the coffin-lid's surface is decorated, from top to bottom, with seven individual metal plates representing biblical texts or visual images. Clarissa's semantic intention in Meditation 6 determines both the selection and the location of these texts and images. What she has to say is expressed by "the principal device," the crowned serpent which is "neatly etched on a plate of white metal," and the subsidiary "ornaments" (VII.311–2; 4.257) inscribed on the six other plates.

Picturing Belford's description, we see that the coffin-lid plates are so positioned as to overlay her corpse top to bottom with biblical texts and religious images which, read as a unitary design, explain what her story means in the context of the "vast eternity" she expects. If we recollect medieval tombs upon which one sees a sculptured figure of the dead person whose remains are contained within, one finds a useful contrast. Clarissa's intent is not to provide a visual image of her person but to give visual and textual aids to reflection that guide the meditation of those who remember her and ponder her history. Because we read English from top to bottom of the page, and the coffin's lid is the final page of Clarissa's earthly history, we advance top to bottom from the "Hour-glass winged" covering her eyes, to the "urn, near the bottom" covering her feet. Above this urn is the assertion that God has "*delivered . . . mine eyes from tears; and my feet from falling*" (Psalm 116, 7–8). The eyes which contemplate the road she follows and the feet which carry her in the journey of life become instruments of God's providential affection.

Clarissa's history is the common lot—the losses and sorrows of time-as-temporality. But hers is also the story of Lovelace's fraudulence, his abduction, her defloration, and her struggles to mend the damage. The clashing of those mighty opposites is shown in the middle of the coffin-lid design, where two opposing visual images are mediated by a reconciling text: the "principal device" of the crowned serpent is appropriately located over Clarissa's own heart; the "white Lily snapt short off, and just falling from the stalk" must (given the positions of neighboring metal plates) be situated close to, if not directly over, the physical seat of honor that Lovelace defiled; lastly, the biblical text is located "between the principal plate and the lily," or over the diaphragm muscles that draw the breath of life: "*The days of man are but as grass. For he flourisheth as a flower . . .*" (Psalm 103, 15-16). In this tripartite configuration, the "sweet and tender blossom" Clarissa is represented as the lily "just falling from its stalk" and as the woman whose name and age-at-death are inscribed within the serpent "emblem of Eternity" (VII.312–4; 4.257–8).

If one briefly turns from the coffin-lid Meditation in order to recall the development of the conventional all-flesh-is-grass metaphor in the bible, one recognizes in its development the same movement through sadness to consolation that occurs in Clarissa's Meditation 6. The lament for mortality that she takes from Psalm 103 is answered in that psalm by peaceful confidence that God is merciful, "as a father pitieth his own children" (v. 13). Isaiah 40 continues this modulation from lamentation into hopeful trust. "The grass withereth, the flower fadeth: but the word of our God shall stand forever" (v. 7). When Jesus says "consider the lilies of the field," his point is to persuade his auditors to adopt the outlook of confident hope that mortality challenges them to take: "if God so clothe the grass of the field . . . shall he not much more clothe you, O ye of little faith?" (Matt. 7, 28–30). As one sees, Meditation 6 is Clarissa's invitation to dwell within those biblical allusions which her coffin-lid's decorations reiterate.

Beyond its role in summarizing her history and exemplifying the human condition, Clarissa's coffin-lid has another function, to commemorate her Christian prudence. Commemoration, as Edward Casey describes it, requires the public ritual during which the commemorating community gather and direct their attentions to the "commemorabilia," the texts and artifacts that are the souvenirs of the dead person; these help them remember. Commemorabilia are public in their "scope and functions" (219), though they commonly are private in their original purpose. Clarissa's coffin-lid was originally used to focus her meditations, but following her death its designs can serve the public function of emblematizing her as she had aspired to live and wants to be remembered: as Prudentia. As commemorabilia, her coffin decorations announce to her public that she has achieved her aspirations and is returning herself to the community of her friends, allowing them to "own" her through the ritual acts of rememberance that she anticipates in a funeral service, should her family agree to her burial in Harlowe Place.

Though Clarissa thinks her coffin may have "shewn more fancy than would perhaps be thought suitable on so solemn an occasion" (VII.312; 4.257), one sees that the ornaments are what ensure the coffin's value for commemoration. One of the ornaments, which is described by Belford as a "crowned Serpent, with its tail in its mouth, forming a ring, the emblem of Eternity," deserves special attention. The serpent encircles Clarissa's name, the day of her flight from home, her age at death. This device may have for its parents the six emblems in George Wither's *Emblemes* (1635) that contain such encircling serpents. All six of these emblems focus on prudence, though the snakes represent various concepts (time, eternity, prudence) and only three of the six are crowned. Three of Wither's emblems are especially pertinent because they help to illuminate Clarissa's intentions.

In the first (Figure 2), the encircling serpent represents time's "*Annuall-Revolutions*" going in "*everlasting rings,*" like seasons of the year, which end "where they first of all *begun.*" But these constantly reiterated cycles do not figure the futile succession of endless temporality because eternity is traveling towards its "full perfection" in God:

> These *Roundells,* helpe to shew the *Mystery*
> Of that immense and blest *Eternitie,*
> From whence the CREATURE sprung, and, into *whom*
> It shall, againe, with full perfection come,
> When those *Additions,* it hath fully had,
> Which all the sev'rall *Orbes* of *Time* can add.

How these tenuous, fading productions of time will be transformed into the glory and permanence of eternity or how the creature and the Creator can be united are mysteries, but Clarissa has learned to accept such mysteries and move forward in confident faith that God's promises are reliable. Wither's text continues:

> It is a full, and fairely written *Scrowle,*
> Which up into it selfe, it selfe doth rowle;
> And, by *Unfolding,* and, *Infolding,* showes
> A *Round,* which neither *End,* nor *entrance* knowes.

In this meditation text, time merges with eternity as the Creator "infolds" His creatures. What is evident here is that creatures, men and women, make distinctive contributions, using their medium of time. Once it is enacted, Clarissa's wish to live the life of moral excellence constitutes a "fairely written *scrowle*" that is not written in ink upon paper, like Belford's history, but graven on her soul when she is taken "up into" the mystery of eternity.

In Figure 3, by contrast, time is not the natural analogue of eternity or a chance to improve it. Time is rather the threat of death, which provokes the action of escaping the state of sin. Wither devotes much the greater part of his versed accompaniment to the picture of the skull-touching child encircled by the tail-ingesting, crested serpent elaborating the process of mutability. He develops the insight that "from

Through many spaces, Time *doth run,*
And, endeth, *where it first* begun.

157

ILLVSTR. XXIII.   *Book.3*

Ld *Sages* by the Figure of the Snake
(Encircled thus) did oft expreſſion make
Of *Annuall-Revolutions*; and of things,
Which wheele about in *everlaſting-rings* ;
There *ending*, where they firſt of all *begun*,
And, there *beginning*, where the *Round* was *done*.
Thus, doe the *Planets* ; Thus, the *Seaſons* doe ;
And, thus, doe many other *Creatures*, too.
   By minutes, and by houres, the *Spring* ſteales in,
And, rolleth on, till *Summer* doth begin :
The *Summer* brings on *Autumne*, by degrees ;
So ripening, that the eye of no man ſees
Her Entrances. That *Seaſon*, likewiſe, hath
To *Winter-ward*, as leaſurely a path :
And, then, cold *Winter* wheeleth on amaine,
Vntill it brings the *Spring* about againe,
With all thoſe *Reſurrections*, which appeare,
To wait upon her comming, every yeare.
   Theſe *Roundells*, helpe to ſhew the *Myſtery*
Of that immenſe and bleſt *Eternitie*,
From whence the CREATVRE ſprung, and, into *whom*
It ſhall, againe, with full perfection come,
When thoſe *Additions*, it hath fully had,
Which all the ſev'rall *Orbes* of *Time* can add.
It is a full, and fairely written *Scrowle*,
Which up into it ſelfe, it ſelfe doth rowle ;
And, by *Vnfolding*, and, *Infolding*, ſhowes
A *Round*, which neither *End*, nor *entrance* knowes.
   And (by this *Emblem*) you may partly ſee,
   Tis that which *I S* ; but, cannot uttred be.

Bach

Figure 2

As foone, as wee to bee, begunne;
We did beginne, to be Vndone.

45

PEDET FINIS ABORIGINE

45

ILLVSTR. XLV.   *Book. 1ª*

When fome, in former Ages, had a meaning
An *Emblem*, of *Mortality*, to make,
They form'd an *Infant*, on a *Deaths-head* leaning,
And, round about, encircled with a *Snake*.
The *Childe* fo pictur'd, was to fignifie,
That, from our very *Birth*, our *Dying* fprings:
The *Snake*, her *Taile devouring*, doth implie
The *Revolution*, of all Earthly things.
For, whatfoever hath *beginning*, here,
Beginnes, immediately, to vary from
The fame it was; and, doth at laft appeare
What very few did thinke it fhould become.
The folid *Stone*, doth molder into *Earth*,
That *Earth*, e're long, to *Water*, rarifies;
That *Water*, gives an *Airy Vapour* birth,
And, thence, a *Fiery-Comet* doth arife:
That, moves, untill it felfe it fo impaire,
That from a *burning-Meteor*, backe againe,
It finketh downe, and thickens into *Aire*;
That *Aire*, becomes a *Cloud*; then, *Drops of Raine*:
Thofe *Drops*, defcending on a *Rocky-Ground*,
There, fettle into *Earth*, which more and more,
Do h harden, ftill; fo, running out the *round*,
It growes to be the *Stone* it was before.
Thus, All things wheele about; and, each *Beginning*,
Made entrance to it owne *Deftruction*, hath.
The *Life* of Nature, entreth in with *Sinning*;
And, is for ever, wayted on by *Death*:
The *Life* of *Grace*, is form'd by *Death* to *Sinne*;
And, there, doth *Life-eternall*, ftraight beginne.

Though

Figure 3

our very *Birth,* our *Dying* springs," explaining that "The Snake, his *Taile* devouring, doth implie/ The *Revolution,* of all Earthly things." Having devoted 26 of his verse lines to reading the emblem physically, Wither in the last 4 lines presents an analogy between the life of "*Nature*" and the life of "*Grace*"; he makes an "in the same way" move that, like a metaphysical conceit, sees similarity in disparate things. Thus the "*Life* of *Nature,*" which "entreth in with *Sinning*" and leads to physical death, is juxtaposed with the "*Life* of *Grace,*" which "is form'd," or begins, "by *Death* to *Sinne,*" advancing then to "Life-eternall." Physical death is used as an analogue of the "*Death* to *Sinne*" which is birth into eternal life—or at least the beginning of the journey that leads there. The fact that the serpent is crested distinguishes it as representing eternity, and not an endless round of physical mutability. The lesson Clarissa has learned through rape, defilement and subjection to sin is the same point as this emblem expresses.

The third Wither serpent emblem (Figure 4) that helps us to read the emblem on Clarissa's coffin pictures the crowned serpent of eternity encircling a blooming flower that Belford says is the "type" of transitory things. Margaret Anne Doody has discussed the pertinence of this emblem to Clarissa, who, she says, is not simply a beautiful girl "who bloomed only to die" but "an heir of eternity," since "it is within time, surrounded by eternity, that the soul works out its salvation" (186). That point is precisely the message insisted on by all six of Wither's encircling-serpent emblems. The Greek words within the boundary ring that contains the flower and its encircling serpent ("aionion kai proskairon"—the eternal and the transient) refer to Chapter 4 of St. Paul's second epistle to the Corinthians, its concluding verse: "we look not at the things which are seen, but at the things which are not seen: for the things which are seen are temporal; but the things which are not seen are eternal."[2] Evidently working with limited space, the engraver selects words that will signal an allusion to Chapter 5, which continues St. Paul's admonition to Christians to live joyfully. For Clarissa's purposes what is most interesting is the exultant desire II Corinthians expresses for the Father's House: "we know that if our earthly house . . . were dissolved, we have a building of God . . . eternal in the heavens. For in this we groan, earnestly desiring to be clothed upon with our house which is from heaven" because "whilst we are at home in the body, we are absent from the lord" (5: 1, 2, 6). Clarissa adopts the prudence emblem convention because it enables her to express her victory in the struggle of Prudentia against the disasters

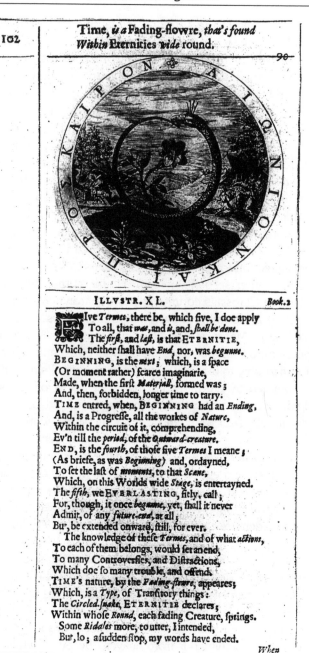

102

Time, *is a* Fading-flowre, *that's found*
Within Eternities *wide* round.

90

ILLVSTR. XL. *Book.* 2

Ive *Termes*, there be, which five, I doe apply
To all, that *was*, and *is*, and, *shall be done*.
The *first*, and *last*, is that ETERNITIE,
Which, neither shall have *End*, nor, was *begunne*.
BEGINNING, is the *next*; which, is a space
(Or moment rather) scarce imaginarie,
Made, when the first *Materiall*, formed was;
And, then, forbidden, longer time to tarry.
TIME entred, when, BEGINNING had an *Ending*,
And, is a Progresse, all the workes of *Nature*,
Within the circuit of it, comprehending,
Ev'n till the *period*, of the *Outward-creature*.
END, is the *fourth*, of those five *Termes* I meane;
(As briefe, as was *Beginning*) and, ordayned,
To set the last of *moments*, to that *Scene*,
Which, on this Worlds wide *Stage*, is entertayned.
The *fifth*, we EVERLASTING, fitly, call;
For, though, it once *begunne*, yet, shall it never
Admit, of any *future-end*, at all;
But, be extended onward, still, for ever.
    The knowledge of these *Termes*, and of what *actions*,
To each of them belongs, would set an end,
To many Controversies, and Distractions,
Which doe so many trouble, and offend.
TIME's nature, by the *Fading-flowre*, appeares;
Which, is a *Type*, of Transitory things:
The *Circled-snake*, ETERNITIE declares;
Within whose *Round*, each fading Creature, springs.
Some *Ridales* more, to utter, I intended,
But, lo; a sudden stop, my words have ended.

When

Figure 4

of time and chance. Her most mature conception of prudence includes both reasoned choice as the guide to action and patient endurance of disasters which reason cannot explain.[3]

The Return to Harlowe Place

As the retribution schema predicts, the Harlowes reap what they have sown. When news that Clarissa is dead reaches Harlowe Place, the family's grief is heightened by "remembrance of their unforgiving severity" (VIII.71; 4.396). Foreseeing the severity of their mourning and realizing that "mercy is seasonable in the time of affliction," she "strengthens" them with her "mouth" (as Meditation 4 expresses it) by composing posthumous letters to the Harlowes, letters that Belford will have delivered to them after she dies. Aunt Hervey, who did not participate in the scapegoat violence, can console the family when the news comes, so Clarissa prepares her by listing comforting thoughts: the family have many blessings left, her tragedy was their first heavy evil, suffering can become a blessing when it is borne patiently, total happiness should not be expected on earth, they need not be concerned about her eternal life, her story when publicized will be more to their honor than to their disgrace, they still have two other children, the family will be reunited in Eternity (VIII.31; 4.366).

Clarissa's posthumous letters show the rhetorical skill that the Harlowes previously feared because of its power to move. Now that they are anguished by self-accusatory grief, her therapeutic arguments are meant to soothe and strengthen. At the moment when her persecutors are shaken by the double blow of losing Clarissa and realizing that they have been responsible for that loss, she offers her forgiveness and consolation. She is as unabrasive as truth will permit, positing excusable motives for acts which were inexcusable. She tells James his "rigorous heart" ought to have "permitted other hearts more indulgently to expand" (VIII.25; 4.361). And she hopes that Arabella's severe virtue will pardon the "little occasions of displeasure" which the elder sister has held against the younger ever since childhood (VIII.28; 4.363).

Although Clarissa can do little with her brother and sister but refrain from accusing, her letters to her parents and uncles offer genuine consolation. She presents herself to her parents as a dutiful child grateful for the benefits they have given her. Tactfully adopting the persona of the forgiving parent, Clarissa addresses her father in the "exulting confidence" that he has now forgiven her. She thanks him for his generosity, his "fond Love" during her childhood and the education in virtue that has brought her to her destination in eternal life. Mr. Harlowe's comfort is to be that he has fulfilled his paternal duties to his daughter. Clarissa advises him to "blot" from memory the last eight months and to remember happier times. She asks his forgiveness for the "fatal error" that removed her from his "protection." Moreover, she tells him that she has had "assurances" that God has accepted her penitent sorrows, which are but "so many mercies dispensed to wean [her] betimes" from the world before a longer life threatens that "blessedness" which she trusts she is rejoicing in "on your reading of This" (VIII.22–3; 4.359–60). To her mother, Clarissa stresses her recovery from "the consciousness of a self-convicted criminal" to the happy confidence she now enjoys, and she offers Mrs. Harlowe this comfort, that "the principal end of [her] pious care" has been reached, "though not in the way so much hoped for" (VIII.23–4; 4.360–1).

Clarissa refuses to blame anyone but herself. She softens the evidence of paternal culpability in the Harlowes' sacrificial rejection of her, emphasizing instead the truth readers never see during the Harlowe Place activities—that Mr. Harlowe's harshness was meant for her welfare. Clarissa now knows that he was driven by overwhelming anxiety that Lovelace would take and destroy her. And her father was right: had she not corresponded with Lovelace, Clarissa would not have fallen in love with him, she would never have believed and trusted him, she would have heard Aunt Hervey's evidence against him on the night of her dream, and she would not have gone in person at night to explain to Lovelace why she would not leave with him. Asking her father's forgiveness is more than a tactful way of forgiving him. It is also the candid confession of a woman who belatedly realizes the extent of her culpability. Clarissa's rhetorical design is to tell the story of her father's vigorous efforts to assure her personal safety and salvation, and her folly in raising obstacles that undermined his paternal care, obstacles which she has forgotten except as they were helpful for "weaning" her from the dangerous world. By this process Clarissa offers her father the gift of expiating his rigorous reactions by recognizing, beneath his "Justly incensed" fury, his affectionate intentions.

Because their concern is familial rather than parental, her letter to her uncles is designed to make the family's bleak story intelligible as a punishment/purification narrative; its moral is that we should suspect the testimony of self-awareness, the sense of personal righteousness whose radical unreliability her history has demonstrated. She tells her uncles that, since Providence is beyond human view, we can only conjecture about God's intentions. We know Providence uses various methods "to bring poor sinners to a sense of their duty." Love draws some people and terror drives others to "their Divine Refuge," and perhaps she herself was too ready to measure her value by "the love and favour of every one." As she tells them, "The merit of the good I delighted to do, and of the inclinations which were given me . . . I was, perhaps, too ready to attribute to myself." The wisdom of Providence always remains unsearchable, even if conjecture offers an intelligible interpretation; the best explanation must be taken as a perhaps. She presents personal qualities "given" her by the accident of temperament as the root of "secret pride" she "had not fathomed"; positing such pride, she can explain her "temporary calamities." It was "necessary perhaps" that something evil should "mortify" that pride and vanity (VIII.29–30; 4.365). Clarissa has learned a lesson, for one remembers the mismatch in her post-rape papers between the prophetic voice accusing her of pride, and the voice of her transparent consciousness, scandalized at having receiving the sinner's reward. She presents for her uncles the foolishness of thinking oneself to be innocent on no better evidence than the testimony of one's self-awareness.

Clarissa returns to her family not only in these letters but in her Will, in which she appears not as the dutiful child nor as the forgiving and consoling parent, but as the responsible adult. "In the disposition of what belongs to me, I have endeavoured to do every-thing in the justest and best manner I could think of," as she tells Miss Howe. "Putting myself in my relations places" and "ordering my matters, as if no misunderstanding had happened" (VII.335; 4.274), she wills the estate which agitated her family to her father, according to the convention of primogeniture that Grandfather ought to have observed from the outset. Yet because the accrued interest belongs to *her*, she does not give it to her father but begs it "as a favour" that Mrs. Norton be permitted to live in her Dairy House and govern her charities, to be funded by the interest which has accrued since Grandfather Harlowe's death.

The next most important items that Clarissa must dispose of are the Harlowe family plate and portraits. Those things operate as the family's lares and penates, for they represent the ethical ideals which

Clarissa's brother and sister and elders have proved themselves less than worthy of. One might infer that Grandfather Harlowe, seeing that other members of the family were indifferent to piety and reverence, willed Clarissa "all the family pictures at his late house," along with the family plate, hoping that she would in time reintroduce those lapsed values. Though she never puts it in so many words, she clearly implies that when she says

> Grandfather having a great fondness for the old family plate, which he would never permit to be changed, having lived, as he used to say, to see a great deal of it come into request again in the revolution of fashions; and having left the same to me, with a command to keep it entire; and with power at my death to bequeath it to whomsoever . . . I thought would forward his desire; which was . . . that it should be kept to the end of *time*; (VIII.100–1; 4.419)

"To the end of time" is an ethical designation which means "over many generations," which parallels the religious expression of a "boundless eternity." The family plate, which Clarissa wills to Uncle Antony with the tactful admonition that he honor "the same injuctions which were laid on me," should be kept whole—a symbol of family unity for however long the Harlowes endure. The family pictures she wills to Uncle Harlowe since he has "a gallery where they may be placed to advantage," but also because, following her grandfather's wish, she thinks he "would set most value by them" (VIII.101; 4.419). Thus the exile returns and reassumes her role as guardian of the hearth and defender of the better values which anger had temporarily eclipsed in Harlowe Place.

Notes

1 Together, the figures of God's wrath and God's conjugal love as spouse of the soul oppose the impersonal punishment metaphor: "the ethical framework of law, commandment, transgression and punishment" is thereby repudiated (Ricoeur 1974, 370); disasters in life are then understood not as impersonal punishments meted out for infractions of commandments, but "nothing else than sin itself," or the condition of separation from God (371).

2 I am indebted to my friend and colleague Clifford Minor for translating the Greek phrases seen in Wither's emblem 90 (Fig. 3) and for pointing out that they allude to II Corinthians.

3 Terry Castle completely dismisses Clarissa's intention: "the coffin allows for an excess of contradictory reactions—one for each new reader" (141); the coffin-lid's "point is unclear," it is "utterly opaque, its meaning indeterminate," while "Clarissa dies without providing any extraneous commentary, any gloss, on her mysterious coffin-text" (139). However, Clarissa's intention is perfectly clear to other characters in the novel, for they do not join Castle in considering reading a "wholly personal matter" or interpretation "a form of solipsism, a mode of estrangement" (141). Mr. Melvill, the clergyman who gives the eulogy at the burial service, for example, knows that Clarissa's coffin-text means, in the words of John Norris, that a "Prudent Christian looks upon this World not as his Home" but "takes care how he contracts any Fondness or Affection for any of its transient Vanities [and] becomes a Traveller, that is here to day and gone to morrow" (340). Melvill's audience, likewise, understand the coffin that way, for when he points to the pew where she "used to sit or kneel," they turn to it with "respectful solemnity, as if she had been there herself" (VIII.87; 4.408). One can infer that they are not gawking but imagining themselves too as being here—then gone. Belford understands Clarissa's coffin-lid, for after perusing Morden's funeral narrative he imagines himself as standing inside the burial vault and numbering "the surrounding monuments of mortality" as he muses on "the present stillness of so many once busy vanities," those ancestral dead whose remains were formerly deposited in the same "poor vaulted nook" as that in which "the symbolic coffin" has been placed (VIII.91; 4.411).

Chapter 9

Lovelace Stripped Bare

Lovelace's pretense to normality is most plausible early in the novel, before readers come to know him well through his cruel treatment of Clarissa and the revelations of his motives found in his narrative to Belford. The more he abuses her, the clearer it becomes that doing so is the only thing that gives purpose to his life. His plots all reduce to repetitions of virtually identical actions, which reveals the pattern of compulsive conduct in which his very small repertoire of moves against Clarissa is reiterated again and again. This pattern shows that Lovelace is not living in time, but outside of it, in a time warp, or time lock, because he acts as if he were condemned to constant repetition of futile gestures which do nobody any good.

Psychoanalyst Roy Schafer observes about people who live in a condition of compulsive repetition that their "autobiographical present" cannot be found because it is "no clear point in time at all." Indeed,

> One does not even know how properly to conceive of that present; more and more it seems to be both a repetitive crisis-perpetuating misremembering of the past and a way of living defensively with respect to the future which is, in the most disruptive way, imagined fearfully and irrationally on the model of the past. (238)

But though one cannot say when their autobiographical present is, one can specify where they are spending it—that is, behind bars. The "imprisoned analysand" is one of the most common stories that psychoanalysts hear from patients who have Lovelace's difficulty; they describe themselves as "always doing time or serving time," because in the imprisonment narrative "time, place, and person stand still" (Schafer 261). This is precisely the condition from which Lovelace has tried to free himself by transferring his own imprisonment to Clarissa, who through his influence is put under house arrest in Harlowe Place, abducted and locked in Sinclair's house, incarcerated at Rowland's and at last compelled to endure the interiorized solitary confinement of shameful defilement and her ruined life. Why does Lovelace do it? Because he is afraid that Clarissa, who in his narcissistic perception *is* his self, will escape from his control, with the result that he would lose control of his life. The rape was meant to keep Clarissa locked up, and cohabitation and marriage—one or the other of which he expects to follow her defloration—are both ways to lock her up.

Lovelace's Unwitting Psychoanalysis

Fortunately for him, Lovelace's friends attempt to free him from imprisonment. Clarissa and Belford, who are the ideal and mirroring selfobjects he formerly used to enable his narcissism, exert their own independence by working to help him become less dependent upon compulsive conduct. To some extent they succeed, putting him through a kind of psychoanalysis. Analysis can help the narcissist to transform "the static, timeless prison into a setting of personal and beneficial change," says Schafer (279), and that is the ameliorative effect his selfobjects' reactions have on him following the June 30 "chevalier in armour" fantasy which pictures imprisonment and despair of living well in time. Before the rape, Belford's role had been to admire the narrative of his grandiose actions, and Clarissa's function was to approve of him by submitting to his unspeakable treatment. Following the rape, neither of them supports his disease, with the result that Lovelace's narcissistic defenses are gradually stripped away and he becomes vulnerable to conscious disappointment and capable of guilt. This stripping is overseen by Clarissa and Belford, who are bound to Lovelace by the emotion he invested in them. They operate as the parents whom he finds it difficult to internalize.

Though Clarissa and Belford have to face a psychotherapeutic situation, they have no understanding of pathological narcissism. Since their conceptual tools are moral, not psychoanalytic, they cannot understand what accounts for Lovelace's behavior and they certainly do not know how to help him. Their intention is good, yet they make serious blunders, the worst of which is pressuring Lovelace to reform. They have no way of realizing that what Roy Schafer calls "the simplistic, partisan" exhortative approach to his conduct encourages Lovelace to "persevere in sado-masochistic fantasizing and acting out" (5); in fact, their direct efforts to help him cause "rebellion or submission, control or helplessness, flattery or insult, seductiveness or rejection" (8). The one way that succeeds with narcissistic persons is to inflict small doses of the "optimal frustration" which helps children to become less dependent (Kohut 1971, 64). Ironically, Clarissa and Belford do administer *this* kind of help despite themselves. When Clarissa withdraws, Lovelace is deeply frustrated, and Belford's narrative role optimizes that frustration by keeping her continually in his view. Together, they function as his unwitting psychotherapists.

Roy Schafer describes psychoanalysts as "people who listen to the narrations of analysands" and help them to transform the false stories they tell about themselves into "others that are more complete, coherent, convincing, and adaptively useful than those they have been accustomed to constructing" (240). By this definition, Belford is Lovelace's analyst. Initially, he merely listens, but eventually he criticizes the falsehoods Lovelace is "accustomed to constructing," and after the rape he harnesses the emotional pain caused by Clarissa's rejection to help release him from narcissistic convictions that are "pathologically confining in their fixedness and narrowness" (Schafer 279). At the outset, though, Belford faces a formidable challenge, because the patient loves his disease. Belford presumes that Lovelace will recognize his inhumanity to Clarissa if it is told with sufficient clarity, but Lovelace cannot blame himself except, as he tells Belford, to "disarm thy malice by acknowledgment" (IV.103; 3.318) and excuse himself. When Belford says "in what an execrable light wilt thou appear to all the world!" (VI.88; 3.307), Lovelace ignores that warning since he is fabricating an edited account of his conduct that will persuade his family to help him coax Clarissa to marry him; his inability to accept guilt is virtually unshakeable.

Even the episodes in which Lovelace appears to feel sympathy for Clarissa are really episodes of self-pity, as in his agitated reaction to her imprisonment: "Hasten, hasten, dear Jack . . . My heart bleeds for her!" (VI.240; 3.420). Since Clarissa functions as the mirroring pool which accurately pictures his intra-psychic turmoil, it is no wonder that he is agitated by her imprisonment, for it is really his own. Lovelace's agitation is genuine; it is the terror of self-dissolution that overcame him after Clarissa's first escape, the fear that made him draw a sword to kill himself on seeing her nosebleed. His anxiety about her makes him attend to the narrative about her imprisonment (VI.247–71; 3.425–50) and evokes his curse of Belford for interrupting that "soul-harrowing intelligence" (VI.281; 3.451). But when

Belford gives Clarissa's self-narrative as a penitent daughter at the Smiths', Lovelace is comforted by the tearful tale since it shows she is regaining her health. Presuming that the recovered Clarissa will marry him, "I rejoice that she is already so much better" that she is able to "hold, with strangers, such a long and interesting conversation" (VI.359; 3.508).

Nor should we mistake as compassion the slow alteration that makes Lovelace able to perceive in Clarissa's sorrow a picture of his own. Because he confusedly realizes that her griefs are his, he begins learning how to appropriate his own hidden sorrows. He begins imitating her, parodying her sufferings and her decline by falling ill himself. On July 26 Belford narrates Clarissa gazing into her mirror: "stepping to the glass, with great composure, My countenance, said she, is indeed an honest picture of my heart," because, as Belford says, she had wanted to reclaim "a Libertine whom she loved" (VI.396-7; 4.9-10). Lovelace's response is to appropriate her gesture and attitude for himself by imitating it ("I stept to the glass: A poor figure, by Jupiter, cried I!—And they all praised and admired me"), which is an appropriation like his response after reading Meditation 2 ("as suitable to my case, as to the Lady's" (VII.118-9; 4.114)). Two contrary impulses are at work in Lovelace: a narcissistic theft of value from Clarissa, but also something new, the desire to learn how to be like her by imitating her. The first is habitual, the second subtly emergent beneath his more familiar response. At this point in the action, though, Lovelace's overriding impulse is to deny the reality that Clarissa is dying and to continue inventing stories which gratify his wish to recover her. When, for instance, Clarissa hears that Lovelace is ill, her words "May he meet with the mercy he has not shown" catapult him from his sickbed ("I am sick only of Love!"), to recover his "*forgiving* angel" (VII.121; 4.116). This magical recovery to health demonstrates his conviction that he is the one who requires healing and that Clarissa will eventually heal him.

Dismayed by his repeated refusals to accept reality, Belford tries to force Lovelace to endure the truth: "thy spirits are so offensively up since thy recovery," he says, "that I ought . . . to reduce thee to the standard of humanity" (VII.169; 4.152), and so he begins "expatiating upon" Belton's dying days, warning that "THOU MUST DIE, AS WELL AS BELTON" (VII.158; 4.144). Lovelace is unmoved by Belton's death, however, because he is ecstatic about Clarissa's "father's house" letter. He is incapable of rational fear about himself such as Belford tries to tap, so when Belford pictures those "sinking jaws, and erected staring eyebrows, with his lengthened furrowed forehead" and remarks that "It is not, it cannot be, the face of Belton . . . whom we have beheld with so much delight over the social bottle" (VII.192; 4.169), the horror of death's realism has no salutory effect on Lovelace. Shielding himself with reductive humor, he shows Mowbray "a passage or two" and they both find Belford "an absolute master of the Lamentable" (VII.195; 4.171). The only thing that raises anxiety in Lovelace is fear that Clarissa will abandon him, and he confesses that his "Levity" is meant to control his "deep concern" at her decline by attempting to "buffet down [his] cruel reflections as they rise" (VII.319; 4.262). Not recognizing that Lovelace's one concern is holding onto Clarissa, Belford continues his effort to provoke in his friend the moral reflection which could lead to penitence and the wish to reform his life—the direct approach that Roy Schafer assures us always fails with narcissists. With these intentions, Belford continues writing the narrative that he hopes will "*find*" Lovelace and "help [him] to reflection" when he is "restored" to himself after Clarissa's death (VIII.35; 4.369). But despite his hopes, his account of Sinclair's death (a "scene to paint, that, if I do it justice, will make thee seriously ponder and reflect, or nothing can" (VIII.49; 4.379)) fails of its intended effect on Lovelace, who is preoccupied with anxiety about losing Clarissa.

Unlike Belford, Clarissa is not involved in direct struggle against Lovelace; instead, Lovelace uses her in his struggle with himself. As she proceeds with her own life, Lovelace responds to everything she does, either copying her as an ideal self or else engaging in symbolic acts that dramatize his needs. So when the Lovelace family call him to account for treating her shabbily, he writes "*And now I enter upon my TRYAL*" (VI.203; 3.393) in mockery but also in imitation of her. When his family have promised that he will be a good husband and written Miss Howe their desire that Clarissa marry him, he sees an end to *his* test: "Did ever Comedy end more happily, than this long tryal?" (VI.228; 3.411) he asks. One sees that the amorous See-saw that transfers his fault to her and appropriates her worth for himself continues operating, since he notices that if she keeps refusing him "all the blame" will be hers, but "the pity of which she is now in full possession" would be "transferred" to him (VII.59; 4.71).

Clarissa's direct contribution to Lovelace's self-stripping is to remain unwaveringly truthful. While he is anticipating the tacit approval that will be implied by her marrying him, Clarissa is indicting him for his "unprecedented and elaborate wickedness" (VII.62; 4.73). That accusation evokes this complaint: "how does she know what Love, in its flaming ardour will stimulate men to do? . . . To think the *worst*, and to be able to *make comparisons* in these *very* delicate situations, must she not be less delicate than I had imagined her to be?" (VII.82; 4.88). Such a complaint is nothing but his usual list of narcissistic falsifications, for it was not "flaming love" that motivated him to rape her; rather, he had intended to "lock up her speech." But Clarissa refuses to conceal the shame of defilement by remaining silent about what he quite deliberately did to her. The "very delicate" situation she has been too truthful about is not the act of rape itself, which Lovelace here misrepresents as an ambiguous action so delicately balanced between force and yielding that blame should be divided, so that—again—he can benefit from "dividing of blame" with her. Her indelicacy is to insist upon his "unprecedented wickedness," when her narcissistic function is to *be* guilty so that he remains innocent. Lovelace's imagination, which pictured Twin Lovelaces at Clarissa's breasts before the Fire Plot, returns to the image of small boys, but "dirty" ones, in reaction to her indictment:

> she has heard, that the devil is black; and having a mind to make one of me, brays together, in the mortar of her wild fancy, twenty chimney-sweepers, in order to make one sootier than ordinary rise out of the dirty mass. (VII.82; 4.88)

The stripping away of Lovelace's self-deceptions proceeds in his narcissistic fantasies, where previously self-praising images are displaced by the more truthful image of a burnt-out and worthless self.

By insisting upon the truth that he refuses to acknowledge, Clarissa helps him bring into consciousness forgotten grievances for which he is still seeking revenge; "unprecedented wickedness" activates in Lovelace's disturbed psyche the infantile suffering which he has never consciously accepted, and his anxieties surge up uncontrollably against her. "I could tear my flesh" (VII.83; 4.88), he tells Belford, for failing to rape her into submission during the Penknife Scene. His vulnerability and his sense that he has been injured are clear in his insistence that his heart is "more tender" than hers:

> I will tear it out in her presence, and throw it at hers, that she may see how much more tender than her own that organ is, which she, and you, and everyone else, have taken the liberty to call callous. (VII.85; 4.90)

Using one's heart as a projectile to attack an uncaring mother is an infantile response, as is Lovelace's complaint that Belford is not only allowed to come near Clarissa, he is "admitted daily to her presence" and permitted "to look upon her, to talk to her, to hear her talk," though Lovelace is "forbid to come within view of her window" (VII.84; 4.89).

Along with telling the truth, Clarissa's role in Lovelace's stripping includes her withdrawal of further direct contact with him, insulating herself every way she can. Her candid accusation of "unprecedented wickedness" was sent not to Lovelace but to his relatives, and when he writes her in answer, threatening that she will be responsible for his damnation when he kills himself after her rejection makes him "desperate," Clarissa does not write him. He writes her again, imitating her religious vocabulary and point of view to evoke her sympathy and compliance. But that strategy has been bankrupt ever since Hamstead. In any event, he is not trying to persuade the social individual Clarissa, but talking to himself IN Clarissa-perceived-as his Ideal Selfobject.

in YOU, Madam, in YOUR *forgiveness,* are centred my hopes as to *both worlds:* Since to be reprobated finally by *You,* will leave me without expectation of mercy from *Above!*—For I am now awakened enough to think, that to be forgiven by injured Innocents is *necessary* to the Divine pardon; the Almighty putting into the power of such (as is reasonable to believe) the wretch who causelessly and capitally offends them. And *who* can be entitled to this power if YOU are not? (VII.86; 4.91)

The phrase "injured innocents," which seems to refer to Clarissa, really points to himself, for she has become the mirror in which he can trace the unacknowledged suffering in his troubled psyche. If her "resentments are so admirably just" that she appears "even in a divine light," the reason is that his self is his divinity. If, paradoxically, he admires her both for mirroring his "injured innocent" self and for resenting what he has done, it is because he wants to own not only the qualities that made him admire, envy and defile her, but also the mercy she can show by forgiving him.

As he imitated Clarissa during the trial before his family, so Lovelace imitates her in the psychosomatic illness which lasts from August 13 to August 15; by the indirection of copying her he is learning to endure suffering. However, the smallest token of sympathy, Belford's report that Clarissa wishes him "the mercy he has not shewn" (VII.120;

4.116), restores him to health. Yet his frustration at her refusal ("She forgives my sin: She accepts my repentance: But she won't let me repair" (VII.129; 4.122)) drives him to ransack the Smiths' home hoping to find and repossess her. There, he engages in three symbolic activities that dramatize his frantic narcissistic hunger to recover the lost self she figures. The first action is a diligent search of the closets, receptacles and cabinets where she might lie. The second is his manipulation of the "pretty genteel lady" he coaxes into the shop; seizing her hand, he "besought her to walk into the back-shop with me," which repeats his habitual catch-and-cage impulse (VII.141–2; 4.131–2). The third and most interesting symbolic action is his attempt to replace Will's teeth: noticing Will smiling with "his teeth out," touched by "conscience" for having done it, he seizes Joseph and threatens to extract "two or three of this rascal's broad teeth, to put them into my servant's jaws" (VII.139–40; 4.130). Though he explains his strange conduct as humor intended to win over the Smiths so that they will not suppose him a monstrous fellow, they understand well enough that he is utterly out of control and they appreciate more fully Clarissa's determination to flee him.

Lovelace's last major attempt to deny Clarissa's abandonment is his optimistic construal of her "father's house" letter, which he takes as signifying his triumph over her will. Like Narcissus talking to his own reflection in the pool, Lovelace addresses his "adorable" Clarissa-self:

> O my best Love! My ever-generous and adorable creature! How much does this thy forgiving goodness exalt us both!—Me, for the occasion given thee! Thee, for turning it so gloriously to thy advantage, and to the honour of both! And if, my beloved creature, you will but connive at the imperfections of your adorer, and not play the *Wife* upon me: If, while the charms of Novelty have their force with me, I should happen to be drawn aside . . . . (VII.178-9; 4.159)

If Lovelace is stripping himself of self-deceit, he obviously has made no headway here, for instead of feeling repentent for raping her, he sees the rape as a necessary "occasion given" to Clarissa so that she can turn her defilement to "the honor of both." She is "ever-generous and adorable" because of the necessary role she will play in the narcissistic future he continues to be attracted by: as his wife, her function will be constant forgiveness of the continuing seductions which enhance his deficient self-esteem, as Morden's letter has illustrated in graphic and lurid detail.

If Lovelace never came to greater self-understanding through his transaction with Clarissa, it would be pointless to describe the tenacity with which he maintains the narcissistic demands he continues to make upon her. But, in fact, although we cannot say he overcomes his narcissism, he does acquire a larger capacity to face reality; the pivotal moment comes in his letter of September 1 when he surrenders the intolerable anxiety raised by impending abandonment and suddenly recognizes that Clarissa is *herself*, not *himself*. What makes this moment pivotal is that Lovelace offers action, not protestations, as the guarantee of his truthfulness. If Clarissa is as near to death as Belford says, and if she would be "*too much discomposed* by a visit; [he] would not think of it" (VII.320; 4.263). For the time being he surrenders any pretense to ownership of her victory and glory: "I know thou wilt think I am going to claim some merit to myself" he tells Belford, but his only claim is that he overlooked her towering moral grandeur, for "occasion had not at that time ripened" the perfections that "now astonish and confound me" (VII.318; 4.262). There is evidence of normal human hurt in Lovelace's reflection that, when last he saw her, she went from him "with an incurable fracture in her heart":

> O Jack! how my Conscience, that gives edge even to thy blunt reflections, tears me! . . . . what would I give that I had not been guilty of such barbarous and ungrateful perfidy to the most excellent of God's creatures!" (VII.320–1; 4.263).

Lovelace's narcissism is weakening here, because he is capable of feeling the sorrow he suppresses and the guilt he transfers onto other people. Soon he will repent of his "reptile envy" based on "consciousness of inferiority to her" and find "no alleviation to [his] self-reproach!" because there is no longer any "dividing of blame with her!" (VII.399; 4.323). One ought also to notice his developing relationship to Belford, who is fast becoming a friend rather than simply his mirror. Earlier, Lovelace would have been too imperiously superior to tell Belford, the day before Clarissa expires, "You have infinitely obliged me . . . by pressing for an admission for me, tho' it succeeded not" (VII.400; 4.323). Thus, the suffering Lovelace, no longer a hunter, newly grateful to his friend, is now able to compassionate with others; he has achieved what Belford calls "the standard of humanity" (VII.169; 4.152).

Unfortunately, the grinding frustration that helped Lovelace to confess Clarissa's independence and superiority catapults him into a frenzy of narcissistic reaction when she dies. During her decline, he has been attempting to re-form his self by imitating everything she does. When she dies, he continues his "Imitation of Clarissa" by mourning his loss, but he is not strong enough to endure the "buffeting of emotion" that mourning demands. Neither can he attain "redefinition" of self and situation (Bowlby 93–4), the aim of successful mourning. Because narcissism protects the borderline personality against psychosis, one wonders if Lovelace can survive self-knowledge. Tiresias's prediction that Narcissus cannot live long if ever he knows himself bodes ill for Lovelace.

Lovelace's inability to endure abandonment by his selfobject is evident from his frenetic determination to possess Clarissa's cadaver, a wish so macabre that Mowbray—disturbed by Lovelace's bizarre conduct—tells Belford to "Get the Lady buried as fast as you can" (VII.42; 4.374). As Lovelace had clutched at her living flesh to overcome his terror of fragmentation, now he intends to control her corpse: "Everything that can be done to preserve the Charmer from decay" shall be done, and when she "cannot be kept longer, I will have her laid in my family-vault between my own Father and Mother." His intention to keep Clarissa's heart "in spirits" (Philippe Ariès informs us that it was "not absolutely exceptional" in the eighteenth century to keep all or part of a beloved's body at home, the heart being the "most sought after, the noblest part" (286, 387)) shows her continuing centrality to him, the absoluteness of his psychic dependence. Unwilling that anyone else should be anything to her, Lovelace declares that her ties to the Harlowes are dissolved ("She left *them* for *me*. She chose *me* therefore: And I was her husband" (VIII.44; 4.375–6)) as he tries to dismiss Belford from his role as her executor. One understands from his demand for possession of her corpse that she still symbolizes the self-possession that his weak self-formation makes impossible.

The psychic implosion that Clarissa's death causes Lovelace dramatizes the insuperable narcissistic problem that he lacks the competent self-structure needed for reform: "The very repentance and amendment wished me so heartily by my kind and cross dear, have been invalidated and postponed . . . Can a madman be capable of either?" (VIII.132; 4.443); "Who can bear such reflections" as his own posttrauma realization that he caused Clarissa's death. As time passes, one sees that Lovelace can neither move ahead in imitation of Clarissa nor regain his earlier grandiose pretenses. Returning to his earlier habit of self-justification, he invents the exemplum that compares Clarissa, who overvalued her chastity, with the miser who once "hid a parcel of gold in a *secret place*" (VIII.144; 4.452). Another Lovelace trick to escape condemnation is to return to his former habit of rejecting guilt and trying to "claim pity" (VIII.147; 4.454), though when that fails he recants that attempt. Unable to find relief, he waffles between enduring and trying to escape his debilitating grief.

Lovelace's curse, and punishment, is to have understood his situation only when it is too late to learn from his mistakes and to be psychically too weak to forgive himself and recover a life. Lacerating himself with sorry reflections about his "*premeditated* ingratitude to the most excellent of women" (VIII.238; 4.522), he is sickened now by his feigned pretenses to passionate love:

> Well might *such* a woman be allowed to draw back, when she found herself kept in suspense, *as to the great question of all,* by a designing and intriguing spirit; pretending awe and distance, as reasons for reining-in a fervour, which, if real, cannot be reined-in. (VIII.240; 4.524)

His severest punishment is to have her "astonishing perfections" keenly alive in his memory alongside grief for having robbed both himself "and the world" of her blessing (VIII.241; 4.524). The objectivity of this assessment shows his success in escaping the narcissistic defense system that used to shield him from sorrow, for he now understands that he has robbed not himself alone, but "the world" as well, of Clarissa. Lovelace has entered mourning.

Conscious mourning is an advance for Lovelace, who has never acknowledged his sorrows but has always protected himself against suffering by the "defensive exclusion of unwelcome information." Although mourning normally prepares one for new love attachments, if a person's capacity to love is already fragile, the emotional distress of grieving may leave the already impaired capacity for love "more impaired than it was before." The most reliable sign of a disordered mourning is an "unusually intense and prolonged" reaction to the death of the beloved, "in many cases with anger or self-reproach dominant and persistent. . . ." If depression continues, as it does with Lovelace, the mourner cannot "replan his life, which commonly becomes and remains sadly disorganized" (Bowlby 1980, 137–40).

What can Lovelace do now? He tells Belford that because he is miserable abroad he will "soon return to England, and follow your example, and see what a constant course of penitence and mortification will do for me. There is no living at this rate" (VIII.241; 4.525). Then he writes to Morden and precipitates the duel in which he is killed. Readers have sometimes supposed that Lovelace's death is suicide, but suicide requires the intent and its performance, while both are absent from the novel. In truth, Lovelace expects to overcome Morden when they fight, for he loves dueling "as well as [his] food" and is not shaken by "revenge and passion" as is Morden (VIII.242–3; 4.525). Possibly, Lovelace is self-deceived in assessing his chances, yet his deceptions always in the past protected a fragile self. He is untruthful from long habit, but after confronting the truth of his disability Lovelace has no more need to lie; perhaps an accurate way of understanding him here is to see him as moved by habitual impatience: he "could not . . . live in suspense" (VII.233; 4.518). If prudence is the wise use of one's time, it is Clarissa's management of unbearable suspense and sorrow that guarantees her success in completing her life; conversely, it is Lovelace's inability to use time properly that makes him unable to bear guilt and anxiety, which causes his death before he learns to govern himself by using his time well.

The Figures of Lovelace's Self-Exposure

As Chapter 4 points out, Lovelace's fantasies always uncover the pathological motives his cover-stories hope to conceal. One could say that Lovelace tells the truth in spite of himself, for his fantasies can invariably be relied upon to discover his self-deception. Because his fantasies are a picture gallery in which one sees an accurate representation of his moment-to-moment self, whenever his transaction with Clarissa causes change in his self, one sees the changes reflected in his fantasy language. Thus the stripping of illusions which proceeds in his late-novel exchanges with Belford and Clarissa is echoed by "the figures of Lovelace's self-exposure," that is, the images that articulate the stripping away of his grandiosity. By mid-novel his early predator figures (Dryden's lion, the infectious Spider) have disappeared by giving way to the amorous See-saw, which itself yields to his despairing chevalier in armour and his Clarissa accusatory laced-hat orator fantasies. What happens when she escapes his power and continues to exert her own influence on him is that Lovelace's imagination pictures both the exhaustion of his unhappy narcissistic self and the beginnings of its healthier reconstitution.

The exhaustion of Lovelace's narcissistic self is figured by two image clusters, one showing the gradual depletion of psychic energy as represented by dogs, horses, fire and similar metaphors of vitality, the other turning the hunt metaphor against himself. To begin with the metaphors of psychic depletion, the dog figure traces the rise and fall of Lovelace's power. When his power is at its crest after his seizure of

Clarissa, his maniacal laughter makes his "dogs conclude [him] mad" (III.30; 1.513); when Belford (once "an excellent *setter* and *starter*" in the pursuit of women, whose ugly face, says Lovelace, frightened them "into *my* paws" (VIII.149; 4.445)) complains about his mistreatment of Clarissa, Lovelace silences him as one does a dog: "Lie thee down, oddity!" (IV.352; 2.490). But as Lovelace's power wanes and his anxieties become more conscious, the dog figure turns upon its master, for when his relatives forbid him "coming into their apartments," he pretends that *they* are *his* "prisoners": they skulk "while I range about as I please. Pretty dogs and *doggesses,* to quarrel and bark at me, and yet, whenever I appear, afraid to pop out of their kennels . . ." (VII.81; 4.87). After that, the dog figures self-accusation, when as Clarissa nears death he asks Belford not to "halloo on a worrying conscience, which, without thy merciless aggravations, is altogether intolerable" (VII.362; 4.295). After Lovelace achieves self-knowledge, he embraces the judgment of his conscience, saying "*To be a dog, and dead,/ Were paradise to such a life as mine*" (VIII.131; 4.442), knowing that his contemptible conduct has earned his being "*pointed at, screamed out upon, run away from, as a mad dog would be*" (VIII.143; 4.451).

Even a better example of a depletion figure running through the novel is the horse, which begins as the figure of Lovelace's initial grandiosity, "a restiff horse [that] pains one's hands, and half disjoints one's arms, to rein him in" (I.168; 1.124). Later on the horse/virility image dwindles to exhaustion. It is corrupted in Mrs. Sinclair's "horse-nostrils" (V.290; 3.196), the bellows she huffs through in the rape. The horse represents deep anxiety when Lovelace fantasizes the post-horse beaten alive and harrowed into living dog's meat (VI.281; 3.451) because Belford interrupts his prison narrative. Thinking that a "time-pacified" Clarissa will marry him, Lovelace reveals his deep despair in the drowsy marriage he calls the "mill-horse round" (VI.313; 3.474). Finally, the horse image expresses the draining of all power, for Lovelace is "chained to the belly of the beast" (VII.284; 4.236) while he waits helplessly for the horse that carries the news of Clarissa's death, Belford has deserved "sousing" in a "horsepond" (VIII.151; 4.457) for failing to warn Clarissa about her danger, and Lovelace tries to "buffet down" his "cruel reflections" with a "horse-laugh" (VII.319; 4.262) when Clarissa expires.

A second image cluster that figures Lovelace's narcissistic depletion takes up those earlier "hunt" figures which emphasized his pursuit of Clarissa (Dryden's lion and the infectious Spider) and advances them to the hunt's conclusion in killing and eating. Having pursued her to consume her, he finds *himself* being killed and shredded in a feast-of-consuming-passion that is dominated by images that show Lovelace eating-his-heart-out, conscience having turned cannibal. As the novel concludes, the man who had tried, and is still trying, to transfer blame to others becomes his own hunter and his own prey. Like the Erinyes who pursue the guilty to kill them (Megaera the envious, Tisiphone the blood avenger, and Alecto the unceasing in pursuit), Lovelace turns his energies into a figurative self-pursuit which annihilates his grandiosity.

In Lovelace's ferocious curse of Mrs. Sinclair and her women for their complicity, and of Belford for interrupting his prison narrative, one can see the termination of a Fury-like pursuit in which the guilty parties, having been hunted down in the sense of being identified and captured, are violently ripped and shredded into fragments. As Clarissa approaches death, Lovelace's denials of responsibility wear very thin, but rather than feel guilty for his actions he blames those who are closest to him, i.e., Belford and Mrs. Sinclair. Cursing the women, he wants the "great devil" to dash them to pieces "against the tops of chimneys" as "lesser devils collect their scattered scraps, and bag them up . . . to put them together again in the element of fire" (VI.241; 3.421). Lovelace's curse of the brothel women is his attempt to deflect blame from himself, for one notes that it is figurally identical to his reaction against Clarissa's indictment for "unprecedented wickedness"; she has "heard, that the devil is black; and having a mind to make one of me, brays together, in the mortar of her wild fancy, twenty chimney-sweepers, in order to make one sootier than ordinary" (VII.82; 4.88). In both figures, Lovelace refuses blame, either by shifting it to Sinclair or by denying Clarissa's charge. And in both cases the incinerated self-state that images the psychic fragmentation he continues to deny are represented by the "wild fancy" which reveals that being Lovelace is like being smashed and battered to pieces, by himself.

Lovelace's curse of Belford likewise concludes an Erinyean pursuit. The post-horse, carrying the prison narrative in which he finds mirrored his own unconscious psychic grief, is harrowed *by Lovelace* into living "dog's meat" to be "devoured peace-meal." As in the curse aimed at Sinclair, we find this fantasy figuring punishment as being continually ripped into fragments and eaten.

Confound thee for a malicious devil! I wish thou wert a post-horse, and I upon the back of thee! How would I whip and spur, and harrow up thy clumsy

sides, till I made thee a ready-roasted, ready-flayed, mess of dog's meat; all
the hounds in the county howling after thee as I drove thee, to wait my dis-
mounting, in order to devour thee peace-meal; life still throbbing in each
churned mouthful! (VI.281; 3.451)

In his "poor hungry fox" fantasy, Lovelace had shifted his self-hatred
onto malicious villagers clamoring in murderous pursuit, though he
later disguises this self-murderous pursuit as "sport." His curse of
Belford shows Lovelace's self-deception dissolving. If fox and hunter
give way to horse and sadistic rider, they both focus on driving to
death, pursuing and dismembering. Lovelace's imagination pictures
himself in all these figures, whether it be fox and hunter, horse and
rider, or the ravening hounds that come "howling after" to "devour"
him like Actaeon's dogs.

The conclusion of the "hunt" that Lovelace's fantasies have pictured comes with news of Clarissa's death. At this point the self-con-
tradiction of being both pursuer and hunted is dramatized by his attempts to escape—and to prevent himself from escaping—out the
window. Long an ambivalent portal for him, the window is associated
with conscience because it was Clarissa, representing his conscience,
who flew out the window when he was designing the Fire Plot (IV.227;
2.400), and the dream-image of Morden figuring conscience comes in
with "drawn sword" (VII.147; 4.136) through a window. When news
comes that Clarissa has died,

off went his hat to one corner of the room, his wig to the other . . . running
up and down the room, and throwing up the sash, and pulling it down, and
smiting his forehead with his double fist, with such force as would have felled
an ox, and stamping and tearing . . . And this was the *distraction-scene* for
some time.

Throwing up the sash to flee and pulling it down to keep himself in
custody, Lovelace attacks himself by "smiting his forehead" as if to kill
the animal ("an ox") that will be cooked and consumed. After explod-
ing into hyperkinetic liveliness, he "sits grinning" like a Bedlamite and
then "creeps into holes and corners, like an old hedgehog hunted for
his grease" (VII.428; 4.344). His grease is the self-substance burned
in self-consuming, and the hedgehog, with its wholly self-protective
surface, is an appropriate emblem for Lovelace because the grandiose
pretenses that used to conceal his self-contempt can no longer be
sustained.

As the hunt ends in the kill, followed by cooking and eating the
dead animal's flesh, so Lovelace's "smiting his forehead with his double

fist" with sufficient violence to "have felled an ox" is followed by cooking. Like the dog figure, the figure of fire also traces the trajectory of
Lovelace's descent from grandiosity to depletion; as fire had imaged
his energy (his soul is "*A fire, which ev'ry windy passion blows*"
(I.200; 1.147)), it now figures exhaustion. And thus Clarissa's prediction about the "evil man," that "A fire not blown shall consume him"
(VIII.125; 4.437), does come true in Lovelace's reaction to Clarissa's
abandonment of him in death: when madness seizes him, his brain,
"all boiling like a cauldron over a fiery furnace" (VIII.47; 4.378), is "on
fire day and night" (VIII.130; 4.441). The "madness" of his narcissistic grandiosity is burned into cinder within his sensory imagination.

One could follow the entire trajectory of Lovelace's psychic alteration in the novel by watching the demise of that "strutting rascal of a
cock" who represented his power over women and their submissive-
ness to him by initiating a contest over a barley-corn: giving it to a
favorite hen with "a chuck-aw-aw-a, circling round her, with dropt wings,
sweeping the dust in humble courtship" as he courted Clarissa, while
the hen demonstrates by "her cowring tail, prepared wings . . . and
contracted neck" (III.122–3; 2.67) that sexual submission will be required from her. The falsehood figured here is that Lovelace can give
food, offer something that sustains life and health, when he really has
nothing to offer any woman. When the "cock" figure reappears, during the psychomatic sickness he suffers in response to Clarissa's decline, it is not the earlier "strutting rascal" of grandiose pretensions to
power but the plucked, disembowled and shredded fowl whose last use
is to be eaten: "I am in no fighting mood just now: But as patient and
passive as the chickens that are brought me in broth—for I am come to
that already," being, he says, "egregiously cropsick" (VII.116–7; 4.113–
4). After Clarissa dies and he recovers from temporary madness and
realizes what he has done to her, Lovelace exclaims "A thousand vultures in turn are preying upon my heart" (VIII.128–9; 4.440). Food is
always the critical issue in these fantasies, beginning with the pretense
that he offers nourishment to women and ending with the experience
that he is self-consuming now that he has lost his psychic defense
against guilt and grief.

Chapter 10

Lovelace's Ameliorative Decline

If Lovelace is crushed by the bad news about himself that he faces after his narcissistic defenses are broken, the news is not uniformly dismaying, since his imagination has begun picturing a reconstituted self which is available, at least as a possibility. The specter of despair begins to fade from his fantasies, while a tentative move toward a less conflicted intrapsychic condition is represented by Lovelace's August 21 dream of Clarissa rising into the heavens and by an August 31 waking reverie about the Carteret funeral monument.[1] His dream of Clarissa rising is evidence of a benign psychic development taking place within him, the fruits of which appear in his September 1 letter in which Lovelace realizes that Clarissa is an independent woman and not his self-extension. His August 21 dream is important because it shows so unmistakably that he hopes and expects, through her mediatorship, to avoid the self-murder he covertly fears. In the dream's text he is engaged in a colloquy with Clarissa, who is "overcome in [his] favour" by his relatives, all of them wearing black "to express their sorrow for [his] sins against her, and to implore her to forgive [him]" (VII.147; 4.136). Lovelace himself is kneeling with naked sword, ready to kill himself should she refuse, when Morden flashes in "thro' a window" with drawn sword to destroy him if he refuses to marry her. When Lovelace stands up in order to "resent" Morden's insult, Lord M. throws his "black mantle" across Lovelace's face, making him vulnerable to Morden's attack. At this point Clarissa graciously "wrapped her arms round [him], muffled as [he] was in my Lord's mantle," asking him and Morden to "spare" each another: "Let me not have my distresses augmented by the fall of either or both of those who are so dear to me!" (VII.147–8; 4.136). This dream shows that Lovelace has reached a point at which denials or transfers of guilt no longer work; although he cannot yet confess or repent, he accepts his relatives' aid.

Morden, who represents Lovelace's conscience, demands retribution, but the self-conflict is neutralized by the Clarissa figure: she rescues him from self-condemnation by demanding that the guilty man and his retributive conscience "spare" one another. So the first of the dream's two points, that Lovelace's self-murder is avoidable, has been made.

Lovelace's dream having made its point about retribution and forgiveness, it suddenly shifts into a different drama, one which features "the most angelic form" he has ever seen. This "angelic form" is *not* Clarissa, and *that* is the message the dream insists upon, because Lovelace has learned to comprehend the difference. From the outset Lovelace has constantly used Clarissa as a screen upon which he projects the faultless self he desires. But now he can surrender her as a narcissistic selfobject because he is able to perceive her as an independent woman, a remarkable woman, one who has helped him to see himself, without her as his reflection. In his dream, we can see Lovelace advancing from the subjectivity of his narcissistic projections into the objectivity of realizing that living in fantasy is unnecessary because one truly can enact the self that one aspires to become, as Clarissa has done. While Clarissa is the exemplar, the angelic form is the symbolic, i.e., the intelligible, form of the "good" which she exemplified:

> the most angelic form I had ever beheld, all clad in transparent white, descended in a cloud, which, opening, discovered a firmament above it, crouded with golden Cherubs and glittering Seraphs, all addressing her with, Welcome, welcome, welcome! and, encircling my charmer, ascended with her to the region of Seraphims; (VII.148;4.136)

If one remembers back to mid-novel, it is evident that Lovelace's transfer of guilt had been imaged by his "laced-hat orator" whose picture-of-the-world vehicle lifts his Clarissa-surrogate upwards in the hubristic act of reforming her Lovelace rake, then dashing her brains out in that grandiose attempt. Now Lovelace has come to internalize his own guilt, or is on the verge of doing so, for his dream shows him forfeiting altitude. He is not positioned in Narcissistic levitation above Clarissa, nor does he stand safely on the ground while she falls; instead, she rises as he plummets:

> instantly, the opening cloud closing, I lost sight of *her,* and of the *bright form* together, and found wrapt in my arms her azure robe (all stuck thick with stars

of embossed silver) which I had caught hold of in hopes of detaining her; but was all that was left me of my beloved Clarissa. And then (horrid to relate) the floor sinking under *me* . . . I dropt into a hole more frightful than that of Elden; and, tumbling over and over down it, without view of a bottom, I awaked in a panic. (VII.148; 4.136)

He falls ignominiously while Clarissa rises in grandeur. And her ascension, far from causing envy and rage in Lovelace, now evokes feelings of reverence and awe. Even though he will be the "enemy of her soul" when he wakes the next morning to renew his pursuit, he has already abandoned self-deceit in favor of self-knowledge.

The other piece of evidence for the change making possible his September 1 letter is Lovelace's August 31 reverie upon the Carteret memorial sculpture, prompted by Belford's comment that Clarissa was "sent from heaven to draw me after her." In reply, Lovelace informs him "I could not for an hour put thee out of my head, in the attitude of Dame Elizabeth Carteret, on her monument in Westminster-Abbey" (VII.305; 4.252). He encourages Belford to "go thither on purpose" to meditate upon the Carteret sculpture (Figure 5):

there wilt thou see this Dame in effigie, with uplifted head and hand, the latter taken hold of by a Cupid every inch of stone, one clumsy foot lifted up also, aiming, as the Sculptor designed it, to ascend; but so executed, as would rather make one imagine, that the Figure (without shoe or stocken, as it is, tho' the rest of the body is robed) was looking up to its Corn-cutter: The other riveted to its native earth, bemired, like thee . . . beyond the possibility of unsticking itself. Both Figures, thou wilt find, seem to be in a contention, the bigger, whether it should pull down the lesser about its ears—the lesser (a chubby fat little varlet, of a fourth part of the other's bigness, with wings not much larger than those of a butterfly) whether it should raise the larger to a Heaven it points to, hardly big enough to contain the great toes of either. (VII.305–6; 4.252–3)

Lovelace's reading of the monument is a typical jest at Belford's expense. The stone lady represents Belford well enough, although the angel Clarissa is "but sorrily represented by the fat-flanked Cupid." Granting "enough in [Belford's] aspirations" to strike his mind with a "resemblance of thee and the Lady to the Figures on the wretched monument," Lovelace insists, however, that, while Clarissa may be preparing "to mount to her native skies," it is impossible for her "to draw after her a heavy fellow who has so much to repent of as thou hast" (VII.306; 4.253).

Figure 5. The Carteret Funeral Sculpture
If thou never observedst it, go thither on purpose; and there wilt thou see . . .

Perhaps the best way to appreciate the importance of this fantasy is to measure by it the distance Lovelace has come since his "affronted God of Love" psychomachia prior to the Fire Plot. There Clarissa was an "adorable *Nemesis*" who deserved punishment, and Belford ("thy lips twisted; thy forehead furrowed; thy whole face drawn out from the stupid round to the ghastly oval; every muscle contributing its power to complete the aspect-grievous" (IV.375; 2.494)) was the mirror wherein Lovelace viewed the angry child of his psychic pathology. Because Belford in his mirroring role is always involved in Lovelace's perception of Clarissa, one can see that a Belford/Clarissa relationship is a representation of a Lovelace/Clarissa relationship, and this psychic connection can helpfully illuminate his "reading" of the Carteret sculpture. Belford had earlier been considered treasonable for his sympathy towards the "adorable *Nemesis*," but now his recognition that she has been "sent from heaven" to help him get there allows Lovelace to recognize her mission as it relates to himself. For Lovelace, a Belford-Clarissa transaction is a transaction between his wish to understand himself without deceit (Belford as mirror) and his aspiration to somehow become a worthier self (Clarissa as ideal).

But such a transaction, still necessarily dependent on those who assist him towards self-competence, is problematic because of Lovelace's incapable self. The sculptor's "wretched" execution, which corresponds to the faulty formation of Lovelace's self, is the problem the two figures are coping with. The lady is not at fault, being herself as much a victim of circumstances as is the Cupid who is trying to assist her. Fortunately, the two figures are not fighting, but cooperating. The "uplifted head and hand" of the stone lady are being "taken hold of" by the Cupid, their joint effort being to "raise" the "bemired" lady. Here, through his Belford mirror, Lovelace sees his own "bemired" situation in the stone lady, while the generous Cupid who "raises" him already has been identified by Belford as Clarissa herself. One can find here nothing of the rankling envy seen in his mid-novel complaint about the "pretty little miss" who did everything well, since now he too admires Clarissa without envying her.

Lovelace's dream and his reading of the Carteret sculpture put to rest his contention with Clarissa. His dream pictures her as victorious in the contest between them when she is "lifted up" by the "bright form" into "a firmament stuck round with golden cherubims" while Lovelace falls into a "bottomless pit." But his fall does not at all resemble earlier fantasies of being crushed, smashed and cooked, for it is cleansing rather than annihilating. His fall permits his rise; he imagines himself "soused into some river" and "purified" of his faults, after which he and Clarissa go on "cherubiming of it and carolling to the end of the chapter" (VII.177; 4.158). Though the stone lady and the Cupid appear to struggle in "contention, the bigger [Lovelace], whether it should pull down the lesser [Clarissa] about its ears" (VII.306; 4.253), his intention to pull her down a little closer to his own level, as he had put it to Belford, has been withdrawn. Cooperation has supplanted contention; the Cupid wins and the stone lady does not lose.

However, more than his rivalry with Clarissa is being put to rest here, for Lovelace's reflections upon the Carteret sculpture signify the end of his long quarrel with the "disdainful mother" image in his own psyche—the mother who refuses him body contact, comfort and feeding. As Roy Schafer predicts, the development of Lovelace's self-interpreting fantasies has been "*toward ever more archaic*" (271) storylines; these return him to the psychic moment of infant trauma, with its pain, but also with its possibility of starting afresh in self-formation. Lovelace's dream and Carteret memorial fantasy are focused upon that possibility. His approach to archaic psychic material can be recognized when he says "to be forgiven by injured Innocents is *necessary* to the Divine pardon" (VII.86; 4.91). And his arrival upon the threshhold of repressed infantile memories is expressed when, as infantile disappointment becomes more nearly conscious, he says about Clarissa's body, "I will have her laid in my family-vault between my own Father and Mother" (VII.44; 4.375-6). Trying to recover after her death, he cannot accomplish the "amendment wished me so heartily by my kind and cross dear" (VIII.132; 4.443); the modifiers "kind and cross" signify that Lovelace no longer takes Clarissa for the disdainful mother of his narcissistic defect who merits punishment, but for the good mother who loves and wishes him well. After his madness has gone, he tells Belford "They govern me as a child in strings" (VIII.130; 4.441), as a pre-toddler being aided to start learning how to walk. Lovelace has come to "ground zero" of the repressed material and figures himself as starting over from the beginning.

One cannot conclude an examination of Clarissa's effect upon Lovelace without taking into account her Christian belief system, because it is the key to her own actions, which set the challenge to Lovelace. At the outset Clarissa had presumed the retribution schema in which good actions are rewarded and evil ones punished. Lovelace shares that stance, since he sets out to punish everyone who has of-

fended him. "Is such a one as he to set himself up to punish the guilty?,"
the indignant Clarissa wonders. "He is, I suppose, on earth, to act the
part, which the malignant Fiend is supposed to act below—Dealing
out punishments, at his pleasure, to every inferior instrument of mis-
chief" (VI.299; 3.464). Yet whether one's effort is to shun evil in order to avoid punishment or to punish others for the evil which one
already suffers is not particularly important, for in either case desire is
held hostage to retribution.

The retribution schema is articulated in what Ricoeur calls "the
'Adamic' myth," which goes beyond the myths of chaos and the
"wicked god" by positing that God is holy and that sin enters the
world "by a sort of catastrophe" that people bring on themselves. This
myth comes at a high price theologically, because "the same theology
that makes God innocent accuses man" (*Symbolism of Evil* 239–40).
The Jewish spirit of repentence that produced this myth discovered
"an evil root" both "individual and collective," which is like a choice
that "each would make for all and all for each" (1967, 214), but which
is not easily assigned to a particular act of individual will. Clarissa too
arrives at something like that conception of evil through her experience of defilement, sin and guilt, followed by penitential suffering.

It is as the fruit of her personal reflections that Clarissa can write
Mr. Wyerley that "there was a kind of fatality [Ricoeur calls it "a sort of
catastrophe"] by which our whole family was impelled, as I may say;
and which none of us were permitted to avoid" (VII.240; 4.204). In
her posthumous letter to her uncles Clarissa clearly assumes that suffering is God's punishment, yet her stress on mutual culpability is
something new and difficult to grasp fully: "It was necessary perhaps
that . . . misfortunes should befall me, in order to mortify that my
pride, and that my vanity. Temptations were accordingly sent. I shrunk
in the day of tryal. My discretion, which had been so cried up, was
found wanting when it came to be weighed in an equal balance. I was
betrayed, fell, and became the by-word of my companions, and a disgrace to my family, which had prided itself in me perhaps too much"
(VIII.29–30; 4.365). Here Clarissa articulates her insight that evil is
"both individual and collective," something like "a choice that each
would make for all."

The problem with the Adamic myth is that the sin revealed by God's
holiness accuses the Creator of having "made man evil," so that "I
accuse God in the same moment in which he accuses me" (1967,
242). The result is that the evil committed leads to the "just exile"

represented by Adam, while the evil that is suffered leads to the "un-just deprivation" expressed by Job. Only a third figure, says Ricoeur, could overcome this contradiction, and that is the Suffering Servant, who would transform suffering from an evil undergone into "an *action* capable of redeeming the evil that is committed" (324). The stage represented by Job is necessary, for without it the need for a Suffering Servant would not become clear. Job is the key. "The suffering of the innocent broke the schema of retribution" because, under the old law, guilt produced suffering as its punishment; Job is needed "to mediate" the shift from punishment to generosity, in order that guilt might be given another horizon, says Ricoeur, "not that of Judgment, but that of Mercy" (325). In the Suffering Servant figure, the relationship between persons rests on the "reciprocity" of a gift responded to by its acceptance. "This alliance supposes that the substitutive suffering is not the simple transfer of defilement to a passive object, such as the scapegoat," but instead "the voluntary 'gift' of a suffering taken upon [one]self and offered to others" (266).

As Richardson's novel approaches its conclusion, a suffering Clarissa suffiently overcomes the disabling power of her mourning to undertake the work of the Suffering Servant on behalf of—who? Lovelace and the Harlowes. Clarissa turns her suffering into the "voluntary 'gift'" she offers them in her posthumous letters and Will. Until now, her family and Lovelace had been unable to hear what she has to say—the Harlowes because he has so falsified her as to destroy her credibility, Lovelace because his narcissistic needs obliterate her reality. But after her death their deafness disappears and her destroyers hear from Clarissa the message they had collaborated in order to silence. The schema of retribution is overthrown in *Clarissa* when Clarissa turns her suffering into "gifts" to those who abused her, thus making the transition "from punishment to generosity" (Ricoeur 1967, 325).

In order to provide Lovelace the gift of her forgiveness and her encouragement, Clarissa must make the distinction between his false self and his true. His false self is the "great fiend" who was unveiled in the Fire Plot, the Satanic demon who long pursued her as "the enemy of" her soul; that demon Clarissa repudiates on September 3 when she says "I am glad this violent spirit can thus creep; that, like a poisonous serpent, he can thus coil himself, and hide his head in his own narrow circlets." She expresses not resentment but disappointment in observing that after mistreating her "as he did," he could "creep to me for forgiveness of crimes so wilful, so black, and so premeditated"

(VII.338; 4.276). She had expected better of him, and Clarissa's complaint here is the anger of his "kind and cross dear," who in her posthumous letter says, "Nor have I yet, as you will see by the pains I take . . . given over all hopes" of his reformation (VIII.125; 4.437).

Having forgiven Lovelace, Clarissa reaches for intercession on his behalf when on September 5 she says, "pray tell him, that if I could know, that my death might be a means to reclaim and save him, it would be an inexpressible satisfaction to me!" Then after a brief space of time, "tell the poor man, that I not only forgive him, but have *such* earnest wishes for the good of his soul . . . that could my penitence avail for more sins than my own, my last tear should fall for him by whom I die!" (VII.377–9; 4.306–7).

The huge irony is that Lovelace, who during the entire novel has demanded "forgiveness" and "generosity" from Clarissa in the debased language that concealed his narcissistic compulsions, is crushed when she freely offers them: "the generosity of her mind display'd in both [her Will and her posthumous letter], is what stings me most. And the more still, as it is now out of my power any way in the world to be even with her" (VIII.224; 4.511). The disparity in moral worth between them which formerly raised envy and anger now provokes in Lovelace admiration mixed with sorrow: "I am, and shall be, to my latest hour, the most miserable of beings. Such exalted generosity!— Why didst thou put into my craving hands the copy of her will? Why sentest thou to me the posthumous letter?" (VIII.238; 4.522). That Clarissa's gift has such a crushing effect is the more ironic because her intention had been to help him to overcome his despair. "To love anybody," says Gabriel Marcel, "is to expect something from him" and at the same time "in some way to make it possible for him to fulfil this expectation . . . [since] to expect is in some way to give." But the opposite is also true, for "no longer to expect is to strike with sterility the being from whom no more is expected" (49–50). Clarissa has continued to "expect something" from Lovelace, and he regretfully recognizes the generosity of that expectation.

Lovelace is devastated by Clarissa's generosity because he cannot ever "be even with her" through generosity of his own: she has died and he is guilty of her death. Guilt has not until now been a part of Lovelace's repertoire. But the psychotherapeutic intervention undertaken by his Ideal and Mirroring Selfobjects has brought him into the ethical register of meaning, Belford's "standard of humanity." He is now capable of guilt, capable of responsibility for his deeds. "Guilt progresses by passing over two thresholds," says Ricoeur, the first of them being "remorse for having been unjust." That is the threshold Lovelace crosses when he sees that breaking the interpersonal bond connecting him to Clarissa, i.e., "the wrong done to the person of another," is more greatly to be feared than what Ricoeur calls the "threat of castration," which is at the root of his criminal behavior. Thus Lovelace learns the Lesson of Guilt from Clarissa. She can teach him that lesson, for she herself has crossed the second threshold beyond which, says Ricoeur, "guilt progresses." She has overcome the temptation to believe that self-evident self-awareness is the criterion of reality. That presumption, which Ricoeur calls "the pretension of empirical consciousness to say the totality," makes her vulnerable to resentment, which is "a very hidden hatred, and a very shrewd hedonism" (1974, 350–1). Thus Clarissa is engaging in important work when she meditates on death: "It teaches me, by strengthening in me the force of the Divinest Example, to forgive the injuries I have received; and shuts out the remembrance of past evils from my soul" (VII.313–4; 4.258).

Lovelace's final action is not the duel with Morden but, as De La Tour says, "a seeming ejaculation" which he "spoke inwardly so as not to be understood," and then the "distinctly pronounced" words "LET THIS EXPIATE!" (VIII.249; 4.530). It is evident from the eye-witness's narrative of "Chevalier Lovelace" that he is no longer the despairing chevalier in armour but a vigorously active man using his remaining moments to talk to the dead Clarissa, who remains very much alive to him and to whom he is praying. Harold Bloom is accurate to say that Lovelace "dies in his own acquired religion, which is the worship of the blessed Clarissa" and that he dies as "a Clarissan rather than a Christian." Yet Bloom goes too far in describing Lovelace's last act as "hardly expiation in any moral or spiritual sense whatever" (1987, 4), even though the sense in which it is expiation needs to be clarified.

One way to understand expiation is to see it as meaning that Lovelace offers his death as an even exchange for the damage that he has done Clarissa. Jocelyn Harris interprets him in that way, and she bristles at his arrogance: "we must ask how this one deed can in reality expiate the avarice, the tyranny, the deceptions, the rape, the misery and the death [of Clarissa]" (1987, 128). Harris has quite precisely formulated the indignation which "LET THIS EXPIATE!" raises in people who continue to reflect upon the transaction between the main characters in terms of the schema of retribution, in which punishment restores the damage done, "makes up for" by giving back something else of equivalent worth. Miss Howe's opinion that Lovelace ought to be "excluded by his crimes from the benefit even of christian forgiveness" and her advice to his family that they join her to "admire" Clarissa and "execrate" him (VII.27–8; 4.48) is the response that the retribution schema requires. Indeed, it is the just response which Lovelace himself embraces, for nobody in the novel is more committed to punishment than he has been from the outset, his self-destructive compulsion being the secret cause of his transference of violence to others. But Clarissa's intervention has changed him by helping him to see and accept his own guilt, with the result that he now understands that *he should* "admire" her and "execrate" himself. And *he does*:

> Exalted creature!—And couldst thou at *such a time,* and *so early,* and in *such circumstances,* have so far subdued thy own just resentments, as to wish happiness to the principal author of thy distresses? . . . "Remorse has broken in upon me. "—Dreadful *is* my condition!—It *is* all reproach and horror with me!"—A thousand vultures in turn are preying upon my heart. (VIII.128–9; 4.440)

When Harris and Miss Howe indict Lovelace for his elaborate and unprecedented wickedness, they do no more than Lovelace himself does once he has become capable of embracing his own guilt. Yet it is important to note that his "LET THIS EXPIATE!" goes beyond the "Exalted creature!/thousand vultures" immobilizing opposition between her admirable goodness and his punishable depravity, for, as De La Tour reports, "his last few words . . . shew an ultimate composure" (VIII.249; 4.530). Upon what is that composure based? If he dies not a Christian but a Clarissan, what would that mean?

To answer such questions one needs to interrogate Lovelace's state of mind during the time between his mid-September recovery from madness and his death three months later. During this time, he experiences continuing remorse and occasional consolation: "I have nothing left me but the remorse" caused by reflecting on his conduct, though "Now-and-then, indeed, am I capable of a gleam of comfort, arising . . . from the moral certainty which I have of her everlasting happiness," despite his efforts "to bring down so pure a mind to my own level" (VIII.241; 4.524). It is clear that Lovelace's conscious state during his final three months of life is totally cleansed of those narcissistic accusations of Clarissa which had constituted his habitual attitude to her; now he wavers in an uneasy balance between his remorsefulness and the "comfort" of knowing that she has prevailed over his wicked-ness and is now happy in post-mortal existence. Thus his continuing mental state is indecisive because he has not decided whether to em-brace self-accusation and remorse as his final stance, or whether in-stead to embrace Clarissa's forgiveness.

That Lovelace vacillates between self-accusation and self-forgive-ness is evident from De la Tour's description. Sometimes he calls out "as if he had seen some frightful Spectre, Take her away!," at other times he addresses Clarissa as "Fair Sufferer" and begs her "Look down, blessed Spirit" (VIII.249; 4.530). One has to surmise that Lovelace is not prepared to die until he has made the decision not to remain bemired in remorse but to accept Clarissa's forgiveness, which he does by lifting his eyes upward, spreading his hands and pronounc-ing the words "LET THIS EXPIATE."

This action—which is the declarative speech act that enacts into social reality the expiation he intends—returns us to the interpretive difficulty posed earlier, since to expiate means to atone. The word "atone" can be understood in either of these two ways: to offer rec-ompense as reparation, or to be reconciled. Lovelace's intention is to achieve reconciliation with Clarissa. He is adapting for his use in the ethical register of meaning the "Suffering Servant" figure Clarissa has enacted in the religious field of meaning. His "Fair Sufferer" becomes a non-narcissistic Ideal Selfobject, the secular divinity or "blessed Spirit" of his invocation, who is the focus of his fervent quasi-religious hope. One can see that Lovelace's "answering" Clarissa by accepting her "gift of pardon" does not depend upon either his being adequately punished or his psychological and moral self being foundationally re-formed. Says Ricoeur:

> Pardon does not appear here as a wholly inward change, psychological and moral, but as an interpersonal relation to that immolated personality . . . this interpersonal relation rests on the reciprocity of a gift ("in place of," "for our sins") and an acceptance ("we did esteem him stricken, smitten of God, and afflicted"). (1967, 266)

In his "LET THIS EXPIATE!" Lovelace abandons his endless remorse and accepts Clarissa's gift of pardon. What de la Tour calls the "ulti-mate composure" of his final moments stems from the offering of his death as the validation of his intention to be reconciled.

Note

1   Lovelace's August 21 dream of "Clarissa rising" has a demonic parody in his
June 20 dream of "Mother H rescuing Clarissa" into a different brothel. That
Richardson intended these dreams to be contrasted is evidenced by the paral-
lelism between them, since in both dreams Clarissa is addressed identically:
"Welcome, welcome, welcome, fair young Lady" says Mother H as she greets
Clarissa to chariot her to another brothel (VI.11; 3.249); "Welcome, welcome,
welcome" sing out the Cherubs and Seraphs who greet Clarissa and accom-
pany her into the heavens (VII.148; 4.136). The pairing of the dreams dramatizes the incremental amelioration of Lovelace's narcissistic problems during
the two-month period that separates the dream of Mother H from the dream
of Clarissa rising.

Terry Eagleton's and Tassie Gwilliam's remarks on Lovelace's dream of
Mother H demonstrate that different interpretive points of view often yield
similar insights, as when Eagleton's Freudian approach produces a very
Kohutian reading focused upon Lovelace's vacillation between "good" and
"persecuting, vindictive" mothers:

> If more evidence were needed of Lovelace's Oedipal difficulties, there is
> always the astonishing dream which he recounts to Belford after the rape—
> a dream in which the figure of a "good" mother changes rapidly into a
> persecuting, vindictive one, and that in turn into Lovelace himself. . . .
> The dream reveals Clarissa as unconscious mother-figure for Lovelace. . . .
> She bears him a son, who is at once Lovelace's own son and Lovelace
> himself . . . . By the end of the dream, he has successfully resolved his
> relationship with the ambivalently threatening and nurturing mother, reaf-
> firmed his own masculine power by impregnating Clarissa, and punctured
> her own infuriating narcissism in the process. Thoroughly narcissistic and
> regressive, Lovelace's "rakishness," for all its virile panache, is nothing
> less than a cripping incapacity for adult sexual relationship. (62–3)

Gwilliam writes from an Ovidian viewpoint ("'Like Tiresias': Metamorphosis and Gender in Clarissa"), as one could say. About Lovelace's continuing
effort to transformation himself, she says "metamorphosis has a problematic
narrative status because it is always both a reflection of genuine impulses"
towards alteration of one's being "and a disguise." Dreaming of Mother H,
Lovelace "imagines himself as the central but absent figure in the scene of
feminine intercourse," their "intercourse" being the "dismal tale" of her rape
that Clarissa tells while lying next to Mother H in the bed. "The intoxicating
moment in which Clarissa finds Mother H. 'turned into a young person of the
other sex' is the quintessential moment of magical bodily change" while in
contrast the "moment of actual intercourse" is "anticlimactic." The dream
continues with Lovelace fathering "Anna's daughter and Clarissa's son," who
will of course eventually marry, since "incest succeeds metamorphosis" as his
way of "incorporating in himself . . . all sexual activity connected with Clarissa's
body" (113–7).

Works Cited

Aquinas, St. Thomas. *Summa Theologica*. Trans. Fathers of the English Dominican Province. 1911. Rev. 1920. Reprinted in 5 vols (Westminster, Md.) by Christian Classics, 1981.

Ariès, Philippe. *The Hour of Our Death*. Trans. H. Weaver. New York: Knopf, 1981.

Aristotle. *Nicomachean Ethics*. Trans. W. D. Ross. *Great Books of the Western World*, ed. R. M. Hutchins. Vol 9. Chicago & London: Encyclopedia Britannica, 1952.

Beebee, Thomas O. Clarissa *on the Continent*. University Park and London: Penn State UP, 1990.

Bloom, Harold. Introduction to *Samuel Richardson*, ed. Bloom. New York: Chelsea House, 1987.

Boswell, James. *Life of Johnson*. London: Oxford U. Press, 1904. Reprinted 1961.

Bowlby, John. *Separation*. Vol. 2 of *Attachment and Loss*, 3 Vols. New York: Basic Books, 1973.

———. *The Making and Breaking of Affectional Bonds*. London: Tavistock Publications, 1979.

———. *Loss: Sadness and Depression*. Vol. 3 of *Attachment and Loss*, 3 Vols. New York: Basic Books, 1980.

Bueler, Lois. Clarissa's *Plots*. Newark: U Delaware P, 1994.

Casey, Edward S. *Remembering: A Phenomenological Study*. Bloomington and Indianapolis: Indiana UP, 1987.

Castle, Terry. *Clarissa's Ciphers: Meaning and Disruption in Richardson's* Clarissa. Ithaca and London: Cornell UP, 1982.

Cicero, M. Tullius. *De Officiis.* Trans. Walter Miller. Loeb Classical Library. New York: Macmillan, 1921.

Coates, Paul. *The Realist Fantasy: Fiction and Reality Since* Clarissa. New York: St. Martin's Press, 1983.

Doody, Margaret Anne. *A Natural Passion: A Study of the Novels of Samuel Richardson.* Oxford: Clarendon Press, 1974.

Dryden, John. *The Works of Virgil in English* (1697). Vol 5 in *The Works of John Dryden.* Berkeley: U Cal. Press, 1987.

Eagleton, Terry. *The Rape of Clarissa.* Minneapolis: U Minnesota P, 1982.

Fingarette, Herbert. *Self-Deception: Studies in Philosophical Psychology.* New York: Humanities Press, 1969.

Flynn, Carol Houlihan. *Samuel Richardson: A Man of Letters.* Princeton: Princeton UP, 1982.

Gillis, Christina Marsden. *The Paradox of Privacy: Epistolary Form in* Clarissa. Gainesville: U Presses of Florida, 1983.

Girard, René. *The Scapegoat.* Trans. Yvonne Freccero. Baltimore: Johns Hopkins UP, 1986.

———. *Job, the Victim of His People.* Trans. Yvonne Freccero. Stanford: Stanford UP, 1987.

Goldberg, Rita. *Sex and Enlightenment: Women in Richardson and Diderot.* Cambridge and New York: Cambridge UP, 1984.

Grotstein, James. "Some Perspectives on Self Psychology." In *The Future of Psychoanalysis: Essays in Honor of Heinz Kohut.* New York: International Universities Press, 1983.

Gwilliam, Tassie. "'Like Tiresias': Metamorphosis and Gender in *Clarissa*," *Novel* 12:2 (1986), 101–17.

Harris, Jocelyn. *Samuel Richardson.* Cambridge: The University Press, 1987.

Hillard, Raymond F. "*Clarissa* and Ritual Cannibalism," *PMLA* 105:5 (1990), 1083–97.

Hyman, Stanley Edgar. *The Armed Vision.* New York: Knopf, 1948.

Kernberg, Otto F. "Further Contributions to the Treatment of Narcissistic Personalities," *Internat. Journ. of Psychoanalysis* 55 (1974): 215–39.

Keymer, Tom. "Richardson's *Meditations*: Clarissa's *Clarissa.*" In *S. R.: Tercentenary Essays.* Cambridge: Cambridge UP, 1989.

————. *Richardson's* Clarissa *and the Eighteenth-Century Reader.* Cambridge and New York: Cambridge UP, 1992.

Kilfeather, Siobhán. "The Rise of Richardson Criticism." In *S. R.: Tercentenary Essays,* ed. Doody and Sabor. Cambridge: Cambridge UP, 1989.

Kinkead-Weekes, Mark. *Samuel Richardson: Dramatic Novelist.* Ithaca: Cornell UP, 1973.

Kohut, Heinz. *The Analysis of the Self: A Systematic Approach to the Psychoanalytic Treatment of Narcissistic Personality Disorders.* New York: Internat. Universities Press, 1971.

————. *The Restoration of the Self.* New York: International Universities Press, 1977.

————, and Ernest S. Wolf. "The Disorders of the Self and their Treatment, An Outline," *Internat. Journ. of Psychoanalysis* 59 (1978): 413–25.

————. "Reflections on *Advances in Self Psychology.*" In Advances in Self Psychology, ed. Arnold Greenberg. New York: International Universities Press, 1980, 473–554.

MacIntyre, Alasdair. *After Virtue: A Study in Moral Theory.* 2nd ed. Notre Dame, Indiana: Notre Dame UP, 1984.

Marcel, Gabriel. *Homo Viator: Introduction to a Metaphysics of Hope.* Trans. Emma Craufurd. 1951. Harper & Row Torchbook, 1962.

Niebuhr, Reinhold. *The Nature and Destiny of Man: A Christian Interpretation.* Vol. I: *Human Nature* [1941], in the One Volume Edition, New York: Charles Scribner's Sons, 1955.

Norris, John. *A Treatise Concerning Christian Prudence: or the Principles of Practical Wisdom, Fitted to the Use of Human*

Life, and Design'd for the Better Regulation of It. London, 1710.

Ovid. *Metamorphoses.* Trans. A. D. Melville. Oxford and New York: Oxford UP, 1986.

Plato, *The Symposium,* Trans. Benjamin Jowett. *Great Books of the Western World.* Ed. R. M. Hutchins. Vol 7. Chicago and London: Encyclopedia Britannica, 1952.

Richardson, Samuel. *Clarissa.* 3rd Edition. 1751. 8 vols. The Clarissa Project. Ed. Florian Stuber, Margaret Anne Doody, Jim Springer Bork et. al. New York: AMS, 1990.

————. *Clarissa.* Everyman's Library. 4 vols. London: Dent (1932), 1982.

————. *Clarissa.* Ed. and intro. by Angus Ross. Harmondsworth, England: Penguin Books, 1985.

Ricoeur, Paul. *The Symbolism of Evil.* Trans. Emerson Buchanan. Religious Perspectives Series, vol 17. Boston: Beacon Press, 1969.

————. *The Conflict of Interpretations: Essays in Hermeneutics.* Evanston: Northwestern UP, 1974. "'Original Sin': A Study in Meaning." Trans. Peter McCormick. "Interpretation of the Myth of Punishment." Trans. Robert Sweeney.

————. *The Philosophy of Paul Ricoeur.* Ed. by Charles E. Reagan & David Stewart. Boston: Beacon Press, 1978.

————. *Time and Narrative.* 3 Vols. Vol. I. Transl. Kathleen McLaughlin and David Pellauer. Chicago and London: U. Chicago Press, 1984.

Rosenman, Stanley. "Narcissus of the Myth: An Essay on Narcissism and Victimization." In *Object and Self.* New York: Internat. Universities Press, 1981.

Schafer, Roy. *The Analytic Attitude.* New York: Basic Books, 1983.

Scruton, Roger. *Sexual Desire.* London: Werdenfeld & Nicolson, 1986.

Searle, John R. *Intentionality: An Essay in the Philosophy of Mind.* Cambridge: the University Press, 1983.

Serres, Michel. *The Parasite*. Trans. L. R. Schehr. Baltimore: Johns Hopkins UP, 1982.

Sherburn, George. "The Restoration and Eighteenth Century." In *A Literary History of England*. Ed. A. C. Baugh. New York: Appleton-Century-Crofts, 1948.

Stevenson, John Allen. "The Courtship of the Family: Clarissa and the Harlowes Once More," *ELH* 48:4 (1981), 757–77.

Stuber, Florian. "Introduction" to *Clarissa*. The Clarissa Project. New York: AMS, 1990.

————. "*Clarissa*: A Religious Novel?," *Studies in the Literary Imagination* 28:1 (1995), 105–24.

Turner, James Grantham. "Lovelace and the Paradoxes of Libertinism." In *S.R.: Tercentenary Essays*. Ed. Doody & Sabor, 1989.

Warner, William Beatty. *Reading* Clarissa: *The Struggles of Interpretation*. New Haven and London: Yale UP, 1979.

Watt, Ian. *The Rise of the Novel: Studies in Defoe, Richardson and Fielding*. 1957. Berkeley and Los Angeles: U California Press, 1967.

Wilson, Angus. "Clarissa," *Samuel Richardson*. Ed. Valerie Grosvenor Myer. London and Totowa, New Jersey: Vision Press and Barnes & Noble, 1986.

Wilt, Judith. "He Could Go No Farther: A Modest Proposal about Lovelace and Clarissa," *PMLA* 92 (1997), 19–32.

Wither, George. *A Collection of emblemes, ancient and moderne*. 1635. Columbia, S.C.: U South Carolina Press, 1975.

Wolff, Cynthia Griffin. *Samuel Richardson and the Eighteenth-Century Puritan Character*. Hamden, Connecticut: Shoe String Press, 1972.

Index